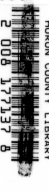

OCCUPIED CANADA

OCCUPIED CANADA

A Young White Man Discovers His Unsuspected Past

Robert Hunter
and
Robert Calihoo

Canadian Cataloguing in Publication Data

Hunter, Robert, date.
   Occupied Canada: a young white man discovers his
      unsuspected past

Includes bibliographical references.
ISBN 0–7710–4295–7

1. Calihoo, Robert.   2. Indians, Treatment of – Canada.
3. Indians of North America – Canada – Ethnic identity.
4. Metis – Biography.   I. Calihoo, Robert.   II. Title.

FC109.1.C3H8   1991   971'.00497   C91–094042–8
E99.M693C34   1991

Quotations from *Forgotten Fathers: How the American Indian
Helped Shape Democracy*, are reprinted with permission from
The Harvard Common Press.
Copyright © 1982 by Bruce E. Johansen

Printed and bound in Canada on acid-free paper.

McClelland & Stewart Inc.
The Canadian Publishers
481 University Avenue
Toronto, Ontario
M5G 2E9

Vive l'Oka Libre

Contents

Acknowledgements   ix

PART I

Chapter 1:   A Good Scottish Name   3

Chapter 2:   Into the Darkness   9

Chapter 3:   Quite a Different World   16

Chapter 4:   Getting Used to Things   22

Chapter 5:   "Not Much Left"   29

Chapter 6:   No Need for a Treaty Card   37

Chapter 7:   "A Meaningful Job Skill"   45

Chapter 8:   The Silent System   51

Chapter 9:   "Say It Fast, Kid"   55

Chapter 10:   "You Know You're an Indian"   64

PART II

Chapter 11:   The Dream of "Iroquois Louis"   75

Chapter 12:   Plagues and Rebellion   81

Chapter 13:   The Taking of the Plains   93

Chapter 14:   Famine and Extinction   101

Chapter 15:   The Gatling Gun and the Indian Act   109

Chapter 16:   "A Just and Honourable Indian Policy"   116

Part III

Chapter 17: A Bold, Distant Pen-Stroke 127

Chapter 18: One Big Claim-Jump 140

Chapter 19: The Empire of Canada 147

Chapter 20: The Beginning of the Holocaust 156

Chapter 21: The Soul-Hunters 168

Chapter 22: The Collapse of the Five Nations 182

Chapter 23: The Great Gift of the Iroquois 190

Part IV

Chapter 24: The Death of Nelson Small Legs, Jr. 205

Chapter 25: In the Belly of the Beast 217

Chapter 26: The Bureau of Indian Control 225

Chapter 27: The Disappearance of a Reserve 236

Chapter 28: The Invisible Wall 249

Chapter 29: The Long Road Home 258

Epilogue 262

Selected Bibliography 266

Acknowledgements

EVEN IF WE HAVE VERY LITTLE THAT IS NICE TO SAY ABOUT THE Indian Affairs Department itself, we are indebted to the Research Branch for its help in obtaining the documents concerning the establishment, the piecemeal surrender, and the eventual enfranchisement of Michel Indian Reserve No. 132.

Also, we owe debts of thanks to the following individuals for assistance in digging up further critical information: Marty Dunn, chief researcher for the Native Council of Canada, for his overview; Grand Chief Joseph Norton of the Iroquois Six Nations Confederacy, for making the essential historical connection; Smoky Breuire, former president of the Native Council of Canada, for encouragement and assistance; and Chief Patrick Alfred of the Nimpkish Band Council of Alert Bay for putting the authors together in the first place.

PART I

Chapter 1

A Good Scottish Name

THE BATTERED GREEN HUDSON WITH THE EXHAUST PIPE DANGLing came backfiring down 103rd Street and stopped for a moment, engine rumbling, in front of Mama's house. Practising aggies carefully, so as not to get dirt on his pressed blue short pants, blue socks, oxfords, blue blazer, and string tie, nine-year-old Robert Royer paused and stared up at the people in the car: long-haired, pigtailed, dark-skinned, not much more than shadows with narrow white eyes gazing back.

Staring, Robert froze. Indians! What were they doing here?

He'd glimpsed Indians before; out at his Uncle Andy's farm just north of Edmonton, a couple of years ago. He and Uncle Andy and Mama had been sitting out on the porch when they saw a couple of men in faded clothes and cowboy hats cutting across a corner of the property, so far away that Robert couldn't see anything peculiar about them at all.

But Mama snapped: "Indians! Get your gun, Andy!"

Robert knew exactly which gun she meant. It was famous in the family. It had been Papa's. Mama had given it to Uncle Andy one Christmas. It was an ancient, long-barrelled Colt .45, which Robert had been allowed to touch now and then. It was too good to be true that he was going to see Uncle Andy use it! But was he going to use it on those men over there? Were those Indians? They looked just like ordinary farm workers, except that their hair was all dark. Mama's anger was amazing. He had seen her get excited before about all sorts of little things, but this was different. She genuinely hated those Indians for some reason.

Uncle Andy just shook his head. "You don't shoot Indians any more, Mother," he said. He had looked at Robert then in a funny sort of way, as though embarrassed about something. Robert squinted at the distant men. He'd seen pictures of half-naked Indians wearing feathers, sitting around their tipis, mothers carrying babies on their backs, and the kids playing with sticks around a fire. It looked like summer-camping all the time, like Cubs and Scouts. These men didn't look anything like that.

Mama often talked excitedly about the trip northwest from Pennsylvania in a wagon train when she was a little girl, and how one of her sisters had been shot and wounded by an Indian. It was a story everybody in the family had heard before. He could tell from Uncle Andy's face every time he heard this story that he didn't believe it for a minute. It was as though she was mad at Indians for some other reason, but she wasn't talking about what it was. Uncle Andy knew, but he wasn't saying anything either. He kept looking at Robert out of the corner of his eye, still embarrassed. . . .

"Don't act like a wild Indian!" How often had Mama said that over the years? Hundreds of times. "Don't sit like an Indian! Don't eat like an Indian! Use your fork!" The wrong way, about anything, was the Indian way.

And now here they were on his own street, actual Indians, engine clunking, dented car shuddering, staring at him in his own front yard.

It didn't seem quite right for them to be here. This was such a neat, freshly painted, orderly, undented place, the rows of black poplar and birch along the street forming a speckled canopy that kept the air cool, even when the prairie sun fizzled and the air was full of mosquitoes. Everybody had

screens on their verandahs. The screen around Mama's verandah, taped in a couple of places where baseballs had torn into
it, was fretted up against the white-painted corner pillar, and
continued along the side of the house right to the kitchen
door where the old hand-pump stood, no longer used but
kept for memory's sake. It was the biggest screened-in verandah on the block. There were tulips and roses and pansies in
the beds beneath the porch. The lawn was large and, like all
the other lawns, never allowed to get more than an inch high;
then little Robert would be out there with the lawn-mower,
even if the grass were still wet and the ground so soggy the
mower left tread-marks.

Likewise, in fall, he had to rake the leaves every day and
burn them so they wouldn't pile up. He didn't mind that
much. The smell of them and the look of them and the smell
of the blue-grey smoke and the way it softened everything in
the distance, making even objects that were close seem far
away, so that he felt he almost had the neighbourhood to
himself, gave him a dreamy feeling of pleasant aliveness.
Time seemed slow and went on forever.

The sidewalks that ran along the street were constructed of
wooden planks, fashionable right after the First World War
when the neighbourhood was built, but the street itself was a
marvel of asphalt, soft to the touch in summer, smooth and
hard as a bonspiel rink in winter. There had never been any
serious accidents that he knew about. Certainly there had
never been any crime. Everything was always the same. Oh,
he grew taller and the other kids grew taller, but the adults
were always adults and the old people stayed old. Sometimes
somebody's dog disappeared or a cat vanished, but that was
about the only change that ever occurred. Everything was
orderly, as clean as humanly possible, cleaner, if Mama had
her way. It was often remarked you could eat off her floors.
The linoleum sparkled. You could see your reflection plainly
in her hardwood. Robert learned early how the silverware
was properly set on the table. He was a good boy.

The world of West Edmonton was serene, respectable, comfortable. Nearby was St. George's Crescent, where the doctors and lawyers and businessmen lived. Robert's chums at St. Alphonse's School and later at St. Vincent Elementary were boys like Tommy McConnelly, whose father owned the big Catholic funeral home of McConnelly, McKinley. Rich kids. Robert wasn't rich, but he was nearly rich. Mama's first husband, last name of Burns, had been an inspector with the police force. After he died she'd married "Papa," John Williams, a mining engineer, who died too. Robert knew that Mama wasn't his real mother, she was his grandmother. She'd told him that when he was just small. But grandmothers were sometimes even better than mothers, she'd added, and Robert was content with that. It didn't matter that Mama and he had different last names. Royer was "a good Scottish name," she assured him, every bit as good as Williams. Anyway, she liked being called Mama, and Robert liked calling her that. She *felt* like his mother.

She had always, it seemed to him, dressed completely in black, with old-style buttoned-up shoes, and she wore a veil on her big black hat and carried her cane whenever she went out, which was usually to church. She was deeply religious, and because she led such a clean, moral life, she was without sin. She was absolutely certain about this, and knew of hardly anyone else about whom the same could be said. She was thin and tall, with silver hair and piercing blue eyes, and had a way, when she came into a room, of taking charge; she could stare anybody down. She was strict and she dominated people easily, and it was only natural to treat her grandson the same way. It was the only way to show love. Real love. Love for his poor, endangered eternal soul. A Catholic, a personal friend of the priest and the nuns, she read to Robert from the Catechism every night, allowing him to sit on her knee, until, around the age of eight, he got too big. On Sunday he had to put on his blue Sunday outfit. He didn't mind as much as some of the other boys did. It made Mama happy.

There was hardly ever any mention of his parents. None at all of his father. As for his mother, Mama's daughter, she had run off. That was the full and terrible extent of her sin. Running off. He wasn't sure whether it was a venial or a mortal sin, but it was right up there, about as bad as it could be. He had a brother and sister somewhere, Harvey and Dorothy, but that was all he knew. He didn't think too much about them.

He had plenty of friends, boys he played aggies and hockey and baseball with. He'd learned early on that he could make the other guys laugh. Funny things just came to his mind at the drop of a hat. He had to be careful not to say all the things that popped into his mind around Mama because she didn't laugh much, and a lot of things she didn't consider funny, especially children that spoke out of place or at the table or whispered in school or at Catechism classes or, God forbid, at Mass. "Be mannerly," she said again and again. "Be civilized."

And he was. Was that why he felt alarmed at the sight of a carload of Indians watching him? How many were there? He couldn't tell. They were crowded together, and the windows of their Hudson were nearly as narrow as tank-slits, and there were furry balls all along the tops of the windows. Dark faces. Hats pulled low.

One of them saw something behind Robert, said something to the driver, and the car jerked into gear. Robert looked over his shoulder. Mama had appeared in the front living-room window. She was wagging a finger and opening and closing her mouth. The car hunched away, the Indians not looking back.

Mama stomped out on the verandah and yanked open the screen door. She was mad, but a little worried too. "You don't talk to them!" she ordered. "You come and tell me if they show up again." She went back inside and Robert could hear her picking up the phone.

As the Hudson backfired down the street, leaving fumes trailing above the asphalt, people looked up from cutting the lawn, trimming the hedges, weeding the gardens, repainting the white picket fences, and then, as one, looked away, pretending not to see the old heap. A few parents nervously called out their children's names. It was as though some big, dangerous animal had lumbered down 103rd. Everybody tried hard to ignore it, but they all knew it was passing through, and they were immensely relieved when it was gone.

Chapter 2

Into the Darkness

IT WAS A DROWSY AFTERNOON IN JUNE 1953, BEFORE THE CAT-
tails had burst or the mosquitoes had hatched, with only two
weeks to go before summer holidays. Robert was walking
home with Tommy McConnelly and a couple of other boys,
their shoes thunking on the old wooden planks of the sidewalk, fresh birch leaves a delicate pale green with silver
underbellies flickering like so many tiny fish above, the
chalk-shrieking boredom of Grade 5's Mercator projection
and memorization tables almost behind them. They were
making plans to build a new fort in the bush behind the
Protestant school, because too many other kids had discovered the whereabouts of the old one. Then they heard the
ambulance.

It was racing along 142nd Avenue, the main artery from
downtown. They could tell from the sound that it was turning
at 103rd Street; that it was stopping just past 143rd, right by the
corner where Robert lived. He started running, excited at first.
Tommy and the other boys galloped along beside him for a
couple of blocks, but once the siren had stopped, they lost
interest and turned off at St. George's Crescent to go home.

There was now silence, except for his oxfords on the
planks, the zip of the wind around his face, the pounding of

his heart, the flies buzzing in the ditch. Robert's excitement began to wane, to be replaced by a cold, belated thought: this was too awfully close . . .

Long before he reached the corner, he could see front doors opening and neighbours coming out on their verandahs. Others stood in their gateways. A few of the smaller kids were sitting or standing on the curb. They were all looking toward his house. And then he could see the creamy white snout of the ambulance sticking out from behind the hedge.

He ran the last block, knowing there could be no other explanation. For all her steel and fire, Mama was in her seventies. There was no one else in the house. He started to pray, but the prayers were shattered by bursts of panic. By the time he pushed open the side gate and charged into the yard, he could tell at a glance that the worst had happened. One ambulance attendant was backing out of the front door, gripping the handles of a stretcher, while another held the verandah's screen door open. There was a plastic mask over Mama's mouth and nose, attached to an oxygen tank. He caught only one glimpse of her as the attendants made their way, crablike, down the front steps: her face was as white and wrinkled as used Kleenex, so white that it was hard to tell where the skin ended and the hair began. It was as if she had aged ten or twenty years since she'd kissed him goodbye and sent him off with his lunch that morning. They had a brown blanket over her and a neatly folded sheet tucked up to her neck. She had always been thin, but now it seemed as though there was barely even a skeleton under the blanket. He didn't run up to her. He stood in the middle of the golf-green lawn, paralysed, knowing with precocious certainty that his life had just changed completely. Mama had been nearly everything. It was as though a plug had been yanked and his world was suddenly swirling down a drain, following her into darkness.

After the funeral, at the reception in Mama's house – his house – something strange happened. Although one aunt came up and put her arm around him for a minute, and an uncle gripped his shoulder and squeezed it to reassure him, everyone else stayed back. His cousins, and there were a dozen of them, would not even look him in the eye. Dimly, he was aware of a space, a physical space, opening between himself and everyone there, as though he had somehow become unhooked from them. No matter how the configuration of people changed, there was always a little circle around him where no one was standing or sitting. He had no idea what it meant. They all seemed to share some secret that they weren't communicating. As an only child, he was used to being by himself. It didn't hurt particularly, because in all the family the only one he had really been close to was Mama. Now that she was in the pale blue coffin with its little clasps clipped shut, lowered into that doorway-sized hole in the ground, with clay thrown in on top, he was just that much more removed from the rest of them, as though he was locked in some sort of invisible box of his own. He waited numbly for someone to say what no one was saying. He overheard somebody remark about "not having the nerve to show her face at her own mother's funeral."

Finally, after most of the family had drifted away, with much hugging and crying and patting and a surprising amount of laughter, an uncle took him out on the verandah and told him he'd be living with his real mother from now on. All Robert could do was shake his head. Real mother? The one who'd run off? The sinner? But his real mother was . . . Mama.

When he started to cry, his uncle said sternly: "Be a man." He was ten.

By the time a taxi showed up a couple of hours later, it was dusk. An uncle and aunt had packed Robert's clothes and toys and school books into two suitcases. He was already dressed in his blue Sunday-best uniform for his first meeting with his mother.

The woman who stepped out of the car was surprisingly young and good-looking. She was slim but not thin, with long, brownish-blonde hair and blue eyes. The man who was driving got out of the car but wouldn't come up to the house. Robert assumed he was the taxi driver. In the back seat were two kids. Robert heard his uncle address the woman as "Mary." That jarred. How could this woman, this sinner, have a sacred name like Mary? She looked down at Robert irritably, indicated his luggage, and said: "Is that it?" When he nodded, she picked up the suitcases herself, saying to him, "Come on, then," and headed back toward the taxi.

Knowing he had been betrayed in some terrible and final way, Robert turned his back on his uncle and aunt and followed her out to the street. The taxi driver took the suitcases and flopped them into the trunk, and Mary held the back door open and introduced the children inside as Harvey and Dorothy. The boy was slightly bigger than Robert, the girl slightly smaller. They showed no sign of joy at meeting him, they were as sullen as Robert himself. Harvey shifted over to make room only when his mother snapped at him. When the driver, a big, moustached man with curly black hair, got back in the car and slammed the door, Mary said: "This is your father." The man looked back at him. "'allo, kid. I call you Row-bear, eh? You call me Fodder." Robert realized with a shock that the man spoke with an accent like that of many of the priests. He was French-Canadian.

He took one last wild look at the house with its huge verandah and the neighbourhood with the wooden sidewalk and the orderly rows of poplar and birch trees. Except for his uncle and aunt, standing on the steps waving tentatively, no one had come out to say goodbye.

As his eyes adjusted to the gloom inside the taxi, he took a couple of furtive looks at his brother and sister. They had black hair like him, although that was the only similarity he could see. But what he noticed most about them was that they seemed afraid of something. Very afraid.

In the days that followed, it didn't take long for Robert to get confirmation from Harvey and Dorothy that "Fodder" wasn't their real father, even though they all bore his last name. His first name was Gervais, which sure wasn't Scottish, even though Mama had said that Royer was a good Scottish name. This man pronounced Royer "Roy-aye."

It also didn't take long to discover what his brother and sister were afraid of: the big French-Canadian had a short fuse, especially when he drank, which was often. He'd grown up on a farm in Quebec, where children were strictly to be seen and not heard. He'd married Mary on the rebound from her first marriage, and he had no patience with "brats." Robert, it quickly became clear, was a brat. Worse, he was, as Royer said, an "instigator." Soon Robert, endowed with a sense of dignity, made the mistake of talking back to his stepfather . . . who promptly sent him flying across the kitchen with a back-handed wallop and an expletive in French. The belt was used often.

For all her strictness, Mama had always treated him as somebody essentially equal, somebody important and central. Suddenly, he was just another mouth to feed. There were only two bedrooms in the wartime prefab house that the Royers were renting on the outskirts of Edmonton. Mary had picked up a second-hand fold-out couch for Robert and set it up in the room the other children shared, leaving scarcely any space to play, even though the three of them were expected to stay out of the way as much as possible.

Robert was still in mourning for Mama. Mary remained a stranger to him, a woman who seemed so weak and unfeeling that she made hardly any protest when her husband was hard on her kids. That was just "his way," she explained to them. The only useful information Robert got out of her was the name of his actual father: Albert. Albert Calihoo. Funny last name. He lived out of town somewhere. That was all Robert could find out.

After several encounters with his stepfather's temper, he started trying to do what Harvey and Dorothy automatically did when Gervais was around: whisper and stay out of the way.

Except he wasn't used to whispering and staying out of the way. In the manner of ten-year-olds, Robert soon progressed from indifference towards the man to passionate hatred. His rebellion moved equally quickly from the unconscious to the deliberate.

Within eight months, Mary had decided that the whole business was hopeless. Robert had been "spoiled" by his grandmother. There was no teaching him anything; he wouldn't listen. He was uncontrollable and disrespectful. He was rude to his stepfather and rude to her. He was always putting them down. Who did he think he was anyway? Worst of all, he was a bad influence on the other children. After he'd run away a couple of times, and the police had had to look for him, she decided what Robert needed was proper discipline. She enrolled him in St. Mary's Boys' Home in downtown Edmonton, a live-in school for delinquents, run by the Jesuits.

For the next two years, Robert endured: up in the morning, wash your face, mass, breakfast, exercise outside, into school, Catechism, noon prayers, school, writing, arithmetic, more Catechism, supper prayers, supper, vespers. At night, the priests would take turns walking back and forth in the hallways, praying and reading, always on patrol. The Jesuits, of course, were legendary disciplinarians. They'd slap the boys with their hands, hit them with rulers and straps. There was a father who was a queer, the other boys warned him, but Robert managed to avoid him. On the whole, he took to the Jesuit brand of education no more readily than he had to his stepfather's theory of child-raising. The hurricane fence that surrounded the asphalt school grounds made the school into a prison, but it wasn't enough to hold him. He ran away half a dozen times; each time he was tracked down by the police and returned to St. Mary's.

In the end, the Jesuits decided he was too much trouble. With his mother's permission, they placed him in a foster home in another section of Edmonton. The Coutoure family was a large, well-established French-Canadian family in a middle-class neighbourhood. While living with them, Robert started attending Sacred Heart Church, but the mass was in Latin and the sermon was in French, and he was soon sick of being dragged there. Life with the Coutoures, after life with Mama with the big house almost to himself on 103rd, was a crowded, suffocating experience, with the whole family involved in one Catholic social event after another, from the Knights of Columbus to the LaSalle Club. Before long, Robert was no less resentful of his foster parents than he had been of his mother and stepfather.

And so, one day he decided to run away for good. Taking a pocketful of change, he slipped downtown, found a phone booth, called the operator, and asked for a listing for Albert Calihoo.

Chapter 3

Quite a Different World

IT TOOK A LONG TIME FOR THE CALL TO GO THROUGH. THE
operator was irritated that Robert didn't know where Albert
Calihoo lived, but she eventually traced him through a provincial directory to a town whose name the boy didn't recognize. The operator there put him through to a number that
rang and rang and rang before a woman's voice came on. Her
speech was slow, and she had an accent Robert didn't recognize. Albert? She'd have to go look for him. There was another
delay, so long that Robert was thinking about hanging up and
trying again, then finally the sound of boots and a man's wary
voice: "Yeah?"

Robert took a deep breath: "Guess who this is?"

"Who's that?"

"This is your son."

A long pause, then: "Yeah? Which one?"

After a few awkward minutes of greeting, and Robert's
explanation that he had run away, the man asked him where
he was and promised to come and get him. The wait outside
the telephone booth was as long as it was agonizing. Not
knowing from which direction his father would be coming,
and afraid that at any minute the police might show up and
drag him back to the foster home, Robert alternated between

16

ecstatic expectation and dread. It was early in the year. He could see his breath. He kept his hands in his jacket pocket and stamped his feet to keep them warm. After a while his ears began to tingle.

When a battered old green Hudson pulled up on the other side of the road it stirred memories, but Robert was too absorbed in the moment to put them together in any sensible fashion. The Indian at the wheel must want to make a phone call, Robert thought. But when the guy didn't get out of the car, a small rush of fear passed through him. What was with that guy? Robert looked nervously up and down the street, hoping there might be somebody else around. There wasn't; the street was entirely deserted. All Mama's warnings about talking to strangers came back. Especially . . . Indians.

An odd memory tumbled to mind: Mama taking him down to Charles Camsell Hospital to have dental work done. It was peculiar that they went to Camsell, since most of the time they went to the General Hospital where Dr. Wineloss and the nuns worked. Dr. Wineloss was a famous and important doctor. Charles Camsell Hospital was a much older place. There were a lot of people there with tuberculosis, and a lot of those were Indians. He and Mama had been kept in a separate section, but they watched silently as the Indians went by. Mama said they were "dying off anyway."

Robert didn't like being watched by dying people. It was almost like being watched by ghosts. He had a pretty good idea of what ghosts would look like. He'd sneaked a look at some horror comics in the drugstore. The ghosts were always like skeletons, with sunken cheeks and staring eyes, and they usually didn't say anything either, just looked out from dark eye sockets – like these Indians. It was scary. He'd hoped they were Catholics so they could get into Heaven. Mama had said mostly they weren't anything. He didn't like going out to Charles Camsell Hospital, seeing the dying Indians. Why couldn't he just go to Dr. Wineloss for his teeth, the way he did for everything else?

"Because," snapped Mama, "it's covered."

As he stood there, thinking now, squirming uneasily under the scrutiny of this Indian in the parked car, yet another odd memory spilled into Robert's mind. A few times when he had brought in the mail there had been some envelopes like the ones that cheques come in, and up in the left-hand corner had been printed the words: DEPARTMENT OF INDIAN AFFAIRS. Mama had always done the same thing with them that she'd done with other envelopes with cheques in them: she had taken them down to the bank. He had often thought it strange, but never dwelled on it.

That Indian in the old clunker of a Hudson was watching him all right, a strange expression on his face. Finally he opened the door and climbed out of the car: a scowling, heavy-set man, dressed in faded, frayed, ill-fitting clothes. Robert tried to ignore him, but he ambled across the road and came straight towards him. Robert tensed to run. The man stopped a couple of yards away and looked down at him.

"Waitin' for an invitation?" he asked.

Robert's fear mounted almost to panic. The Indian was huge and terrifying, yet there was a note of amusement in his voice. Something was extremely funny. And the voice, yes, he recognized the voice. He knew exactly whose voice it was. He had just heard it on the phone. His mind had gone blank. He wasn't reacting. "You ain't figured it out yet, eh?" the Indian said. "Guess your Mom didn't tell you much."

All Robert could do was stare, stunned. He managed to shake his head.

His father sighed, then said: "Come on." He headed back to the car. Numbly, Robert started after him. He had been given a command. He obeyed. He climbed into the car, still without saying a word, and sat there for a long time in silence, trying to find out if he had any feelings at all other than the fear that clutched his heart.

The drive took an hour. Albert wasn't inclined to talk much. Robert couldn't think of anything to say. They headed out Stony Plain Road, west towards Jasper, past Cheap Charlie's Garage, with piles of rubber tires and old wrecked threshing machines in the lot, past brand-new stucco motels, old slouched barns with their red paint flecked and peeled, past Spruce Grove and towards Edson, the land starting to canter as the prairie rolled in like waves of drifted soil on the slopes leading to the Rockies, the great checkerboard fields of wheat and rapeseed giving way to clumps of birch, spruce, willow, and black poplar. Albert, in a rare burst of speech, explained that it was on account of those bushes that the Woodland Cree got their name. "We're Cree," he said.

The only other information he volunteered was the story of how he'd come to marry Robert's mother, Mary. She'd been an adopted kid. Turned out to be a hellraiser. "Mama" had kept her until she was a teenager, but by then she had so many problems with her she put her in a convent for wayward girls, a place called The Good Shepherd Home. There, Mary had met an Indian girl named Florence. They hatched a plot to escape over the wall. They got away and ended up going to a dance together at a reserve. There Mary met Albert. She was sixteen. If a girl got married, she couldn't be taken back to the convent, so Mary became Mrs. Calihoo. They'd had three kids. But Mary couldn't tolerate life on the reserve, eating rabbits all the time, so she left while Albert was away, met this Royer guy, took off with him and the other two kids, leaving Robert with his grandmother. "Your grandmother didn't mind you too much 'cause you looked white." That was about it. Albert lapsed back into silence.

Long scallops of shadow fanned out from behind the hills in the late afternoon light as they drove. The snow packed on the north slopes was blue. Windbreaks made of wired-together wooden pickets were rolled up along the road ready to be put up against the serious snow and wind to come. A purple-blue haze thickened over the hills so that the horizon to the west became a smudge. The grass was the colour of a lion's hide. In the copper light even the bare white birch trees were tan, giving the whole setting a dun-coloured texture.

Albert turned off the highway onto a gravel road, and then off the gravel road onto a one-lane trail called, for some reason, Correction Line, which was not much more than a couple of pot-holed ruts. The bottom of the car crunched repeatedly. Ahead, Robert saw a faded wooden sign nailed to a fencepost – "Michel Band Reserve." Beyond that, a low cluster of tiny log cabins and tarpaper shacks hunched against the earth. There were bent, rusted buckets outside the shacks, garbage strewn about on the hard-frozen ground, the stripped-down remains of several old cars, including a Model T Ford, weeds and junk everywhere. Empty liquor bottles were piled up in pyramids of broken glass. A couple of emaciated dogs that looked like they had been skinned alive ran yapping beside the car as Albert bumped out of the ruts and came to a halt in front of a structure, not much more than ten feet by twenty feet, made of logs that were scarcely more than thick branches with clay packed between them. A cracked window was covered over with cardboard. Robert thought at first they had stopped at the barn. He was still looking around for the farmhouse when Albert said: "We'll see your Granddad first. See if he eats you alive."

When they got out of the car, the blast of wind whistling across the barren plain cut through Robert's jacket and he shivered. But it was more than just the wind chilling him. He still felt as if he were walking in a dream, except that the dream had become a nightmare. The buckets outside the cabin were filled to the brim with shit. Albert had to duck his head to go through the door. They stepped down into a darkened interior, the air thick with smoke from a stove made out of an old gasoline drum. Robert could see a tattered blanket dividing the cabin in half, a table covered with oilcloth, a few kitchen chairs, mattresses on the floor, the remains of a meal, and . . . faces. Small dark faces, streaked with soot, staring at him. How many? He couldn't count. It was crowded; there were maybe a dozen kids. The first thing that struck him was the smell of smoke that hung around them. Their hair was uncombed, their eyes huge, their nails long and dirty. Most of them were barefoot. Some were wrapped in faded blankets as they huddled around the stove. There was the smell of urine and something else, something dead.

A huge Indian – so tall his head seemed to touch the ceiling – lurched to his feet, dwarfing Robert's father. The giant wore his hair in two long black braids. There was a terrible scar across his face, and his nose had been turned almost on its side. He had seen the look of horror on Robert's face as he scanned the crowded, smoke-filled hovel.

The enormous Indian's mouth twisted and the words grated out of him: "This's what it means to be Indian."

Chapter 4

Getting Used to Things

"THIS IS WHAT IT MEANS TO BE INDIAN." IT MEANT THAT BATHS, as Robert thought of them, were a thing of the past. When he asked where the bathroom was, the other kids pointed outside. When he asked about a tub, they pointed to a pail in which the handful of cracked dishes and bent pots and pans and utensils were stacked in greasy water. What about a toothbrush? They sombrely shook their heads.

It meant not being able to find anything to read except a few tattered old magazines that were brought in as fire-starter. It meant listening to the wind keening across the plain, like a fist beating at the cardboard over the window and tearing at the tarpaper on the roof.

It meant getting used to being hungry most of the time, except when Granddad or Albert came back from hunting, usually with rabbits, but every once in a while with a deer or – so seldom that it was a major event – a moose. It meant letting his hair get longer and longer because nobody was inclined to cut it.

It meant getting used to bedbugs, and waking up one morning on the old spring mattress on the floor, scratching his head, and discovering that he had lice.

It meant dirt under his fingernails and toenails, and wearing the same unwashed clothes for months at a time.

It meant going to bed every night and praying that when he woke up in the morning this would be over. He'd be back home at Mama's, with the sparkling linoleum and the hardwood you could see yourself in and the warm baths and his great big bed all to himself with clean sheets and pillows and Mama's cooking.

But there was only the wind, the thin crackling of the fire in the converted fuel drum, the coughing of the other kids, the itching in his hair, the hunger in his belly. And most nights the adults were drinking and yelling and groaning and howling and falling down. Outside, there were sounds of fights and breaking glass, and men and women cursing in the strange, sibilant Cree language that he had quickly come to hate, even as he strained to understand it.

This must be purgatory, he thought bitterly. Maybe he had died, halfway died. He sure wasn't in the world as he knew it any longer. Time and again he started across the rolling plains with the idea of trekking to Edmonton, but it was a long way to the horizon and he knew he would freeze to death on the way. He would have to wait until spring, then he'd make his escape. There was absolutely no doubt in his mind. This was all a mistake anyway. He wasn't one of these people. He didn't belong. He was white. He could sing "O Canada" and "God Save the Queen" and recite the Lord's Prayer. This wasn't what was meant to happen to him in life. It couldn't be. He prayed relentlessly – for a month or so. Then it sank in that the prayers weren't working. They were as useless as most things were around there. Nothing worked. Everything was broken, potholed, threadbare, left-over, dulled, worn down, tattered, rusted, crumbled, plugged, jammed, cracked, frayed, bent, busted, rotted, patched, jury-rigged, stripped down, picked over, chewed. It was as though everything had been ground up and swallowed and spat out. And it was not just the buildings and the machinery and everything inside

and outside that was like that, the adults were like that too.
The reserve was a pounded-down junk heap at the very ass-
end of Indian history.

And yet, bit by bit, he began to adjust. He adjusted to the
feeling of hunger; he got thinner, and he simply didn't eat as
much. He got used to being dirty, to not changing his clothes,
to not having clean socks and underwear. He got used to his
hair being long, his fingernails and toenails unclipped. He
got used to bedbugs and lice. He even got used to having a
runny nose and colds all the time. Everybody had some kind
of disease, after all. By early summer, he had gotten used to a
lot of things. He was starting to understand a bit of Cree, even
to speak some, and without anyone around to correct his
English, his grammar had slipped. Mama would not have
been pleased. The Catholic thought patterns, of course,
would be there forever at some level.

It hadn't taken too long for him to realize that, for the most
part, Indians were a non-verbal people. There was no need to
fill the air with banter and babble. He could still crack jokes,
but the shorter the better; one word was ideal. The people
around him dealt with each other largely through eye contact
and body posture and lip movement, and few words were
uttered.

When the adults were around, the kids stayed quiet.
Nobody started teasing or pulling hair. Adults were the centre
of the world, no doubt about it, whether they were playing
cards, drinking, singing, or just sitting talking. Gervais Royer
would have loved it. Rather than making trouble about this,
Robert picked up from the other kids the habit of avoiding
collisions with the adult world. Being reticent was the appropriate style.

The other kids, being Indian, withdrew shyly from Robert.
He was dressed differently, after all. He looked like a white
kid and talked like a white kid. Also, at first, he was pushy in
a way none of them could understand. The Indian kids didn't
tell anybody where to go or what to do. They watched to see
what Robert would do, but didn't help to guide him. Thanks

to them, however, he wasn't Robert any more. From the first day, nobody would call him Robert. He was just plain Bob. After a while, he got used to it. He even started to think of himself as Bob. As for his last name, that good Scottish name bequeathed by his French-Canadian stepfather, it just faded. He was one of the Calihoo kids, that was all. Bob Calihoo, if anybody asked.

However, by then one thing had finally happened that made life different in a way he liked – in a way he more than liked. It began to make life on the reserve seem bearable after all. Albert started teaching him how to hunt.

It was the kind of hunting the Woodland Cree had been doing since . . . forever. They'd approach a clump of trees that showed all the little trails that the game had made to all the possible hiding places in the midst of the clump. On one side of the bushes, father and son would set snares at the entrance-ways to the trails, then they'd go around to the other side. With sticks in hand, they'd start yelling and whacking the bushes and trees as they marched forward. The rabbits would head the other way, naturally. In the average clump of trees, even in the lowlands down around the swamps and creeks, they'd snare two or three rabbits at a time, and sometimes with a bit of luck they'd snare a grouse as well. Bob learned that you had to keep well back from the grouse and try to herd them along, otherwise they'd take off and that would be the end of it. There was no point wasting a shot on them. Bullets were far too precious to be used except for a sure thing. Bob learned to hike as much as twenty miles to bag a duck, rather than waste a bullet. It was not uncommon to go that far either.

It was lean, meagre hunting, but it was hunting, and for Bob it opened up a whole new world. He had only been looking at the landscape before that. Now he began to understand it. Sometimes, when they were hunting, he and Albert would go into the bush and sit still for an hour, hardly breathing. The birds would spot them right away, and screech at them, and every animal that could run would run away, and the others would hop and slither and burrow and flap away. But, little by little, the bush would come back to life. One by one, the animals would return. They'd still be angry at the intruders and know they were there, but they would grudgingly come to accept them as being a harmless new part of the environment.

The land seemed to spread out forever. Yet his Dad – he was even starting to feel comfortable with the idea of the big, fierce, strange Indian named Albert as "Dad" – seemed to know every corner of it. He didn't talk much when they were out hunting, because that wasn't what you did, but the odd story came out. There was the story about how Albert had run away himself when he was a kid, younger than Bob. He ran away and built himself a shelter in the middle of the bush and survived for a whole winter alone with no gun, just a knife, setting snares, catching fish through the ice, keeping a fire going, just like "them old-time Indians." Once, during that winter, he swore he saw a buffalo off in the distance. That was in the late 1920s. A buffalo running loose? In the old days the woodlands on the edge of the Rockies were as far west as the great herds came. This was the outer edge of their domain. It was the only time in his life that Albert had ever seen a wild buffalo. There had been a few still in his own dad's day, at least when he was a kid. But by the time the First World War came, there weren't any buffalo anywhere except in the parks, and if an Indian tried to hunt one they'd lock him up and throw away the key, "like it was our fault or somethin'."

Another time, Albert recalled when he'd gone after moose with Miles, his hunting partner, up north of the reserve. They had split up, each lugging his Lee Enfield. After a while, Albert heard a shot. Thinking Miles must have bagged something, Albert headed over to join him. At the edge of a natural salt lick he saw the moose lying on the ground. No sign of Miles. Must have gone after another one. Albert went over, laid his rifle against the moose's flank, and sat down on top of it to start rolling a cigarette. Suddenly, the moose was up on its feet, dumping Albert, the gun, and the cigarette makings, and charging away into the bush. Sometimes moose will lie down when their horns are drying. Albert had been quite wrong to assume it was dead.

He laughed at the fancy new rifles with scopes brought along by the hunters up from the States in their Jeeps. Albert's thirty-dollar three-ought-three was all he ever needed. Scopes were no good in the bush anyway. Sometimes he'd hire out as a guide and lead the Americans around in the bush for two or three days. He knew where the moose were all along – he could have taken them there in an hour – but the idea was to go camping with them for a few days and get paid. Back before the game got "scarced out," it used to be hard finding places to take them where there weren't any moose.

There were moments, indeed, when it occurred to Bob that, despite the hunger and the poverty, there was a plus side to his father not being able to find work. He had lots of time on his hands, and so they could hunt together. For a kid who had been raised with no father around, to have one around day after day, and to go stalking the hills and lowlands and bush with him in search of game, was a feeling that at moments flared up almost into pain, it felt so good.

At first, when they hunted, it seemed that the land rolled on and on forever. His Dad knew all the animal trails hidden along the edges of lakes and creeks and swamps, and these were what they usually followed. But every now and then, when game was scarcer than usual and they had to wander farther, preserving those precious bullets, they came across dirt roads, and sometimes gravel roads, and sometimes fences. Albert never hesitated, either hunching down and pushing himself through holes on all fours, like the prairie-dogs and coyotes and grouse had already done, or sometimes straddling the barbed wire, holding it down for Bob to clamber gingerly up and over. A few times, they spotted farmers in the distance on their tractors. Dogs barked and started toward them, but were called back. Bob was reminded uncomfortably of Mama seeing Indians cutting across Uncle Andy's property and wanting him to shoot them, but Albert didn't show any sign of being worried. He just ignored the farmers and they ignored him, and he kept on going.

The eastern boundary of the reserve extended along open undulating prairie interspersed with groves of poplar, hay marshes, and bottom lands. Southward, the land was much the same, getting hillier and more densely wooded toward the western edge. The northern boundary passed through low and gently heaving country, covered with clumps of willow, spruce, and more poplar. Along the western reaches, a thick canopy of fir trees moved down from the foothills. There was a sixteen-mile stretch of rolling prairie in the middle with good dark soil. A small river that was some twenty-five feet wide and just deep enough so Bob had to cling to his father's shoulders to wade across it drained into Sandy Lake, a two-mile-wide, six-mile-long sheet of water ringed by bulrushes, where the duck hunting was best. There were fine white sand beaches with a bed of sandstone extending a hundred feet out into the water. Pike and jack-fish were always easy to catch.

It occurred to him one day that a thousand years ago all this would have been the same. The thought pleased him deeply.

Chapter 5

"Not Much Left"

IN THE SEVEN TARPAPER-AND-LOG SHACKS ON THE RESERVE, there were seventeen adults and a score of kids. The Chief was Bob's Uncle Rod, but Sam, his grandfather, was the natural leader, the opinion-shaper. Sam was not only a big man with a mean temper, he was a legend. He was reputed to have beaten up twenty-seven Mounties once, and they still couldn't restrain him, so they had to deputize a dozen Indians in order to get the handcuffs on him. That's how tough he was. He had been drunk on that occasion, not surprisingly. Indians, of course, weren't supposed to drink alcohol, period, but to make matters worse Sam had been drunk during the annual pilgrimage to Lac St. Anne, when thousands of Catholic Indians and Métis from all over North America gather at the shore of the holy lake. It was odd: miracles were said to have occurred at the lake, and the Virgin Mary had been seen here by a child years before, but in Cree the name of the place was Devil's Lake. Maybe that was what brought out the bad side in Sam, although it came out often enough, anyway. It came out whenever he drank – which was as often as possible.

Bob could understand why his own father, Albert, had run away in the middle of winter and braved the blizzards to avoid

Sam's alcoholic wrath. But even without booze, Sam's whole
personality could change at the drop of a hat. Mostly, he was
Sam Calihoo, FBI – FBI meaning, he said, "Fucking Big
Indian." But sometimes he was somebody else, somebody
from another time and place who spoke a language all his
own and did not recognize even his own kin. When Sam
changed like that, everybody gave him a wide berth, pretending they didn't hear him or see him, and hoping to hell he
wouldn't notice them either.

Bob could see that when his own father got drunk, he
sometimes drifted like that a bit too. He wasn't himself. But he
wasn't nearly as bad as Sam. Albert's self might forget where
it belonged, but it would never float much farther than a few
inches away. Sam's self, when it disappeared, vanished
totally. This other guy who got into his head, no one had a
clue where he came from – or where he went. But it was easy
enough to tell when he was there in Sam's place. A strange
light appeared in Sam's eyes. He looked down on people like
people looked down on dogs. This was what Albert had
meant when he said: "See if he eats you alive." You got the
feeling he just might. And Sam, in everything but name, was
Chief of the Calihoos. He had a lot of influence on the reserve.
Everybody was scared of him. So when Sam started talking
about something called "enfranchisement," people listened;
they didn't dare not listen.

Sam, in turn, had been listening to Johnny Rodgers. Johnny
was the illegitimate son of an Englishman. His mother, a
Calihoo, had come back to the reserve pregnant some forty-
odd years before, and the council had voted to adopt her son
as a full band member. So Johnny had voting rights – the same
voting rights Bob was told he'd have when he turned twenty-
one, and the same voting rights as his nine half-brothers and
sisters, Albert's children with his second wife, Phyllis.

The talk about enfranchisement had been going on since
long before Bob arrived at the reserve, but it hadn't gotten
anywhere. It was hard to get the seventeen adults together;
somebody or other was usually off hunting ducks or fishing

or in Edmonton, probably blind drunk. That's where most of the other Calihoos who didn't live on the reservation were, too, although some had wandered away as far as Calgary, and a few to distant Vancouver.

Bob had asked: "How many Calihoos are there?"

His Dad had shrugged. "A lot more'n there is here."

"Why don't they come back?"

"Nuttin' to come back to."

Another time he asked: "How big is the reserve?"

"Used to stretch to Banff," Albert replied.

"Yeah, but now?"

Albert shrugged: "Not much left. Twenty-one square miles."

"How come it got so small?"

But his Dad lapsed into silence. For whatever reasons, the reserve had been shrinking steadily, Bob gathered. It had once been a mighty thing. Now it was this barren little garbage heap, surrounded by farms and roads.

"How many Calihoos were there?"

"Hard to say. Maybe a hundred."

"What happened to them?"

A bitter look, another shrug, more silence.

The past was one of the subjects nobody mentioned much, although Bob picked up oblique references now and again. There had been a great-grandfather who had owned the biggest ranch in all of Alberta and had married one of the daughters of Simon Fraser, the explorer. That was before the Calihoos "took treaty," whatever that meant. And there was somebody named "Iroquois Louis," the forefather of them all, who had done something great once upon a time, but Bob couldn't pin anyone down as to what exactly it was. And why was he named "Iroquois Louis" if they were Cree?

Tales in which the Indians triumphed were rare, but there was one good story about an Indian who had spotted a white man stealing stacks of upland hay he'd left along a trail to feed his own horses. The Indian had sneaked up behind the white man, who was carrying the hay on his back, lit a match, and set the hay on fire. The white man dropped the burning hay and ran, never looking back.

But mostly the past was like the purple-grey haze that often spread out over the rolling hills in late afternoon into which everything faded, leaving only the worn warped tabletop of the present. There was a glint of reflected light here, a nugget-glimmer there, the glow of dying coals. But everything now was ash and dust and hard muck and shit.

That's why everything Granddad was saying, when he was himself and not drinking, made so much sense. There was "no percentage" in staying on the reserve. Sam said it again and again. "You want to die of pneumonia?" he'd ask. "What if you cut off your arm or a finger with an axe and bleed to death before you finally get to hospital?"

Sam and Johnny Rodgers made their rounds of the shacks, arguing the case for enfranchisement in English and Cree: "You stay here and you take a chance on killing your kids. There's nothing for Indians on the reserve. This is a hopeless place. You can't live here in poverty, with disease and lice and unsanitary conditions. We could do better if we had some money. Then maybe we could buy a farm or a business and get away from this."

Johnny Rodgers would go on at great length about something called the "double mother clause." According to Johnny, if your mother was a white woman, when you turned twenty-one you could be enfranchised, which meant you could vote in Canadian elections, something Indians still weren't allowed to do. And then if you married a white woman, your kids were automatically enfranchised, whether you had been enfranchised or not, because they had had a white grandmother as well as a white mother. It didn't matter what you called yourself, or whether you were in line to be hereditary Chief, or even if you *were* the Chief; under the law you and your kids were automatically and officially white. It was like your Indian blood got drained out of you, leaving you pale forever.

The Indian Affairs Department was going to pass a law

making all Indians white anyway, Johnny Rodgers said. He'd been told so by the Indian Agent, Mr. Lapp. Mr. Lapp had said the same thing to Sam and to Albert, whose kids would all be affected by the double mother clause, since both his ex-wife and his present wife were white. Bob heard Albert quoting Mr. Lapp as saying: "Your kids are going to get cut out if you don't surrender this reserve. Then they won't get anything."

Albert didn't know what to think about it all. He didn't want to hang around arguing about this and that; he just wanted to go out hunting and trapping and drink a little wine and beer, maybe some spirits if he could get them.

Albert's second wife, Phyllis, didn't think much of enfranchisement at all. She didn't believe a word Johnny Rodgers said, for one thing. Or Sam. What did Sam know anyway? Sam was crazy. As for Johnny, Phyllis pointed out, since he had been adopted by the band he was on the Indian List all right, but his father hadn't been a Calihoo or even an Indian, and unless his kids married Indians, they wouldn't be band members. With things going the way they were, with most of the band members already gone, Johnny's kids would probably marry off the reserve. It made good sense, Phyllis said, for Johnny to urge enfranchisement now, so that he could get a piece of the action; there wasn't likely to be anything in it for his own kids later. But that was his own sad story; she couldn't see how it applied to Albert or Sam. They had both had Indian fathers, they were both Indians, and their kids were Indians, even Albert's half-white kids. But nobody paid much attention to Phyllis. She was white, a second wife, and just a woman after all.

However, there was one thing about enfranchisement that Albert definitely did understand, and so did Sam, and so did every other man left on the reserve. If you gave up being an Indian, accepted being a Canadian citizen, you could vote, sure, and that was great. But you could also go into a beer parlour or a bar and drink, instead of having to hide in the bushes or in a back lane, gulping down booze you had to get some white man to buy for you or guzzling bootleg all the time. Most of the guys who landed in jail ended up there because they got caught drinking, it was as simple as that. Drinking was the big crime that Indians committed and white men didn't, because for white men, it wasn't a crime. If you wanted to take a white girl out, where could you take her? Not to a bar, that was for certain. Pretty hard to impress a girl if you can't even buy her a drink.

As an advocate, Johnny had one thing going for him that nobody else on the reserve had. He claimed to have read the Indian Act. If he said it said something, who could argue? They could always ask Mr. Lapp when he came to visit, but that wasn't very often. Maybe once a year he'd show up, and then he'd go into a shack with Sam and Johnny and Uncle Rod and maybe a couple of the other men, if they weren't away hunting. They'd talk for a few hours, then the Indian Agent would emerge, climb into his car, and drive away.

He seemed to know the farmers in the area better than he did the Indians. His car could be seen parked outside their houses now and then. Of course, most of the farmers were leasing reserve land, and although they didn't pay much for it, it was something regular, so maybe Mr. Lapp had business with them, making sure the Indians were getting a fair deal and all. Phyllis sneered at this. "He's workin' for them," she said. "Think he ain't?"

The deal with enfranchisement, as Johnny and Sam pointed out, was that everybody would get some money for the reserve land. It could be as much as $20,000. Now that was a lot of money. With that kind of money, a man could do pretty well in the white man's world. Not only would they get to vote – and to drink – but they'd get paid for the privilege! And what was the point of sticking around here on this god-forsaken tract of barren land, the game scarced out and most of the trees gone and no services and no future? Still, Albert shook his head.

"What about the treaty?" Phyllis demanded. "Didn't it say something about having the use of this land for as long as the sun sets and the rivers flow or something?"

Sam glowered at her. Johnny sneered. But Bob thought about that. The shacks were awful and conditions inside were like a nightmare. But out on the land, it was different. It was clean. Being out there, alone, with the wind in your hair, listening for the small sounds in the bush and watching for movements that might betray a groundhog in the waving grass, easing up quietly toward the top of the hill to peer down the other side and see if anything was moving, swimming in the lake – even if it was still so cold it took your breath away – lying on your back on the still-damp, still-cold earth, looking up at the clouds gliding over the tops of last year's dry grass, a whisky-jack bucking the west wind . . . or at night with all the universe up there hanging like broken chandeliers or falling with infinite slowness toward you, that was something special.

By late summer, Bob had been on the reserve less than a year, but thoughts of running away to Edmonton were gone.

He had shot his first duck, and the moment would remain with him all his life. The sudden stillness all around as the shot echoed away across the lake, the dog Butch whining with excitement at his side, the duck tumbling in the right direction towards the bulrushes, Butch tearing loose through the reeds, Bob's dawning realization that he had crossed the ancient line from boyhood to adulthood. He had a sense, for the first time since his world had been shattered by the death of his grandmother, of being in the right place, doing the right thing. He felt a new seriousness, an actual flash of pride. He was a Woodland Cree alone on the vast land – hunting. This was almost like the pictures he had seen in books. It was the very first time he'd felt good about his Indianness.

By now, he was comfortable with his longer hair, too. He liked the way the wind moved it caressingly around his head and neck. Worries about having regular baths had long since passed from his mind. Although he was dirty, he didn't itch any more. If he found a louse, he picked it off casually and flicked it away. No big deal. He had discovered that if he was nice to some of the older women, they'd share their precious supplies of ginger root or muskrat root, which eased a sore throat. A few drops added to warm water were also good for earaches. Once, when he had had a fever, one of the old women had boiled wild mint and given it to him and brought the fever under control within hours. When summer came, he began gathering lady's-slippers for the women to dry for medicine.

Summer meant, above all, more to eat. Rabbits were everywhere. Fish were easier to catch. When there was some money from slash-burning or odd jobs at the various farmers' places, the men and women of the reserve came back with fresh vegetables as well as booze. And everywhere there were blueberries, crowberries, and cranberries to be picked. Summer was a good time to be an Indian.

Chapter 6

No Need for a Treaty Card

IN AUGUST, THE DEBATE OVER ENFRANCHISEMENT CAME TO A head; a big meeting was called. A "committee" was involved – a couple of priests, Indian Agent Lapp, several local farmers, a lawyer, and a judge. All seventeen adults from the reserve attended. Sam Calihoo and Johnny Rodgers did most of the talking.

The meeting was held in the schoolhouse just outside the reserve, since none of the shacks were big enough to accommodate everybody. Sitting cross-legged on the sidelines with the other kids, young Bob Calihoo, Robert Royer in a previous existence, found that he could follow most of the arguments easily enough as they went back and forth.

Something of tremendous importance was happening. A vivid memory of a colour picture in a schoolbook came to Bob's mind: Indians all decked out in feathers and blankets, muscular young men carrying rifles, so many of them that the horde faded into the distance across the prairies. Facing them was a fat white man in a pith helmet, sitting under an awning, surrounded by flags and red-jacketed soldiers standing at attention.

It seemed to him that this enfranchisement business meant something as awesome as that: a great treaty-making powwow. Once, the text in the schoolbooks had said, the Indians had been mighty and numerous, then a handful of white men had come and made them bend down on their knees. This little situation in the schoolhouse could hardly be compared to the great battles of old. There were no heroic warriors. The Mounties didn't even bother to come. But it was the same thing, really. The land itself was involved. A part of Bob felt as though an earthquake was coming; the land was shifting underneath them all. Now, just as he was feeling at home. It seemed like more terrible unfairness. Was it because he'd sinned? Was it his fault? Bob was still a Catholic, and guilt came readily to him.

Bob understood what his Granddad and Johnny Rodgers were saying. He could see that making a living on the reserve was impossible, unless you were willing to stay hungry forever. He was lucky. He still had some body fat. Everyone else was lean and chronically weakened. He remembered how fabulously rich life had been in West Edmonton. That had been another country compared to this. Why would anybody want to put up with this any longer?

Yet something felt deeply wrong. He couldn't ignore the fact that a crazy old man and a bunch of drunks were talking about something that was going to affect his whole life. As for the white men involved, he was amused to notice that none of them gave him a second glance. They had him figured for just another scruffy, long-haired Indian kid. He was kind of proud of that. It was a secret he had: he knew what it was like to be white. It was like knowing somebody's language when they don't know you know.

Although he didn't have it with him, Indian Agent Lapp explained that he had been "in receipt" of a letter from the Premier of Alberta, Ernest Manning, giving permission for the Calihoos to apply for enfranchisement. It had been sent in response to a letter from Sam, urging the provincial government to hurry up and make a decision in this matter. This was more than slightly surprising, since Sam could neither read nor write. It was presumed that Johnny Rodgers had written the letter for him. In any event, the agent said smoothly, Sam's letter to Manning was merely a formal legal requirement. The province had a "revisionary interest" going back to the British North America Act, which meant that the province had to give its official permission before reserve land could be turned back over to it.

There was a brief discussion of who had voting rights and who didn't. A look through the Indian Register showed there were some fifty-three Michel Band members listed. Shouldn't they all have a vote? No, said Mr. Lapp, because they weren't on the reserve any longer, and therefore they had lost their voting privileges. This was all in the Indian Act, he assured everyone. As it turned out, nobody happened to have a copy of the Indian Act handy, but that's what it said. No doubt about it. It was right there in "black and white." Later, these words would seem laughable.

One of the priests pointed out that this was a bit strange. If the non-resident band members had lost their votes concerning reserve affairs, they certainly hadn't acquired any voting rights off the reserve to make up for it. The short answer from Mr. Lapp was simply that they'd lost their status by leaving the reserve. They were non-status Indians now. Non-status Canadians, too, the priest countered. He was answered by shrugs. That was just the way things were. The judge who was present didn't argue with this. In point of fact, he admitted, he hadn't read the Indian Act himself. It wasn't something that was taught in law school. He was counting on the lawyer and the Indian Agent to know, intimately, what provisions it contained. They assured him that they did.

The two priests were the only members of the committee opposed to enfranchisement. The reserve wasn't owned by any individual, they argued. It was held in trust for future generations. It belonged to Calihoos who hadn't been born yet, not just the ones who happened to be living there now. No one had the right to make a decision like this. The land, one priest explained carefully, was "held in reserve common." It belong to Her Majesty the Queen for the use and

benefit of the Indians. It didn't belong to any individual, he
repeated. Permission from Premier Manning wasn't enough
to override a federal agreement.

That was what Phyllis had been saying all along. But after
the priests had had their say, Johnny Rodgers carried on as if
they hadn't said anything at all. The lawyer and the Indian
Agent acted as though they hadn't heard a word either. The
judge announced that he was under the impression the band
members were "anxious" to enfranchise, and the only question was whether they were eligible to or not, according to
their "stage of development."

To arrive at some sort of conclusion about this, the judge
turned to the local farmers, who solemnly offered the opinion, one after the other, that the Calihoos were good people,
capable of taking care of their own affairs. "You buy them a
wagon," said one, "and they'll do just fine." Some Calihoos
even went to church near the reserve, another farmer pointed
out. Yessir, the white men all agreed, these Calihoo folk could
speak good English. Nothing there to stop them from acquiring all the rights, responsibilities, and privileges of other
Canadians.

The judge didn't ask about the employment histories or
arrest records or medical backgrounds or possible alcoholism problems of these eager, responsible, church-going,
English-speaking aspirants to citizenship. Only Phyllis tried
to protest, but she was hushed. Nobody asked, "Just what are
you going to do once you're enfranchised – with little education, no training, no inheritance, no contacts in high
places?" In other words, how will you make up for the years
of living outside the framework of rights and privileges?

The figure that the Indian Agent dropped into the air was
$100,000 for the reserve, with occupied land to be deeded to
the occupiers, if eligible. This meant that the farmers who
were already leasing most of the reserve would have first
option to buy the land from Indian Affairs. No price was
mentioned for this. The "surplus" land, meaning the area
currently still being used by band members, would be sold to

the Department of Indian Affairs. Each band member would receive a share of the total. For some families, depending on the number of family members, this could mean as much as $20,000 in cash. Hardly anyone on the reserve had ever seen more than $100 in a lump sum at any one time in their entire lives. It seemed like a dizzying amount of money. There were murmurs and smiles, and visions of wealth passed through people's minds.

However, most of them, like Albert, were under the impression that this was all just a discussion, nothing more. They were here to learn what the terms of enfranchisement were, and after that they would go back to life as usual, and there would be more discussions, more arguments. When a vote was called, fifteen of the seventeen adults put their hands up in the air, thinking they were agreeing to further discussion. The meeting broke up. The judge, the lawyer, and the Indian Agent shook hands all around and drove away, followed by the farmers and the priests. Only the priests shook their heads.

Sam and Johnny walked around afterwards with big grins on their faces. Somebody broke out the bootleg. There were parties on the reserve that night. But then there almost always were parties – and fights. It was no big deal. The next morning, nursing a hangover, Albert went hunting as usual, taking Bob and Butch with him. A month later, a cheque arrived, made out to Albert Calihoo, for $22,000. A couple of days after that, Indian Agent Lapp arrived and asked for Albert's green treaty card. He wouldn't be needing it: he wasn't an Indian any more. "Congratulations," Mr. Lapp said.

He hadn't voted for it, and he didn't particularly want to leave his familiar world behind, but once Albert had the money in his hand, it was impossible to resist the possibilities. This was going to be the beginning of a New Life. Phyllis herself, now that the money had arrived, began to think things might just work out for the better. As far as the kids, including Bob, were concerned, they were rich.

The rest of the Calihoos took their disbursements and

headed straight for the bright lights. A couple of the boys took a taxi to Vancouver, loaded down with wine, using up almost every red cent in the process. Most of the others disappeared to Edmonton.

Albert and Phyllis were going to do it differently. They shopped around and bought a garage toward Jasper, just outside Edson at a place called Mulborough, a tiny Métis settlement surrounded by five lakes in mosquito-infested lowlands. There were thirty to thirty-five shacks, a post office, and a pool hall, where practically all the Métis and Indians played. The little houses were lit by smoky lanterns and the sounds of guitars and fiddles came from them at night. There were other Calihoos there, people whose forebears had not taken treaty in the late 1800s, continuing to live in what was now Jasper Park until they were kicked out by the Mounties in the 1920s and 1930s.

They were not the most affluent or reliable set of customers a garage-owner might hope to have. But then, as a service-station operator, which was what he now proudly titled himself, Albert left something to be desired as well. For one thing, he knew scarcely anything about mechanics. For another, he knew nothing at all about balancing books or even how to keep track of cash. Phyllis tried to handle that end of things, but Albert kept taking cash from the till to pay for booze. Thinking himself a man of means, he also went out and bought a brand-new car.

However, one thing had not changed. To his dismay, he discovered that, when he marched into a bar and ordered a drink, the bartender and other customers still considered him an Indian. He explained that he didn't have a green card any longer. He had been enfranchised. He showed them his ID. He was a Canadian citizen. To them, he looked like an Indian, therefore he must be an Indian – and it was illegal for an Indian to drink. He was bounced.

There was no Indian Agent to go to now, either. Eventually, Albert had to hire a lawyer to write to Indian Affairs to have them send him a letter, stating that he had been enfranchised and was no longer an Indian. Only then could he get into a bar. He carried this letter around, carefully folded up in his wallet.

Bob, meanwhile, found himself back in school, along with his half-brothers and sisters. While he had the enormous advantage of already being able to read and write, for the others the experience was as short-lived as it was useless. By Grade 10 most of them had left for the streets. All the boys had learned was how to endure the strap without flinching. The girls had detentions nearly every day. Bob didn't like school any more here than he had in Edmonton, when he was living with his real mother or in the foster homes or with the Jesuits.

For his family, the adventure in the fully privileged Canadian lifestyle was over in less than two years. Albert drank away any money that Phyllis didn't manage to hide. The service station went bankrupt. The car was repossessed. Phyllis and the kids had to go on welfare. Albert wandered off to the town of Hinton, where he got work for a while. Eventually he disappeared into the squalor of Vancouver's notorious Skid Road district. Nobody in the family would see him for the next ten years.

It was easer to collect welfare in Edmonton than in Mulborough, so that's where Phyllis moved, encouraged by the social workers who wanted to keep their own lives simple. She took the kids, including Bob, with her. Full circle for Robert Royer, now Bob Calihoo.

In Edmonton, Bob wandered through his old neighbourhood and along 103rd Street. He saw a few kids he knew, but nobody recognized him. If they looked at him at all, they glanced only briefly, and then looked away. He was just some dirty teenaged Indian kid hanging around.

He tried looking up his mother and Harvey and Dorothy, but found they had moved to Jasper Place, just outside Edmonton, with Gervais Royer. He walked by St. Mary's Boys' Home, spotting some of the Jesuits who used to try to beat the Catechism into him, but they took no notice of him either. He paused outside the Coutoure family's house, where he had stayed as a foster child for a while, and it was the same: nobody noticed him, nobody recognized him. He was invisible.

It was strange, he thought, how in the country at least you left a footprint. It got rained on and drifted over and it blew away, but it lasted for a little while. Here, on the cement and cinders, not a trace was left. Not for a minute. You were here and then you were gone. You might as well never have been.

It wasn't long before he connected with other Calihoo kids from the reserve. Some of their folks were bootlegging. Most of the girls had started hustling. The boys were doing break-and-enters, petty theft. Through them, he met a lot of other distant cousins, most of whom had already done time, usually in the jail at Fort Saskatchewan. He even started using the name Royer again. A new life had, indeed, begun.

Chapter 7

"A Meaningful Job Skill"

BOB'S CREE BY NOW WAS FAIRLY GOOD. HE COULD SPEAK THE Métis patois. He was fluent in English. Since he could also think like a white man, he was useful in situations where somebody had to cool things out. And there were plenty of those.

As Bob began to get used to life on the streets, the first thing he learned was that the enemy wore a uniform. It was common practice, he discovered, for the Edmonton Police to harass tough young bucks to test them out, then, when they fought back, to charge them with assaulting a police officer. It was the routine way of getting them off the streets and safely behind bars. In short order, there was not much left of little Robert Royer, who had not complained about wearing his dress suit on Sundays because it made Mama happy.

Bob got odd jobs where he could, but finally, just after he turned sixteen, he landed a good one with a roof-repair outfit. It was hard, cold work, and at times was dangerous, since there was the risk of slipping on frozen shingles, but the pay, especially for someone his age, was good. He was still living with Phyllis and the other kids, but it was crowded, and Phyllis was having a tough time making ends meet. Bob helped out by babysitting, and he chipped in money when he had it, but the real need was for regular money, and up till now a steady job had eluded him. After all, counting the year in Mulborough, he had only a Grade 6 education. He had high hopes for the roof-repair business.

He'd been on the job for only a week, though, when several of the guys from the reserve decided to head out to a party they'd heard about at a community skating-rink. The rink was in Jasper Place; Bob's mother and her family were living in Jasper Place. Maybe he'd run into his brother and sister.

Sure enough, at the rink, there was his sister, Dorothy, and she was even unhappier than she had been when Bob had left. Their stepfather hadn't changed. He was still prone to taking out his anger on everyone around when he was at home. Dorothy wanted desperately to run away, and Bob would happily have taken her in, but Phyllis could hardly be expected to welcome another hungry mouth. Maybe after he'd been working a while, he thought, he'd be able to afford a place of his own, then he'd be able to help her out. She was still only fifteen, and if she made any attempt to escape, she would be grabbed as a runaway and put into a home. From experience, Bob could tell her this was no solution.

However, his sister's problems were not the only thing on his mind at the rink. Bob spotted a flaxen-haired white girl, and she seemed interested in him. Her name was Mary, and she had arrived from Scotland only a few months before. Scotland? Well, now, Royer was a good Scottish name, was it not? Bob turned on the charm. Mary had no inkling that he was part Indian, and there was no reason for him to be eager to point it out. They went into the community hall to dance. A job. Maybe a girl. Life was taking a distinct turn for the better.

Bob was feeling pretty good when he got a signal from some of the guys that he had come with; it was time to sneak out for a drink in the ravine behind the rink. Bob looked around to make sure no one was watching, scuttled across the snow, through a clump of bushes, and down into the ravine after his friends. There, in addition to his buddies, was one of his uncles from the reserve. Since Bob and all his friends were minors, he was the one who'd procured the bottle of wine. In the manner of Indians grown used to drinking quickly to avoid detection, they took turns swigging from the bottle. It wasn't just a matter of chug-a-lugging it so they wouldn't get caught in the act; it was also important to get rid of the evidence.

Young Indians were always being watched. Someone must have noticed them sneaking off and noticed a "white kid," Bob, tagging along. Although the wine disappeared quickly, they weren't fast enough with the bottle; it was still in somebody's hand when two Jasper Place policemen came crashing over the edge of the ravine, waving their guns and yelling: "Don't move!" This wasn't just an ordinary case of Indians drinking, and drinking outside a licensed establishment, subject to penalties under both the Indian Act and the Criminal Code; this looked like a case of contributing to the delinquency of minors – and one of them a white minor at that.

Within minutes, the paddy wagon had arrived. A small crowd gathered outside the community hall. Bob had a glimpse of his sister, looking frightened, and of Mary, looking rather impressed actually. Then he was inside with the others, being whisked downtown. His uncle explained urgently that if Bob or the others admitted anything to the cops, it could mean a couple of years on a contributing rap. The uncle could face a couple of weeks with no problem, but he could do without a couple of years, thanks.

Downtown, Bob, whom they obviously thought was white, was separated from the rest and taken to a room downstairs. The wine, gulped in a hurry, had left his head spinning, as two detectives began to question him. "Those other people that you were arrested with, did they buy you liquor and give you liquor?" one detective demanded.

"No, sir."

"Well, you have been consuming liquor. Where did you get the liquor?"

"I got it at the dance."

The other detective slapped him, knocking him out of his

chair. They hit him half a dozen times, but when that didn't work, they went back to question the others. Left alone, Bob pushed a table up against the wall, hoisted a chair on top of it, and clambered out through the basement window of the Jasper Place Police station. He was just small enough to squeeze through the bars.

It wasn't until he was outside that it struck him that he had done something serious: he had escaped from prison! Terror overcame him. He started running. He had always been a fast runner, but he had never run as fast as he ran now, through the snow, under the street-lamps, his shadow stretching out ahead of him, shortening, shrinking to a blot, vanishing beneath his flying feet, another long shadow leaping out ahead. There was no point running home to Phyllis, he reasoned. She had her hands full. So where could he go?

A plan leapt to mind. For the last couple of days the roofing company had had him working at a business in Jasper Place called Paramount Cleaners. He remembered that they'd left the skylight open, waiting for some putty to dry around the edge. Paramount Cleaners was where he headed. Dodging into the alley beside the building, he found the iron fire-escape ladder leading to the roof and scampered up. Sure enough, the skylight was till ajar. Lifting it, he eased over the edge and lowered himself as far as he could before letting go and dropping, hoping he would land on top of the delivery truck.

He did, and the keys were in the truck. It was a simple matter to unlatch the sliding front door of the building from the inside. He had never driven a truck on his own before, but Albert had let him drive the old Hudson around the reserve a few times, and later, at the service station, he'd started cars up and bumped around the parking lot when nobody was paying attention.

Gears grinding, engine screeching, he lurched out onto the street and hung a wide, awkward left. He had decided that if he was going to make a getaway, he would save his sister while he was at it, so he aimed the truck as best he could for the

Jasper Place skating-rink. Several cars blinked theirs lights at him before he finally figured out which switch to pull to get his own headlights on. On a Friday night, with the police out in force and with him weaving all over the road, the odds against him making it back to the rink unnoticed were astronomical, but he made it. Leaving the truck for a moment, he ran into the dance and grabbed his sister. The Scottish girl, Mary, was watching, but there was no time to think about a girlfriend now. He was on the run.

Mary wasn't the only one watching. Everybody there had seen him being hauled away in the paddy wagon with the Indians. Now here he was, out of breath, storming into the dance hall, grabbing a girl, and running outside again. Dorothy was happy to go with him – it was her dream come true to be rescued from the life she was living by her big mysterious brother. However, as they climbed into the truck and Bob fought the gears, trying to figure out how to get the truck in reverse, a crowd gathered. Everybody watched the truck rumble haltingly back onto the road. Inside the dance hall, someone was already dialing the police.

In the truck, giddy with excitement, brother and sister made frantic plans. They would head for the west coast. Maybe they'd find their father in Vancouver. Maybe he'd straighten out. When Bob made some money, they'd send for their brother Harvey. It wasn't until they were out on the highway, with the lights of Edmonton behind them, casting an orange glow on the underbelly of the clouds, that Bob got around to checking the fuel gauge. The needle registered nearly empty. By this time the effects of the wine had worn off, and he could see that this wasn't such a good plan after all.

Dorothy cried when he turned the truck around. He felt close to tears himself, but there really wasn't much choice. He wasn't sure how far it was to the next town, but out here on the prairies it was likely to be a long way. Their chances of making it were just about zero. And even if they did, he had only a couple of bucks and Dorothy had only a quarter.

He dropped her off at home and drove back to Paramount Cleaners. He parked two blocks from the building, leaving the key inside, and started walking. He got only a block before a squad car pulled up and a policeman's voice bellowed: "Don't try to run!"

When he was led into court the next morning and charged with theft of a motor vehicle, the judge asked: "Who's responsible for you?" Bob didn't see any point in naming poor Phyllis. She was just his stepmother, he figured, and she couldn't afford to take a day off. Why burden her even more? If he mentioned his mother, Mary, Dorothy would be implicated in the theft.

"My Dad, I guess," he replied.

"Where is he?"

"Drunk in Vancouver, I think."

After a brief discussion with the Crown, the judge announced: "This boy needs to learn a meaningful job skill. For his own good. I therefore sentence him to one year in Fort Saskatchewan Provincial Jail."

This is a mistake, Bob wanted to scream, a terrible mistake! But there was no point. Instead, he concentrated on fighting back the tears.

As they were fixing the handcuffs around his wrists and leading him out to the bus to be taken away, Bob told himself that at least he'd learn a trade. And after the Jesuits and his stepfather and that winter on the reserve, what could they do to him that could be worse?

Chapter 8

The Silent System

THE FIRST THING THEY DID WAS MAKE HIM TAKE HIS CLOTHES OFF so they could hose him down. Then they sprayed him with disinfectant.

It was 1959. Fort Saskatchewan was still run on the Silent System. Prisoners were not allowed to talk to each other. There was no radio. There were no newspapers. There was no canteen. You couldn't even buy toothbrushes. In the silence, sixteen-year-old Bob stayed in a cell for twenty-two hours each day. There was a sink that flowed into a toilet with no lid. The steel door had six little windows at the top. The glass was heavy, unbreakable, imbedded with wire-mesh. The bottom of the door had holes for ventilation.

The only exercise he got was an hour in the morning when he and the other prisoners were herded out of their cells, taken to an inner courtyard surrounded by high stone walls, and forced to march single file in a circle – silently – watched over by guards armed with rifles. Prisoners always marched counter-clockwise. That was the rule.

A lot of the guards were retired farmers from the surrounding area, and a few, Bob could swear, were demented. Sneaky Pete was, for sure.

Sneaky Pete was a night guard, so named because he alone

of all the guards wore rubber-soled shoes, enabling him to move soundlessly along the tier. The other prisoners – and soon Bob as well – played a game with Sneaky Pete, bending down by their doors and yelling such remarks as: "Hey Sneaky, you phoney prick!" Because of the echo, Sneaky wouldn't be able to tell which cell the voice came from. It was a dangerous game. Prisoners who got caught were beaten up and taken to the Hole – solitary confinement. Sneaky would glide silently from cell to cell, sometimes, like a hunter in the bush, flattening himself against a wall and waiting, hoping the caller would think he'd moved on, that it was safe to yell, and then he'd have the bugger. The trouble was, the prisoners could look out through the little windows on the door and see across the tier. Someone could always keep him in view. Hand signals, passed back and forth along the tier, kept every-one informed of his every move. When he realized he was being tracked, Sneaky would get beet-red and start panting like an animal. It was rare for him to catch anyone.

But there was an exception shortly after Bob's arrival. Sneaky Pete managed to jump a new kid who'd just yelled out some abuse. The kid must have been Bob's age, but he looked only about twelve. He had a baby face.

Watching through the crack between his door and its steel frame, Bob saw the boy being taken from his cell into the rotunda to the maze of cages next to the main office. There, Sneaky Pete and two other huge guards beat the little fellow unconscious.

On the reserve, Bob had thought for a while that he'd died and gone to purgatory. Now, as he watched in horror, hearing the kid's futile pleading, his cries of pain, the sound of his head hitting the concrete, the sound of Sneaky's knuckles landing on his skull, the splash of his blood on the floor, he thought that maybe he had slipped over the line from purga-tory into hell itself.

Fort Saskatchewan had always been known among ex-cons for its goon squad of five or six big guards who would take troublesome prisoners out of their cells, work them over, and toss them in the Hole for three days at a stretch. A beating such as this would never normally have attracted much attention, but times were changing slightly, and there was a new warden in charge. Perhaps because of the victim's child-like appearance – or former appearance – this particular beating drew attention. The warden came around asking questions. Realizing the risk, Bob nonetheless went ahead and told him everything he had seen. Other prisoners might have seen it. Maybe he was the only one. He never knew. Even if prisoners had been allowed to talk to each other, he knew better than to discuss this with anybody. Within a couple of weeks, Sneaky Pete was gone, and Bob lived in terror, expecting retaliation from the other guards. That little flash of justice, Bob was to learn, was the exception, not the rule.

One thing he had noticed right from the first day he was marched into the inner courtyard for exercise was that roughly eight out of ten of the inmates were Indians. This was a shock. He had never seen so many Indians together in one place at a time. He had no idea what percentage of the population on the outside was Indian, but his experience of city life told him that it was only a fragment. What were they doing here in such numbers?

It would have been a good question to ask, had he dared. But he had learned that the Silent Rule was serious. Once he made the mistake of whispering to another inmate during exercise. Marching back to his cell, he was suddenly grabbed from behind, yanked out of line, punched in the stomach, kicked, and, when he tried to get up, kicked again. "No talking means no talking," one of the guards snarled. Gasping for breath, Bob was hauled back to his cell and thrown in. It had been expertly done. There was no blood, nothing was broken.

Month after month passed. The peeling walls of his stale little cell seemed to hug him when he closed his eyes. The blunt lines of the bars on the window etched themselves into his brain. A year was turning out to be a long, long time. It soon seemed as though he had spent most of his life in that dank, cold box, where the only sign of natural life was the thin strip of moss clinging to the outside of the cell window and the lime-coloured mould that grew, despite monthly hosings, on the pipes of the sink. He could hear the rats chewing on the other side of the cement wall against which he lay every night, although he never actually saw one. The prison cats were as efficient at their job as the guards.

Not many men had ever escaped from Fort Saskatchewan. The open plain stretched out in every direction around the fortress. The guard towers provided superb vantage points. With their binoculars, the guards could see anything larger than a prairie chicken moving for six miles along every point on the compass. The handful of crazies who did get over the wall had either been shot down like ducks in a shooting gallery or picked up effortlessly within a day. Running through the waving grain fields, it was impossible not to leave a trail that a blind man could follow. Bob thought about it a lot. The walls themselves he figured he could scale, but he remembered those wheat fields all around. Not a chance!

Doing time hurt. It was like having an operation. They took something out of you and threw it away. You were emptier, irreparably older. The damage was done for good. The kicks on the backside were just part of it: the steel cage door slamming shut; the screams coming from the Hole; the sound of some guy bashing his head against cement as hard as he could, but finally having to give up, not being able to break his skull.

He kept trying to tell himself it wasn't real. That this wasn't the same plane of existence as he had known on 103rd Street. It was a bad movie, set in the past, that had somehow trapped him. He strained to wake himself up. This couldn't be Alberta, for God's sake! But then he had thought that a couple of times back on the reserve too.

The white picket fences of West Edmonton seemed further away than ever. Far, far, far away – and fading.

Chapter 9

"Say It Fast, Kid"

BACK IN EDMONTON AFTER HIS YEAR OF "LEARNING A MEANING-
ful job skill", Bob began to circulate in an area known as "The
Drag." He had new status now, having been to the Fort. Any
way you cut it, a year there was a lot of time. By now, he had
earned a reputation as a solid kid who wouldn't rat on you,
and he had a loathing for the fuzz, the courts, the screws, and
white society in general. He carried a switchblade.

In addition to the Indians he already knew from the reserve,
he had new friends from jail, guys he'd gotten to know despite
the Silent System, guys like himself: no home, a record, problems. And then there were the hookers, drifters, thieves, hustlers, boosters, pimps, con-men, drug addicts, pushers. A few
old Indian hookers who had known his father helped him out
from time to time, kept an eye out for him. But by now, he was
used to getting into fights. He had to fight, he knew, otherwise
people would push him around. He'd learned a neat trick: if
he was playing cards and didn't like the way the game was
going, he would just grab the table by the legs and start
hitting people over the head with it. Worked every time.
Once, he had to pull his knife, but that ended the trouble right
away. Lucky.

During this period, there was another part of his life that

was thoroughly separate and apart. These were the evenings and the weekend afternoons when he courted Mary, remembering all the manners that Mama had taught him, remembering, as well, the importance of neat appearance and politeness. She had, as yet, only a vague idea of the way the rest of his existence worked. The courtship would last more than five years, although much of that time they would be separated by bars.

It was hard to find a place to live. Finally Bob ended up staying with a guy and they got to stealing to pay for the room. Within a matter of months, he was back in the Fort, facing sixty days for possession of stolen property. Then, he was back in for a year for breaking and entry and theft. After that year was up, he started hanging around with much more experienced people. When he went back to prison this time it was for "deuce less" – two years minus a day – plus various amounts of remand time for possession of nitroglycerin and safe-breaking instruments. He had learned a thing or two, after all. His mentors had been the very best in the underworld. Unfortunately, they hadn't taught him how to control his impulsiveness, and his fatal tendency to make decisions while drinking.

It was in this state that he decided one night to break into a Safeway, a job he wanted to do with style. Accordingly, he stole a tow-truck: this wasn't going to be a break-in so much as a frontal assault on a fortress. He roared onto the parking lot, swung the truck round so that its rear end was facing the nearest plate-glass window, slammed it into reverse, and stepped on the gas. The truck screeched backwards over the asphalt, bumped over the curb, and shattered the window. Bob was out in a flash, churning through the broken glass and into the building. His alcohol-induced plan had been to loop the towing chain around the safe and use the winch to pull it free. But it took longer to get the chain in place than he expected, and by then he could hear sirens in the distance. Oops! Time to skedaddle! He hopped back into the cab of the truck and tore off across the parking lot, the chain sending sparks flying as it lashed about behind. He passed the squad cars as they drove towards the Safeway, nobody suspecting that a tow-truck could be a getaway vehicle. He ditched the truck later.

And that might have been the end of it, except that a couple of nights later, once again after having had too much to drink, he found himself becoming obsessed with the notion that the scam would have worked if he had just had the nitroglycerine ready, and had blown the safe first. Such a beautiful job it would have been! And then he got thinking how nobody on earth would expect a crazy stunt like that to be pulled twice. So he went back.

Again, he'd had a bit to drink. He stole another tow-truck and hit exactly the same Safeway, but this time, he backed the truck through the boarded-up window, sending splinters of ply-wood flying. The stuff didn't shatter as neatly as the glass had, which slowed him down a bit as he clambered through the wreckage. Also, this time the cops were a lot faster in their response. He blew the safe all right, but he was still trying to get the chain around it to winch it outside when the Edmonton Police burst through the shreds of plywood, waving their guns.

Back in Fort Saskatchewan, he found himself in the remand section, Block "A," where you landed if you were facing an offence warranting bail but couldn't raise the money. There you stayed on remand until your trial. He sat there doing dead time for several months before a trial date was set, even though he had not yet been convicted of anything.

For the first time, the specific injustice of the remand system got to him. Oh, he had been wracked with a bitter aware-ness of the injustice of life ever since his grandmother had died: whether it was his stepfather beating him or the Jesuits trying to pound their mysticism down his throat or the hun-ger and cold of the reserve, madmen and drunkards making decisions that affected his life, cops slapping him around, prison goons kicking him; these were all part of a generalized unfairness and rottenness that, as far as he could see, was characteristic of the business of being alive. It was the shits.

He had learned to think in terms of "us" and "them": "us" being the Indians, the Métis, the street people, the poor, the physically crippled, the emotionally crippled, the under-achievers, and the peripheral people, and "them" being respectable white society and its enforcers. It was all unfair, of course. Each aspect of the unfairness was more or less the same as any other aspect. It all stemmed from "them" having all the power and "us" having none.

But this remand business was beyond anything he'd seen yet. As injustice, this really took the cake. First of all, he was in a cell-block with one hundred cells, and at least eighty of them were filled with Indians. A lot of the white guys, as far as Bob could tell, ought to have been over at the Oliver crazy house. They had no business even being in prison. They were all sitting there twenty-two hours a day in their cells with nothing to relieve the boredom, and many of them would sit there for years before getting a trial.

The problem, especially for the Indians, was that they didn't own any property. The reserves were supposed to be Crown land held in trust. Nobody could put up a chunk of a reserve in order to get bail, and without property there was no hope of bail. They could therefore be held without charge. They couldn't sign their way out. Indian Agents weren't in the habit of coming to the prison to bail Indians out. So they sat there and rotted. Indians had learned, virtually as a matter of routine, to plead guilty to whatever they were charged with. If they pleaded not guilty, they would be remanded, and it could take four, five, six months, sometimes up to two years before they would get to court trial – time that could not be counted against their sentence. Such was the pace of justice in Alberta. At least the guys who were convicted got to work in the fresh air. Indians generally were given all the outdoor jobs like sawing wood and cleaning the piggery and taking care of the horses, because "they were good at that" and, as everybody knew, "Indians like it better outside." The "classy" indoor cleaning jobs went to whites.

Bob seethed and raged, and – now that the Silent System

had been abolished – found himself making speeches to the other prisoners. Not just once, but over and over again he went over it, until his outbursts resolved into a set speech. It went like this: "Well, this is bullshit. This is real bullshit. We're being exploited. Just think about the reality. We're only charged, and the reason we're rotting in jail is because we're too fucking poor to sign our way out. We're not being treated equally here under the eyes of the law or any kind of justice. There's no way we can bail ourselves out. The Métis people have got fuck-all in their pockets, and the Indians, where are they going to get bail? Is some white guy going to put up his fucking house? It'll never happen in your life. So you're going to face up to two years in jail on dead time – on top of any sentence – simply because you're accused of a crime. No sir, we're going to have to take up this matter of how we're treated behind bars. At the very minimum we should be allowed to have anything that's not going to endanger the security of the prison. Magazines. Books. You know, whatever. Radio . . ."

Finally, his speeches touched a nerve, and he was elected spokesman for the prisoners. The following day, when the time came to go back to the cells after exercise, some eighty Indian and Métis prisoners refused to leave the courtyard. They weren't going to budge, either, until the Inspector of Jails had a meeting with their spokesman. And who might that be? Over there: Bob Royer. Feeling a lot more nervous now than when he'd been making speeches, Bob nevertheless relished his first taste of political power.

The guards had never been faced with a situation like this. It was all the fault of that new goddamn warden. In the old days, this never would have happened. The guards tried prodding the prisoners out of the courtyard, but, by agreement, they all sat down. The idea of carrying them back inside physically was out of the question. Word went upstairs.

The protest had begun in the morning. It wasn't until mid-afternoon that four guards finally filed into the courtyard and summoned Bob to follow them. The Inspector of Jails wouldn't see him, one of them announced, but the Assistant Inspector would. Bob looked around for guidance. Most of the prisoners nodded. This would do. He stood, his knees feeling weak, as much from excitement as fear.

The elation of victory lasted about two minutes, just long enough for Bob to be marched from the courtyard to the rotunda outside the cell-block. There, lined up in rows, were some sixty waiting RCMP, many, but not all, in full riot gear: helmets, shields, jack boots, weighted billy clubs. They had obviously been hastily assembled; either that or they simply didn't have enough equipment on hand. The result was that about a third of them were wearing football helmets and shoulder pads and shin pads, and a few were carrying bats instead of billy clubs. All of them were armed with revolvers. They almost looked like a visiting team of ill-equipped players straight off the farm. But they were big, all of them, and from their faces Bob could tell they were looking forward to cracking skulls. The youthful spokesman for the prisoners was mightily impressed.

Nevertheless, he had a speech to give. He was marched smartly into the office of the Assistant Inspector of Jails. A heavy-set, white-haired cop, with a face as hard as the stones out of which the Fort had been carved, the Assistant Inspector growled: "Whatever you've got to say, kid, say it fast."

Summoning up all the politeness he could remember, Bob gave his pitch: "We don't think that it's quite right that so many Indians should be charged to begin with, and be in jail in this situation, because a lot of them are just committing crimes because they have to kick in windows sometimes in wintertime because they've got no place to sleep, and it's cold outside, and nobody else wants them, and the way Canada keeps their reserves, jail is like a palace . . . "

"That's fine, that's fine," the Assistant Inspector interrupted. "You just shut up."

Bob shut up.

"You go back and tell those men that they've got five minutes to get back in their cells." End of interview. Bob was marched back, past the assembled Mounties, limbering up with their billy clubs and bats, into the courtyard.

Bob's exact words to the other prisoners were: "Holy fuck, I'll tell you we better pack this shit in."

But the Indians just shook their heads. The general response was: "Fuck 'em."

With that, the prisoners turned and began running up the metal stairs leading to the cells. The plan was to retreat to the top floor, the fourth, where the Mounties could only come at them up two staircases at a time. Men started breaking their beds apart so they'd have something to swing.

A whistle blew, as though it was the start of some kind of game, and the Mounties in their riot gear stormed up the staircases. The Indians put up a fight, but it took all of forty-five seconds for the Mounties to break through at the top of the stairs and start beating up everyone in sight. There was no escape. Every single prisoner was grabbed, beaten, and hauled or kicked down the stairs back into their cells. The doors were locked behind them.

Once everyone was back in custody, the guards took them out one by one and made them run the gauntlet, working them over with bats, sticks, boots, and fists. When Bob's turn came, he was hammered with special ferocity as the mouthy punk who had started the trouble. He collapsed part-way through. A guard dragged him slowly the rest of the way, while the others worked off their anger on his ribs and buttocks and shins. When it was over, he was hauled down to the Hole and heaved inside.

The Hole. Five and a half feet by six and a half feet, completely bare except for a pot in the corner. No windows. No glass at the top of the door. Ventilation holes at the bottom of the door, that was all. There were heating pipes running along the ceiling, making it unbearably hot. Six slices of bread and a glass of water that evening. Cement floor. No bed. One blanket. No lightbulb. Six more slices of bread and a glass of water in the morning.

The prisoners were all to be arraigned on a variety of

charges relating to the riot. When they got off the bus in Edmonton a few days later, they were a sorry spectacle: beaten, cut up, covered with bruises, and many were missing teeth. One guy had a complete bootprint, by now turning yellow and green, on his chest. As they were hauled along, manacled and usually in twos, from the holding cells to the court, they urged each other to refuse to enter a plea, to demand a hearing instead. Everyone did just that, causing chaos.

Word of the riot had gotten out. The courtroom was full of reporters, and the physical evidence that the prisoners had been savagely beaten was too overwhelming to ignore. Within days, the Attorney General called for an inquiry into conditions at Fort Saskatchewan. A year later, as a result of the inquiry, the Bail Reform Act was brought in, eliminating the requirements for property in order to obtain release pending charges.

By then, Bob was out again and doing quite well by the standards he'd gotten used to. He had joined the ranks of the criminal elite. He was in charge of a swindle-sheet operation that spanned the prairie provinces. The routine involved "stealing" heavy oil equipment, such as pressure valves and wheel casings and stainless-steel rods and brass valves, and then unloading it on scrapyards. The operation involved pay-offs to oil-company suppliers, who would get their money back from the insurance companies, also pocketing a percentage of the take from Bob. He, in turn, would make his money on the sales to the scrapyards. It was a cosy arrangement. The only people getting hurt, Bob argued, were the insurance companies, who eventually uncovered the operation and put the Mounties on his trail. But while it lasted, it was a heady experience. A small convoy of trucks zig-zagged back and forth across the prairies, transporting stolen oil-rig parts, slipping past Mounties, dodging other freight-carriers, making stealthy drops and pickups behind chain-link fences, paying off crooked suppliers, scrap-dealers, and security men alike. At the peak of his career, Bob was driving a brand-new Buick. He'd gone from being a halfbreed street kid to being a devious and clever thief, operating on a mammoth scale.

Freedom lasted a year before he was nailed for grand theft and found himself being sentenced to seven years in the Drumheller medium-security penitentiary. He also received notice from the Attorney General that he was being investigated as a possible habitual criminal, who could be detained indefinitely. His first impulse was to laugh that off. At twenty-one, he had the distinction of being the youngest person ever threatened with habitual criminal status in Canada. But it was beginning to dawn on him that, at this rate, he just might wind up spending the rest of his life behind bars.

Chapter 10

"You Know You're an Indian"

DURING HIS APPRENTICESHIP AS A CRIMINAL, BOB HAD PICKED UP the philosophy of the old rounders: "Don't hang out with clicks, pricks, and politics." Although he had a distinct sense of "us and them," "them" had no political shape at all. He was comfortable with street people and cons, knew the police strictly as goons, and thought of white society, when he thought of it at all, as a collection of institutions and attitudes that had spat him out a long time ago, and that continued to grind down Indians and outsiders. He hated the law and he hated the authorities. White society as a whole was his enemy. He could steal a white man's money or cut his throat. He wanted retribution as much as he wanted wealth, but if he could steal it, he knew he would enjoy it more, because it would be a blow back at "them," at all of them. To him, by then, "Canadians" were all white and all targets. He had no more allegiance to them than he did to Africans.

By the same token, he felt no particular allegiance to Indians, either. It wasn't just that he could pass as white when he wanted. In order to gain the respect of the old white rounders, the Damon Runyon characters who had taught him his safe-cracking skills, he had acquired the habit over the years of making fun of the Indians – the bush Indians in particular, with their mixed-up French-English-Cree accents. Not letting on that he spoke Cree, he could do a terrific take-off on an Indian accent that would get the boys howling with glee. Sometimes he felt guilty about it.

Accordingly, when, in Drumheller, a number of Indian prisoners announced the formation of the Native Brotherhood and started holding meetings, Bob kept his distance. All he could see was that they would get together and whine about their situation in life, and he couldn't see how that was going to do any good at all.

But then Donny Yellowfly cornered him one day. A natural, charismatic leader, Donny was a Cree who was doing time for murder. He'd been elected first president of the Brotherhood, which he explained was based roughly on the dictums of the black-power movement in the United States. They just replaced the word "nigger" with the word "Indian." It fit perfectly. Donny had been reading Malcolm X and all the Black Panther literature he could get his hands on, and he didn't buy Bob's efforts to stay aloof.

"You know you're an Indian," he said. "Why don't you come down and help us? You've been around the streets. Maybe you've picked up something that we've missed. You have a white background. Maybe you learned something there. Anyway, why don't you come in, and we'll do what we can?"

His first Brotherhood meeting changed Bob's life. Everything that Donny Yellowfly and the others were saying rang true. The problem, they said, was lack of pride, lack of dignity, lack of a sense of who you are. "Apparently the white man knows more about us than we do," Donny said. "So we'll make it our lifetime vocation to research our history and our culture and find out what our people were and what they said. By doing that we'll regain a sense of identity, and from that we'll develop a sense of pride and dignity, and from that we'll develop a sense of motivation instead of apathy."

The gospel was brotherhood among the Indians, regardless of tribe or band. The gospel was a rebirth of Indian culture and a rediscovery of Indian history. Said Donny

Yellowfly: "You can't stop a movement that has begun in the hearts of men because they live under depressed and oppressive conditions that violate their human rights every day." He added: "You are in charge of your own fate, your own destiny, and you can accomplish anything you want to accomplish." The first efforts of the Brotherhood focused on being allowed to perform traditional dance and to carry out traditional religious practices, such as the Sweat Lodge, while in prison. White prisoners laughed at first, but not for long. After a few noses were punched, the jokes stopped.

Prison authorities took quick exception to the Brotherhood and tried to break it up by transferring main spokesmen like Donny Yellowfly to other prisons, but in the long run all they succeeded in doing was spreading the Brotherhood out across the country. A whole generation of Indian leaders was in fact forging a network that would sustain them when they took to the streets seeking change. In the meantime, at least one man's life had been touched by the spirit of the Brotherhood: Bob Royer went to the prison library, got out a copy of the Indian Act, and began to take charge of his destiny.

Destiny. There was destiny, he decided after a while. It was the net effect of all the things that had gone directly before you. He was the product of his father and mother, who were products of theirs. If they were scarred, you were scarred. Whatever nonsense they believed, you'd believe for a while, and then maybe you'd create a new you who didn't believe, and then your kids would take a different position. But there was a thread running through. The word, he learned, was *causal*. There was a causal relationship over time between himself and his situation and what had happened to his father and his grandfathers and his great-grandfathers. This wasn't sentimentalism. This was observable fact. How could it be otherwise? No personality is formed in a vacuum.

His had come close, however. He had been "Indian" in a lot of ways, even when he was running around in the Little Lord

Fauntleroy costume that Mama used to make him wear on Sundays. Not rebelling against her wishes had been one of the ways he had been Indian. Indian boys were good boys as a rule, at least until they started to be driven crazy as they got older. Yet he had adapted almost flawlessly to Mama's world. Did this mean he was schizophrenic? When he thought about it, the answer was: probably. If he hadn't started out that way, he sure felt it now.

For instance, there was all this bullshit about "justice." People acted as if it was something that really happened – and not only happened, but happened all the time in this country. God, it was incredible! There were white people running around who bought that! And at some level even he still expected it to be true, against all evidence to the contrary.

Destiny. The more he thought about it, the darker the idea got. It began to obsess him. If he hadn't gone to the reserve, he'd sure as hell never have gone to jail. Shouldn't say that. Ninety-nine per cent sure as hell. Something wrong there. Why should the reserve weigh so heavily as a great big negative in his, or anyone's, destiny? What was a reserve anyway? A gateway to jail, that's what it was. And why? Why weren't the happy Indians smoking peace pipes outside their teepees while the kids rubbed sticks together and the squaws plucked corn?

The more he thought about being locked away in Fort Saskatchewan Jail for a year when he was sixteen for stealing a truck he took back within hours, the dizzier he felt. This *was* his life, yet it couldn't be happening in the modern world. Hell, Dylan was singing out there! And Bob was rotting in here. It was real, all right. Kick a wall. Rattle a steel door handle.

His life had been ruined, he was sure, not just because he was caught in the middle of a protracted racial war, terrible as that might be, but because of what felt to him like a clerical error. He was sure that somewhere, somebody had put his name in the wrong ledger or file. How else could he have been imprisoned when he was only sixteen? All these fateful after-effects were magnifications of the original tiny, bureaucratic slip-up. This little error that had cast such an appalling

shadow over his life, how could he find it and correct it?
Could it be fixed? The one thing he did know was that nobody
was going to do anything for him. He'd have to do it for himself. And that was a valuable thing to learn.

His first taste of the truth that knowledge really is power
came soon after he began foraging through the Indian Act. He
discovered a simple, incredible fact – a fact that he could use
as a lever to try switching his destiny around 180 degrees.

In 1951, he learned, the "Red Ticket Act" had been passed.
Until then, when a woman left a reserve taking her minor
children with her, she could apply to be enfranchised and to
have her children enfranchised automatically too. It was her
right. But after 1951, the rules changed; Indian children of an
enfranchised woman did not necessarily have to be enfranchised along with their mother. It wasn't until after this that
Bob's mother had been divorced from Albert Calihoo and had
married Gervais Royer. Until the divorce, she and the children
were covered under the Indian Act. She had had Bob, Harvey,
and Dorothy enfranchised at the time of the divorce, and by
doing so, Mary was in fact in violation of the Red Ticket Act.
Somebody should have pointed out that she couldn't do that
any more. But no one had.

The price for Bob and his brother and sister had been
immediate impoverishment. When the Michel Band reserve
was broken up and sold, none of their names were on the
Band Register, since they had been struck from the list when
Mary became enfranchised. Accordingly, nothing had to be
put into a trust account for them, and nothing was. Whereas
Albert's other children were awarded small pay-offs from the
sale of the land, Bob, Harvey, and Dorothy got nothing. Moreover, none of the treaty obligations, such as the right to a free
education, applied to them. Also, although Bob hadn't
known it then, when Mary applied for enfranchisement,
Mama had stopped receiving those cheques from Indian
Affairs. And there was another unique, peculiarly Canadian,
twist: although they weren't officially Indians any more,
because they had been born on the reserve, they weren't regis-

tered as Canadian citizens either. Taking his first halting steps in search of his official identity, Bob Royer discovered that he literally didn't have one. He existed in a kind of legal limbo, neither Canadian nor Indian. In later years, when he had found out a bit about the real history of Canada, he would think: "This makes me about as truly 'Canadian' as you can be. Neither conqueror nor conquered, master or slave."

His first political act was to write to the Minister of Justice of the Province of Alberta, pointing out that he had been illegally enfranchised and demanding his Indian status back. Writing skills were handy, after all, especially in one of the "founding languages." Months later, a letter came back from the Minister, referring the matter to the Deputy Minister. More months passed, but eventually a letter from the Deputy Minister arrived, acknowledging that Bob was entirely correct – he should never have been enfranchised as a child. So the answer was yes, he could be reinstated as an Indian.

But there was another Canadian catch. The problem, of course, was that his reserve had disappeared between the time he had been enfranchised and the time he had been disenfranchised. (The words, applied to land, meant the opposite of what they were supposed to mean, he noticed.) The Province of Alberta was happy to make him back into a status Indian with the wave of a bureaucratic wand, but the rules clearly stated that to be a status Indian you had to belong to a specific reserve. Bob spent quite a few nights laughing raggedly alone in his cell over this one.

The solution arrived at, after a lengthy exchange of letters, was for the Deputy Minister to invent a new category of Indian, so Bob, his brother, and his sister could be redefined. Thus was born the "Alberta General Indian List." It had four names on it – the three of them, plus another Calihoo, one who had been declared incompetent and was in fact in the Oliver home for the mentally ill. Bob now began to joke that he was "Chief of the General Indians."

However, it was, of course, much more than a joke. Bob Royer could now attempt to break out of the cycle of poverty by obtaining a university education, guaranteed under treaty to the Indians (even General Indians, apparently), should they wish to avail themselves of it. It was something that none of the Métis back in Mulborough could hope to afford, or any of the street people he'd got to know in Edmonton or in Fort Saskatchewan.

Okay. Step one, he was an Indian. Now he would become an educated Indian. An Indian with access to power. Toward that end, he signed up for courses to complete high school. It had to be done in his leisure hours, but there were plenty of those.

As Bob began to study, he also began to read voraciously. His understanding expanded rapidly, guided by the realization that it was up to him to dig himself out of this deep hole he had tripped into. Time and again, although it made his eyes droop, becoming in fact, his favourite way to put himself to sleep, he returned to the prison library's thumb-worn *Indian Act of Canada*. Having hauled himself on board as an Indian, he knew he had to play henceforth by the rules of the Indian Act. He had, as yet, no idea what set of legislative canons and edicts determined the behaviour of white Canadians. It didn't matter. For Indians on the reserve, there was another set of laws entirely. Bound like a mummy by the red tape of the Indian Act, an Indian, Bob quickly realized, might as well be living in a different country. In effect – no, it was more than that, it was in fact – Indians did not live in the political realm known as the Dominion of Canada. They clung to some five hundred shards of land left over, like broken debris, from the vast age-old nations that had existed prior to the arrival of European invaders. And in those tiny fragments of Earth known as *reserves*, the laws were thickly meshed. The Indian Act contained within it, as if in a jar of formaldehyde, the body of the captive Indian. It was meant to keep him in a state of *rigor mortis*.

Bob's patient combing of the Indian Act brought up another strange and precious nugget. He could see that what had happened to his family's reserve wasn't supposed to have happened. Indeed, absolutely never should have happened.

The whole point of the exercise of which the Indian Act was supposed to be the ultimate expression was to reserve, as in "preserve," the land, not to parcel it out to wealthy takers.

Then one night it hit him: the dismemberment and the sale of his reserve had been no less proper than had his name being struck from the Indian Registry! It was like that tiny bureaucratic error haunting not just him but all the Calihoos. Except that this error, if error indeed it was, had turned into an earthquake, scattering Calihoos far and wide. They had been stripped, jettisoned, and abandoned. But he had seen small sparks of justice twice before. Maybe there could be more; maybe they could be bigger. If one illegal act could be reversed, maybe another could.

What he had to do now was to find out for himself how it had happened. And that meant learning the whole story. Where had they come from? Who were they? Why had they fallen? How, for God's sake, had this come to pass? He knew the scale of the disaster, but he lacked the details that would make sense of it. Only if he could fully understand what had happened, he realized, could he hope to muster the strength and certainty to put his shoulder against the enormous wheel of history that had ground his people under, and try to force it backwards just far enough to start over.

Drumheller Penitentiary was a grey concrete tower-rimmed fortress in the middle of nowhere. With five hundred men crowded inside, it was a volatile, dangerous place. The atmosphere was thick with tension and fear. It was an inauspicious place to begin an education, but Bob had no other starting point. During the days he made the rounds of the plumbing shop, welding shop, machine shop, body shop, and boiler room, eventually picking up a fourth-class engineer's certificate. Nights he read. Once he got started, he never stopped reading. The more he found out, the more he realized he didn't know. Obvious enough, but for a mixed-blood in Canada, there was an extra dimension to the axiom.

This wasn't something that hit him right away. Rather, it grew in him as he read and watched television and listened to radio and saw movies and talked with people – other Indians, Métis, half-breeds, and later a few professors and dozens of social workers and people with degrees in political science; with cops, criminals, hoods, hopheads, hippies, lawyers, activists, and archivists. He spent a lot of time putting two and two together, and he saw things the way he eventually came to see them largely because he started from a different premise. He was not reading Canadian history as it is written, namely as a triumph over odds, a pilgrimage, a pageant, a victory, a "building" of something great and eternal. He was not seeing it, to begin with, as a "peaceable kingdom." He was seeing it from inside one of its prisons. He was seeing it as someone who, upon being sent to jail for a year for "borrowing" a truck, was a political prisoner first time around. Everything he did afterwards was shaped by that experience.

When he read books or articles, he read them like an Indian. He read between the lines. He peered behind the bold declarations. He assumed that whoever was talking was lying. He took it for granted that the historians themselves were apologists for the victors. When he looked for a book that would tell him what had happened to the Indians, he couldn't find one. The fate of the Indians had been all but buried. The truth was an embarrassment to a country that knew in its heart it was built on wrong-doing, and so proclaimed loudly, over and over again, that it was just and clean and innocent and good.

So Bob fished around, getting a little bit of information from here, a little bit from there, trying to see, over the years, if he could make out any pattern. Indeed, he could. All in all, he could see, Canadian history was an enormous whitewash job. Knowing as he did how his family had ended up, he went back into the history of his people without any distracting illusions about how fairly or democratically they had been treated.

Again he began to read . . .

PART II

Chapter 11

The Dream of "Iroquois Louis"

AMONG THE VOYAGEURS PADDLING WEST IN A HUGE BIRCHBARK canoe with Alexander Mackenzie in 1793 were two brothers from the Iroquois village of Caughnawaga, Louis and Bernard Karhiio. By the dawn of the eighteenth century, the mighty Five Nations Iroquois Confederacy had suffered its final military reversals at the hands of the soldiers who had followed Cartier and Champlain. Surrounded and outgunned, the Confederacy had gone into decline as a major power on the North American continent, and, worst of all, had seen its cultural defences breached by the Jesuits. Along the St. Lawrence, the Iroquois survivors of the great plagues, once the most feared and respected soldier-citizens of all the Indian peoples, huddled together at Caughnawaga, outside Montreal, where they had been subjected, as forced converts to Christianity, to brainwashing by Jesuits for two whole generations by 1793, oppressed first by their enemies the French, and later by their "friends" the English, whom they had led to victory over the French in 1760.

Treated literally as "children" by the bureaucrats who had gained administrative control over their lives, the Iroquois had been enduring the bad taste of the European occupation for what must have seemed by then a painfully long time. In

1763, the Royal Proclamation had been issued, dictating that all lands for future settlement and development must be cleared of Indian title by Crown purchase. This process, which would culminate in the Robinson Treaties of 1850, meant that the tiny parcels of lands on which the Iroquois of "British America" were now squeezed would remain their only land forever and ever. The freedom they had enjoyed before would never be regained. On top of everything else that had befallen them – plagues, priests, and alcohol – the Iroquois were now limited by law to their small holding areas in Caughnawaga and St. Regis. It was claustrophobic and unbearably restraining. Old people could still remember how it had been. The dream of once again being free had not quite died, and Louis and Bernard Karhiio had inherited that dream.

To get from Montreal to Fort Chipewyan, the Karhiio brothers canoed up the Ottawa River, down the French River into Georgian Bay and the North Channel of Lake Huron, on through Sault Ste. Marie into Lake Superior, and eventually to the Lake of the Woods. From there, the route across the Great Lone Plain was along the Winnipeg River to the mouth of Lake Winnipeg at Elk Island, across the lake, braving sudden winds, through the Grand Rapids into Cedar Lake, to Fort Cumberland. From there, most traders pressed on via various water routes all the way to Fort of the Prairies, later to be known as Fort Edmonton. Mackenzie was aiming to make the more arduous journey along a network of waterways and portages to the Athabaska River, and from there to Lake Athabaska and Fort Chipewyan.

It took them half the summer just to reach Fort Cumberland.

The Karhiio brothers' knowledge of French, Mohawk, and English was not likely to be helpful to Mackenzie from there on, so they disembarked to let two local Indian guides, probably Salteaux, take their place in the canoe for the historic journey beyond Fort Chipewyan into the maw of the mysterious Rockies. While Mackenzie and his party were busy clawing and splashing their way to the Athabasca River, heading up to the lake of the same name, and plunging from there down the avalanche-haunted Peace, "making history," the Karhiio brothers, with time on their hands before they could freight any furs back east, decided to take a look around the peculiar treeless countryside that lay before them.

They were not the first Iroquois to make their way this far from their ancient homeland along the St. Lawrence. Many others had worked as voyageurs. But none, so far as is known, had ever penetrated further west on their own with the specific intention of exploring.

Louis and Bernard made their way through a seemingly peaceful land along the Saskatchewan to Fort of the Prairie, amazed, naturally, by the endless ocean of grass and the thundering, equally endless herds of buffalo. The deserted look of the land didn't fool them for a minute. It would never have occurred to them that there was anything "uninhabited" about that land, vast as it was. They were looking at it through different eyes than were the white explorers who had passed this way. For one thing, they were looking for something very different: the white men wanted furs and a route to the Pacific – ultimately China; the Karhiio brothers, however, hoped for land. Land that was truly uninhabited. Land that they wouldn't have to fight anyone for. Land that was free for the taking because it had not been claimed.

The chance of finding such land, they were aware, was probably zero. They understood Indian territorial boundaries, without having to ask a lot of questions. They knew when they passed out of Cree lands and into the land of the Assiniboines. They knew when they left Assiniboine territory and entered that of the Blackfoot. They kept their heads low, moved quietly, and did not linger in any one spot. This was, after all, foreign – possibly enemy – territory. Less than a hundred years before, the Iroquois had been at war with tribes as far west as the Mississippi River, and although peace treaties had been signed, one could never know. They were strangers in a land where guns and alcohol had only recently been introduced, hoping against hope that they could rebuild the lost utopia of their ancestors. It had to be a place beyond the pale of European influence, where they could live under their own rules, according to their own wishes, rather than being told by white men at every turn what they could or could not do.

Reaching Fort of the Prairies, they left their canoes and pushed on by foot. Now they were so close to the Rockies, they must have felt a certain element of despair, since they were obviously running out of space, yet were still in well-established tribal territories – by this time that of the Sarcee. It is possible, however, that they had picked up rumours by talking to people at the Fort, or in conversation with other Indians they met along the way. In any case, whether they stumbled across their great find, or whether they were guided to it by somebody else, doesn't matter. So far as they knew – and as historians confirm, they were right – there was no area of North America that wasn't claimed by one Indian nation or another, from the Arctic to the Gulf of Mexico, from the Atlantic to the Pacific. Yet here, just to the west of Fort of the Prairies, was the one section of the continent, except for the mountain peaks themselves, to which no tribe laid claim, and which the white men had not yet spotted. Starting in the woodlands of the foothills and extending into what is now Banff, they found a tract of several hundred square miles between the headwaters of the Athabaska and Saskatchewan rivers, which was the last niche of unoccupied land anywhere on the entire land mass.

While their old boss, MacKenzie, was pushing on laboriously through the Rockies, past hostile spear-waving Carriers in the Interior, and into the face of volleys of arrows fired by angry Bella Coolas on the west coast, the Iroquois paddlers from Montreal had stayed behind in what is now Alberta and had made what was for them the greatest discovery of all: uncontested land on the edge of the Great Lone Plain.

It is not known how much time the Karhiio brothers spent exploring their "hidden kingdom," but they headed back east –

probably the next spring – knowing full well the outlines of the terrain of the woodland utopia that they dreamed of building on the old democratic Iroquois model, out of reach of the white man. They certainly kept it a tight secret from the voyageurs with whom they paddled back to Montreal.

Once at home in Caughnawaga, Louis and Bernard talked about their discovery very quietly with their immediate relatives. Although no Iroquois family had ever been known to move as a group beyond the Ottawa Valley, there was no express prohibition against it; people could do as they wanted. No Iroquois had wanted to do this before, but then, never before had the Iroquois endured nearly a century under a conqueror's heel.

It is not known how long it took before a number of Karhiio Iroquois decided to pull up stakes and head west, just as the white people would do en masse almost a century later. It was possibly much more than ten years before they could pull together the resources to make the move – and it is not known exactly how many of them there were who made the move. Some estimates place the exodus at as many as seventy people, some at as low as two families. What is known is that within two generations – by the time of treaties in the west – there were 231 Karhiios.

The Karhiio Iroquois were fed up with being hemmed in on a small slice of land, tired of life under class-obsessed European rules of conduct, and sick of constant prying and bullying by Jesuit overlords. Led by Louis and Bernard, they set out on a unique voyage to seek the refuge of a new, free land in the west. It must have felt good, very good, to be off with their families on the great water highway heading west, leaving behind all the prejudice and discrimination and economic slavery.

In the hills beyond Edmonton, a small new nation began to take shape as the Karhiios clambered with what belongings they had been able to carry into the lovely, lonely woodlands along a section of the Rockies near Jasper.

By 1820 Louis Karhiio had married a white woman, Marie

Patenaude, daughter of a Hudson's Bay factor at Fort Carleton. They had a son, Michel, whose name would eventually become the name for a whole tribe, the first and last new tribe to come into existence in the shadow of the white man's advance. Quietly spreading out, they took possession of an area ranging south along the spine of mountains as far as what is now Banff National Park, one of the most magnificent natural settings in the world. They had found the last unclaimed niche of territory in North America.

And there – oh, so briefly – they prospered.

Chapter 12

Plagues and Rebellion

THE GREAT EXPANSE OF STEPPE BETWEEN THE EDGE OF THE
Rockies and the Red River seemed to form a natural barrier to
European settlement, almost as good as the rocky one against
which the Karhiio had placed their backs. The trouble that
was brewing on the prairies was on the far eastern side, and
the Karhiio could hope that it wouldn't spread to their corner.
With luck, they might remain slightly above the fray.

Paddling through, en route to the far west, the Karhiios had
seen for themselves the tensions between indigenous Plains
Indians and displaced Métis from the east, who had fled, as
the Karhiio were fleeing now, onto the prairies. The difference between the Métis and this small band of Iroquois had
been not only one of numbers: the Iroquois were just passing
through; the Métis were staying. To worsen matters considerably, the Métis's new turf was now being penetrated – taken
over – by Europeans coming from the north through Hudson
Bay, bypassing the eastern bottleneck of towns and settlements where they might otherwise have been absorbed.

In the summer of 1812, twenty-three Scottish refugees had
arrived at the Red River, courtesy of the Earl of Selkirk, who
had bought 116,000 square miles of central British America
from his fellow Hudson's Bay Company stockholders for a

token ten shillings. These settlers, the first of many to arrive, were crofters, evicted by their Highland landlords to make way for lucrative sheep pastures. Everything that could go wrong at Red River had gone wrong. It was the first time the Métis had come into close contact with a colony of whites, as opposed to traders who were there for only a while. The Scottish leader, Miles Macdonnell, made mistakes early. There were some five thousand Métis living by then in what the Selkirk settlers called "Rupert's Land." They outnumbered the whites ten to one. Yet Macdonnell, worried that his colonists might not have enough food to make it through the winter, had the gall to announce to the Métis that henceforth they wouldn't be able to sell their pemmican to the customers they chose; they'd have to sell it to the settlers first. He also imperiously commanded that the Métis stop hunting the buffalo on horseback.

Tensions came to a head in 1816, when the Red River Colony's new governor, Robert Semple, led twenty-six armed men out from Fort Douglas to intercept a Métis raiding party heading along the Red River towards the settlement. When the Métis spokesman shouted at him, Semple grabbed the man's bridle. Colonists and Métis began firing at the same time. Semple went down with a bullet in one thigh. The Métis killed all but three colonists, who managed to crawl back to the stockade.

After that outburst of bloody-mindedness, the Métis turned contrite for a while.

In their new homeland, the Karhiio were busy putting up extremely "modern" Quebec-style log houses, dovetailed at the corners, with dormer windows in a high, pitched roof. Barns, corrals, and outbuildings were erected. Horses were purchased with fur traded at Fort of the Prairies – newly renamed Fort Edmonton. The Iroquois soon became familiar figures at the Fort, along with Saulteaux, Cree, Assiniboines, Blackfoot, and Métis. Energetic and skilled, the Iroquois in

fact behaved exactly the way later waves of European immigrants were encouraged to act. Not only did they build, but
they started domesticating the land. They cut and burned
woodlands to expand the pastures for their horses.

Happily and industriously engaged, they enjoyed only a
little more than one precious generation before the priests
they had escaped in Caughnawaga and the traders they had
left slightly behind in Fort Edmonton caught up with them –
and, in fact, passed them. To reach a fishing station set up at a
lake called *Manito Sakahigan*, "Devil's Lake" in Cree, the
traders and other Indians and Métis got into the habit of
following a natural overland route between the lake and the
fort to supply themselves with food. Groping their way a step
further, beyond the lake, the traders also established another
post called Jasper House, inside the mountain shield itself. In
the trader's wake came a Quebec priest, who donned his
surplice and stole and waved a crucifix over Devil's Lake
when he set up his mission in 1844, renaming it Lac Ste.
Anne after his favourite saint. What with the priests, the fish-
suppliers, and the traders going between Jasper House and
Fort Edmonton, there was steadily growing traffic on the trail,
which became famous as the Lac Ste. Anne Trail. Unfortunately, the trail cut right through the northwest corner of the
lands the Karhiio had adopted as their own. Once more, as
much by accident as plan, the French priests – "Black Robes,"
as they had been known – had thrown a spanner into the
workings of an Iroquois dream.

The Karhiio resisted by building new barns and corrals
across the trail, and by digging up the grassy parts, seeding it
with oats, and fencing it off. It was to no avail. As often as not,
passersby ended up stealing the crop. Short of taking up arms
against the travellers, which would have triggered punitive
raids from Plains Indians as well as from white men, the
Karhiio had to submit to regular trespassing as a fact of life.
They were too small a force to put up a serious fight.

And at first, it was only a trickle of people. Nothing, perhaps, to get really worked up about – unless one knew what

was happening on the other side of the plains, where events were rushing towards a climax that would unlock a flood of white immigration.

By 1849, when the Karhiio were probably at their peak population, about 250 strong, with plenty of horses, well-built and well-kept homes, and a stable economy, there were 4,369 inhabitants at the distant Red River Settlement, the majority of them still Métis. Among them was a man known as the "Miller of the Seine." To increase the flow of water over his mill wheel, the miller had dug a nine-mile channel from the Red River over to a creek that was named after the famous French river. His name was Louis Riel, Sr., and he had planned to build a woollen factory, but the mighty Hudson's Bay Company frowned on industry in fur country.

Likewise, the Bay's directors had frowned upon Lord Selkirk's crazy notion of an agricultural colony in the midst of a much more lucrative trade. Luckily for the directors, when the laird had died in 1820, his heirs, less than thrilled to be pouring a fortune into the support of a distant colony of low-born peasants, had been happy to begin negotiations to transfer the territory back to the Hudson's Bay Company. As fur became the dominant enterprise in Rupert's Land again, men like Louis Riel, Sr., were left out in the cold.

Its monopolistic instincts reinforced, the Hudson's Bay Company began issuing edicts to the still-more-numerous Métis. One such rule forbade trade with the Yankees in the thriving new city of St. Paul. When the company's directors brought a Métis named Guillaume Sayer to trial for "smuggling" in May 1849, a crowd of three hundred Métis, led by Riel, Sr., surrounded the courthouse. Sayer was found guilty, but released. For the next twenty years, the caravans of Red River carts continued to squeak and squeal back and forth unimpeded between the Red River and St. Paul. Widespread trade in pots, kettles, stoves, farm implements, and liquor grew year by year until, in 1867, it topped two thousand caravans a year.

By then, imperialism was astir in the east. That year the four British provinces – Nova Scotia, New Brunswick, Ontario, and Quebec – had federated into the Dominion of Canada. The urge to expand was upon them. The first Canadian Prime Minister, Sir John A. Macdonald, generally so slow to make decisions that he was known as "Old Tomorrow," was fairly quick to decide that "if Englishmen do not go" out to those settlements on the edge of that enormous plain, "Yankees will." The Americans had just bought Alaska, and there was political agitation in the upper midwest states to annex Rupert's Land. The end of the American Civil War meant that there were eight hundred thousand out-of-work American ex-soldiers drifting around, looking for excitement.

Of this the Karhiio knew only what reached the trading posts at Fort Edmonton and Jasper House or the mission at Lac Ste. Anne, but this was enough to confirm what they already knew about tensions between the Yankees and the Canadians, both of them breathing hard at the sight of the unplucked prairie prize.

Tensions were serious – serious enough that by 1869, a deal had been struck between the wily old Hudson's Bay Company and the fledgling Dominion of Canada, whereby Canada bought Rupert's Land for £300,000. Of the 120 million acres stretching from Fort Garry to the rim of British Columbia, the Bay kept control of six million acres, plus fifty thousand more acres around company posts. Ottawa borrowed the money from the Crown – all very tidy, except that by now there were 6,000 French-speaking and 4,000 English-speaking Métis living in the region, alongside 1,600 white settlers. Not one of those 11,600 people was told a thing about the deal until it was done. There was deep foreboding among the Métis, but for the moment they were leaderless.

Louis Riel, Sr., the miller, had died in 1864, survived by a twenty-year-old namesake, a son who was just barely Métis himself: one-eighth Chippewa. Louis Riel, Jr., had excelled at school in St. Boniface and had been sent on a scholarship to a

Montreal seminary. There, he had briefly flourished as a brilliant scholar, before being rejected by a girlfriend's parents, who refused to let her marry a mixed-blood. He headed back to Red River, disconsolate and disillusioned, only to find that the region had filled up with Protestant Orangemen from Ontario who called themselves "Canada Firsters." They were clamouring in the pages of their newspaper, *The Nor'Wester*, for annexation by Canada, and they fully expected "the indolent and careless, like the native tribes of the country, [to] fall back before the march of a superior intelligence." Orangemen boasted openly that they were going to take over. They thought nothing of using whiskey to buy land from Indians who had neither title nor right to sell.

Given all this, it should have come as no surprise on October 11, 1869, when a survey party sent by Macdonald from Ottawa to outline a new system of square townships along the Red River, ran into a party of fifteen Métis led by young Louis Riel, who stepped on the surveyor's chain and said: "You go no further!"

While the political fate of the prairies was being shaped by events at the western edge of the Great Plains, the autumn of 1869 saw pestilence – in the form of smallpox – coming to the rest of Rupert's Land.

The Hudson's Bay Company had all but abdicated authority, and Canada had not yet imposed its will. Riel and his men were struggling to control the Red River Settlement, nearly oblivious to the holocaust crossing the border into the westernmost lands of the Piegans, Sarcees, Bloods, Blackfoot, and the newly-arrived Karhiio, whose Golden Age was over as quickly as it had come. By the time the long winter was through, the Piegans had lost a thousand tribe members, the Blackfoot and Bloods six hundred each.

The epidemic saw whole families die in blizzards, trying to flee their lodges. Such was the horror for the proud, healthy Indians of finding themselves disfigured by the foul-smelling pox that young men killed themselves and others killed their families and then themselves to avoid the shame and agony of decay. Some victims stacked the bodies of their dead on the windward side of traders' forts, hoping to give the pestilence back. Others, seized by delirium and rage, threw themselves at the barricaded gates, rubbing their open sores on anything they could, including door handles.

The Karhiio appear to have weathered this epidemic fairly well, perhaps thanks to the exposure their ancestors had experienced in the previous centuries in Quebec. Some resistance must have developed; the fact that they were relatively isolated was little defence in itself. Certainly it had not helped tribes in the past, nor would it in the future – no matter how remote. The epidemic in the far west also proved to be no barrier to another kind of pestilence.

That same year, two Montana hustlers set up a cluster of log cabins near present-day Lethbridge, at the forks of the Old-man and St. Mary rivers. This became known as Fort Whoop-up. In the first six months of operation, they earned $50,000 selling rot-gut whiskey to the Indians. The buildings burned, and were quickly replaced by a squat ugly bastion, with cannons mounted in the corners and narrow slits for guns. By the time the winter of smallpox had run its course, the prairies were ripe for madness in whatever form it could be found.

In the wake of the plague, the Plains Indians were left virtually leaderless, since elders as well as children were prime victims. Numbed and doubting their destiny, the survivors were especially susceptible to alcohol's promise of ecstatic forgetfulness, and the scenes that swirled around places like Fort Whoop-up, and its smaller versions, Robber's Roost, Fort Slideout, and Fort Standoff, were out of a nightmare, the kind of insanity that is reported to have seized huge numbers of survivors of Europe's fourteenth-century bubonic plague.

Once the booze began to flow through the barred wickets of the squared-timber forts, chaos ensued. Warriors thrust furs, robes, and pemmican inside in exchange for rifles sometimes, but mainly for high-proof liquor that often included such ingredients as red ink, tobacco, and Jamaica ginger. When they had nothing left to trade, the crazed warriors – those who had not been killed outright by poisoning or shock – would try to sell their horses, wives, and daughters, in exchange for more fire water. They tried to scale the walls of the forts, but were repelled with long poles kept specifically for the purpose. In the end, the drunkards turned on one another. Mothers lost their children, who either froze to death or were torn apart by starving dogs.

Two plagues, then.

Again, thanks to being somewhat cloistered in their woodland retreat, the Karhiio were spared exposure to the worst of this second pestilence. Their homes and farms remained intact. They continued to ranch successfully right up until Louis Riel led the resistance on the prairies. The Karhiio played no direct part, but they watched from the foothills with abiding interest. From the bitter experience of their Iroquois ancestors, they were not very optimistic about Riel's chance of success, although he operated at first with amazing finesse. The Karhiio cheered the reports that fed back to them.

First, he blockaded the American border and guarded it with forty armed Métis to prevent the arrival of the governor sent to Red River by Prime Minister Macdonald – a dogmatic, inflexible man named William McDougall. Under the banner of the *Comité national des Métis*, Riel gathered another four hundred French-speaking Métis at Fort Garry, something that was not too difficult to do out of a total population of six thousand such men, women, and children. (Riel's four thousand English-speaking Métis compatriots sat on their hands.) Without firing a single shot, Riel and his men took over.

When McDougall pushed over the border to an abandoned Hudson's Bay post, Riel sent well-armed and determined Métis to expel him. If the Métis were to join Canada, they wanted some guarantees, he proclaimed, and not just from the upstart, imperial capital in Ottawa, but from the Parliament in London. Among these, quite naturally, were guarantees of a democratic voice in government and protection of the Métis language, land, and religion.

At first there was not much they had to do, other than publish their List of Rights. In late November, when Governor McDougall equipped his aide, Lieutenant-Colonel John Dennis, with three hundred rifles and sent him over the border from Minnesota into Rupert's Land to raise an army and overthrow the Métis by force, it was not even necessary for Riel's men to venture forth. Only some sixty-odd Canada Firsters rallied to McDougall's banner. The four thousand English-speaking Métis, whom Riel had derided for not taking sides, again could not make up their minds to take sides, leaving Lieutenant-Colonel Dennis with insufficient force to mount an assault. When the small band of Canada Firsters assembled to march against Riel on their own, led by Dr. John Christian Schultz, publisher of The Nor'Wester, they found themselves facing two hundred men and a cannon, which Riel trained on the door to Schultz's storehouse, where the volunteer militia, including loudmouthed Irish-Ontarian Thomas Scott, whose life and death would prove costly, were gathered. Wisely, the Canadians surrendered. As prisoners, they were marched over to Fort Garry, where Riel a short time later raised the flag of his provisional government: a fleur-de-lis on a white field.

On January 5, 1870, a smooth-talking Hudson's Bay official, Donald Smith, arrived, a delegate from Prime Minister Macdonald, to assure the Métis that the new nation of Canada wanted union on the basis of an accord "among all the classes of people of this land." Smith thereby gave the provisional government enough credibility that the English-speaking Métis finally decided to stand up and be counted along with their French-speaking kin. Together, they were ten thousand strong. On February 9, at a convention representing all of the Red River settlers, white and mixed-blood alike, Riel was confirmed as leader of the provisional government.

However, within a matter of weeks, he had committed the

blunder that led to his ultimate defeat: the particularly offen-
sive and unrepentant prisoner Thomas Scott had been
charged and tried for bearing arms against the state, and on
March 4, he was shot by a firing squad in the courtyard of Fort
Garry. Scott's death turned him into an undeserving but
potent martyr in Ontario, where John Christian Schultz had
fled, spreading lies about Scott being tortured unspeakably.
The fury of Scott's fellow Orangemen was such that when the
Red River government's delegates reached Ontario in mid-
April, they were arrested and charged with murder. Quickly
released, however, they pressed on to Ottawa and presented
Sir John A. Macdonald with Riel's eighteen-point List of
Rights, including the demand that the Red River settlement
enter Confederation as an equal province, not as a colony.

Within weeks, Parliament grudgingly passed the Manitoba
Act, incorporating most of the eighteen points. Conspicu-
ously lacking, however, was amnesty for criminal acts committed during the insurrection. As well as allowing for a
governor to be sent into the settlements, the Act called for the
dispatch of twelve hundred soldiers, not as military conquerors but as a "constabulary," whose function would be to "protect" the colony.

It took ninety-six days for the force from Ontario to slog
through the muskeg, and during that time, M'sieu le President Riel stayed in Fort Garry, intending to hand power over
formally. It was only at the last moment, when the weary,
glowering troops appeared, tramping along the Red River,
scores of them bent on avenging Scott's "murder," that Riel
finally listened to advice from a white friend and escaped out
the front gate of the fort as soldiers were closing in from
behind. He ran for the States, where a decade-long exile
began. In absentia, he was elected to Parliament three times,
but when he tried to sneak into Ottawa to sign the register for
the House, he barely escaped with his life.

Once the troops were in place, the fine promises of the
Manitoba Act vanished into the air. Newly arrived vigilante

Ontarians murdered four of the Thomas Scott jury and left a fifth, badly beaten, for dead.

By that time, anarchy stretched across the entire plain from Fort Garry to Fort Edmonton. Wolfers, men who made their living by strewing the prairie with strychnine-laced buffalo carcases in the hope of poisoning wolves for their pelts, fought private gang wars against whiskey traders, because the traders sold guns as well as whiskey to the Indians. Since the wolfers as often as not poisoned Indians' dogs instead of wolves, and the Indians relied on their dogs as essential beasts of burden, it was inevitable that some of the newly purchased rifle should be employed to take down a wolfer now and then. In addition, by the early 1870s, as many as five hundred hardened American Civil War veterans were roaming Rupert's Land. Forced out of Montana by laws that prevented sales of either arms or whiskey to the Indians, they roared into the vacuum left by the Hudson's Bay Company, a vacuum that Sir John A. Macdonald, having chased off Riel, now decided to fill by stationing a full regiment of 550 mounted soldiers at strategic posts across the Great Lone Land. The original name of this regiment, the Mounted Rifles, was changed to Mounted Police to avoid any impression of militaristic manoeuvring above the 49th Parallel.

As fate would have it, the Cypress Hills Massacre occurred at almost the same time as the bill creating the police force passed without opposition in Ottawa, giving Macdonald a perfect excuse to move with uncharacteristic haste. A gang of Montana wolfers had crossed the border in pursuit of lost or stolen horses, and after a night of drinking, they came across an Assiniboine Indian encampment. Joined by half a dozen Canadians, the wolfers attacked the Assiniboines with repeating rifles. The Assiniboines, also believed to have been drinking, counter-attacked three times. When the gunpowder settled, one white man had died – and thirty Assiniboines.

In Ottawa, Old Tomorrow used this as the excuse to order

the immediate enlistment of three hundred men to be dispatched to the untamed, murderous North-West.

Having resisted a shattering epidemic while managing to avoid the worst influences of the whiskey traders, the Karhiio could be forgiven for feeling slightly triumphant at that point. Little did they realize what lay in store for them.

Chapter 13

The Taking of the Plains

IT WAS GENERALLY EXPECTED AT THE HIGHEST LEVELS IN Macdonald's Ottawa that the Plains Indians, though mortally wounded, might rise one last time in a spontaneous convulsion and sweep the white man and all his plagues from the west. United, especially if allied with the Métis, the Indian nations of the prairies were a serious military consideration.

The vast arena between Red River and the Rockies was itself barrier enough to expansion of the Canadian empire. Bloods and Blackfoot, according to fictitious reports, were still scalping Crees and Assiniboines. At the same time, the resources of the new Dominion of Canada were strained. It had to sit on top of a barely apprehended insurrection in newly claimed Manitoba, and cling to this beachhead long enough for a wave of English-Canadian immigration to arrive and swamp the Métis. There was a lingering fear, too, that the scattered but always formidable American renegade war vets might not like having their lucrative whiskey profits cut off. Couldn't they be expected to fight back?

A simultaneous consolidation along the edge of the westernmost Ontario forest and an advance into the fields of grass were what was required, and this is what the conquering Macdonald exerted himself to do: the North-West Mounted

Police would be deployed from Dufferin to Winnipeg, Swan Lake, Fort Ellice, and Fort Edmonton, and would establish pivotal Fort Macleod near the American border.

At the time of this decision, top military leadership in Canada consisted of a man who had served with the British army in South Africa, a Confederate Army veteran, and a mercenary from Italy's peninsular wars. Their small army of three hundred men was spared the laborious portage through the muskeg north of Superior by an American decision to allow them to travel by train from Chicago to Fargo, North Dakota – providing they wore civvies. As Ogden Tanner records in his book *The Old West: The Canadians*, one officer observed that he doubted any expedition "ever undertook a journey with such complete faith and such utter ignorance." It was intended as a backhanded compliment.

From Fort Dufferin, sixty-five miles south of Winnipeg, the small army of spit-and-polish horsemen, wearing their scarlet jackets, armed with Snider-Enfield carbines and long-barrelled revolvers, and hauling field guns, began their 850-mile trek to the mountains. Expecting a forty-per-cent loss of horses due to mosquitoes, flies, wind, dust, hailstorms, anthills, locusts, heat, and lack of forage because of recent prairie fires, the men bent Job-like to their ordeal, plodding under the scorching prairie sun behind a Boundary Commission survey party that was marking the United States–Canada border as it went.

When the Mounted Police did finally encounter the maddened hordes of armed Indian warriors they were expecting, it was to discover themselves face to face with thirty weary, hungry, dirty refugees, mostly women and children, who arrived chanting a dirge. The only possible sign of guerrilla tactics being used came when the obligatory powwow was over and the Indians had gone. The entire Canadian regiment found itself infested with fleas.

Likewise, the vaunted confrontation with the Civil War vets who were running the whiskey forts proved anticlimatic. At Fort Whoop-up, the Yankee traders had heard the thump of horses moving in disciplined rows vibrating through the drum of the plain. In the crunch, they were as pragmatic as Riel, and, like him, they hurried across the line. They at least closed the fort door behind them, leaving a hired hand to offer the Mountie army a meal and a farewell on behalf of the owners, who had taken their whiskey with them – although the trade itself continued.

The occupying force had its own problems, however. When whiskey couldn't be found to confiscate, the hard-core drinkers among the soldiers resorted to stolen bay rum, rubbing alcohol, and even ether. A whole troop of drunk Mounties terrorized Lethbridge one night, while the hazard presented by drunken troopers in town for the night became a familiar one in the settlements springing up in the wake of the redcoat advance. The desertion rate among soldiers rose as disillusioned conquerors went AWOL, fleeing into Montana to work in the gold mines. Fitful mutinies shook the barracks as boredom took its toll.

But the Mounties' main assignment, of course, was to smooth relations with the tribes and sign them to treaty contracts that would pin them down, thereby opening the rest of the land to a flood of Canadian-controlled immigration, and despite the problems, between 1871 and 1877 the first seven "numbered treaties" were signed. The main impetus for Indian expressions of interest in the treaties was the fact that the buffalo were vanishing before everyone's eyes – along with all the big game.

The Karhiio were affected, but, again, not so drastically as the Plains Indians. The buffalo had never been part of their diet; they relied instead on the animals they found in abundance in the woodlands. As they had through the first major western smallpox epidemic, they managed to survive with relative impunity. Encroachment along the Lac Ste. Anne Trail was still a problem, but the Karhiio's objections to travellers passing through their area was lessened somewhat by the discovery that, as traffic increased, so did the number of customers for their livestock and farm produce. The Iroquois had always been great farmers. Horticultural skills had been the key to their political sophistication – they had had the time, even in the remote past, to ponder in leisure the problems of living with their fellow humans.

For the Indians of the Plains, however, the nightmare was deepening rapidly. As the food chain began to dissolve around them, the Indians who had lived at its apex for so long suddenly found themselves facing mass starvation. It was as though all their "stores" were closing down, going out of business. Into this suddenly barren land crunched the British-style Mounties with their field guns. It only made sense for the Indians to seek treaties to protect themselves, especially since the food supply itself was being swept away.

Between 1871 and 1875, five treaties were made between Treaty Commissioner Alexander Morris (who was also lieutenant-governor of the North-West Territories) and the Indians of northwestern Ontario and southern Manitoba and Saskatchewan, although the government had dragged its heels in accepting the need to begin the treaty-making process. It was only when the Saulteaux of tiny Manitoba turned back settlers trying to move west of Portage la Prairie and the Ojibwas of the North-West Angle started charging rents, as well as threatening settlers crossing their territory, that Ottawa acted at all.

The initial government offer to the Saulteaux and Ojibwas was simply for reserves and a small cash annuity. The Ojibwas threw the offer back twice, while the Saulteaux upped the ante, demanding horses, wagons, and farm tools and equipment. Treaty Commissioner Wemyss Simpson wrote down these demands in the form of a memorandum (now in the Public Archives of Canada) titled "outside promises," which he promptly forgot to include in the original Treaties One and Two. It was only in 1874, after angry Manitoba Indians protested the non-delivery of the goods Simpson had promised, that an inquiry was launched, and the "outside promises" were added to the documents. From that point, Canada included such promises in all treaties.

Again, it was pressure that motivated the government to act in the Qu'Appelle and Saskatchewan districts, this time from the Plains Cree, who intercepted a party of men from the Geological Survey of Canada and prevented telegraph construction crews from setting to work. The Cree had known since 1870 that their land had been "sold" by the Hudson's Bay Company to the Dominion of Canada, and they took the position from the start that they would not allow settlement of their lands until Cree rights had been recognized. They also took the position that any agreement had to include assistance in helping the Cree make the transition to an agricultural style of survival. The Cree had adapted before; they could do it again. But they would need the tools, which otherwise were simply not available.

Traders had been telling them for years that treaties would be offered any moment. With starvation and overcrowding looming, the Cree weren't in any mood to put up with the activities of illegal surveyors and pole-stickers. The Geological Survey of Canada was stopped by the Cree at the elbow of the North Saskatchewan in July 1875, and that did it. A treaty was promised for the following summer. The Indians were to assemble at Fort Carlton and Fort Pitt.

Accompanied by a hundred splendidly tailored and armed Mounties, Treaty Commissioner Morris ventured forth from Fort Garry on July 17, 1876 – smack in the middle of the season when the people had to be out hunting for their winter supply of food. At Duck Lake, Chief Beardy of the Willow Cree told Morris that he wanted the treaty signed right there at the lake, but the commissioner shook his head and pressed on grandly to Fort Carlton, arriving on August 15 to meet the head chiefs of the Carlton Cree, Mistawasis and Ahtukukoop, and about two thousand of their people. The Duck Lake Cree stayed behind, thus cutting themselves out.

At Fort Carlton, a gorgeously adorned pipe was brought out by the medicine men, pointed to the four heavens, and passed around. The Indians had absolute faith that in the presence of the sacred smoke nothing but the truth could be uttered, and any commitment made was binding for eternity. The pipe signified that this was The Deal. The pipe ceremony, moreover, meant that the undertakings were henceforth laid at the feet of the Great Spirit. This was religious ceremony mixed with business.

There was a need for the Indians to prepare for the "diminuation of the buffalo and other large animals" by making homes and gardens for themselves, Morris proclaimed, as noted in "Treaties of Canada with the Indians of Manitoba and the North-West Territories." When a chief suggested that taking steps to preserve the buffalo might be a better route to go than simply giving up and turning into farmers, Morris did little more than nod solemnly. In fact, the Cree had been urging laws to preserve the buffalo since 1850, when they first had noticed a drastic decline in the herds. The logical solution, they had noted then, would be to restrict buffalo hunting to Indians alone. By themselves, the Indians had never threatened the existence of the herds, nor would they now. But this wasn't a notion that sat well with white politicians, any more than it did with white settlers or white hunters.

Morris's serenity was shattered only once when the Cree warrior Poundmaker, not yet a chief, but a powerful orator, stood and said: "The government mentions how much land is to be given to us. He says 640 acres, one mile square, for each band, he will give us, he says." Then, shouting, Poundmaker delivered his point: "This is our land! It isn't a piece of pemmican to be cut off and given in little pieces back to us! It is ours and we will take what we want!"

Poundmaker's followers screamed in Cree: "Yes! Yes!" The head chiefs restored order, although Treaty Commissioner Morris was left visibly shaken in the face of Poundmaker's succinct statement. In the various reports on the meeting, nowhere does Morris address the issue raised by Poundmaker, which was the question of cessation of land title. In its finished handwritten form, Treaty Six would have some very specific things to say about title, but none of this came up during Morris's flowing oration, except when Poundmaker raised it. The closest Morris came to responding to the land question was by saying that the reserves would protect the Indians from being crowded out entirely by the settlers. In fact, the text of the treaty, also quoted in Morris's paper, called for the Indians to "cede, release, surrender and yield up to the Government of the Dominion of Canada for Her Majesty the Queen and her successors forever, all their rights, titles and privileges whatsoever, to the lands included . . . and also their rights, titles and privileges whatsoever, to all other lands, wherever situated, in the North-West Territories, or in any other Province or portion of Her Majesty's Dominions, situated and being within the Dominion of Canada."

There is some doubt as to whether the interpreters read the treaty aloud to the assembled Indians in Cree or whether it was read in Saulteaux and Assiniboine as well. The record simply says it was read "in Indian." In any event, there is nothing at all in the recorded speeches of the commissioners about any voluntary surrender of the Indians' land. The subject was simply avoided. Some sort of a sharing of the vast land was all any of the Indians thought was involved, and even then they were only giving up surface rights, which were explained as the land required for farming.

With Poundmaker getting little political support, regardless of the fact that his comments had cut to the heart of the matter, and with the Duck Lake Cree having isolated themselves by refusing to show up at Fort Carlton, Morris could take his time and leave the head chiefs stewing. In the end, Chief Mistawasis turned to the opposition, led by Poundmaker, and demanded: "Do you have anything better to offer our people?" Chief Ahtukukoop reasoned with even deeper resignation: "Surely we Indians can learn the ways of living that made the White man strong."

When Poundmaker continued to object, Morris made the point that what was offered was a "gift," since the Indians still had their old way of life. Although he was to vow that the

Governor General and the Council of the North-West Territories would examine the feasibility of a law to preserve the buffalo, it is evident that Morris wasn't taking Indian fears about the effects of the disappearance of the buffalo all that seriously. He did repeat his assurance, however, that Treaty Six Indians would be free to hunt and fish throughout the territories as they had done prior to signing the treaty, provided they didn't destroy the settlers' crops.

Blithely handing out uniforms and flags to the chiefs and headmen, after they had signed or had had their "x's" affixed to the Treaty Six document, Treaty Commissioner The Honourable Alexander Morris, Lieutenant-Governor of the North-West Territories, steered his entourage on toward Fort Pitt for the next round of negotiations, knowing that he had served his ambitious Conservative friends in Ottawa well. The new empire had gobbled up another batch of sovereign states.

Chapter 14

Famine and Extinction

THESE WERE TERRITORIES THAT THE TRIBES HAD ALL FOUGHT over at various times. The Assiniboines ("people that cook with hot stones"), for instance, had probably separated from the Dakota Sioux only a few generations before the arrival of white men. By the eighteenth century most of them had moved up from the Lake of the Woods and Lake Nipigon area into the forests around Lake Winnipeg, where they were in regular contact with the Cree, while others had moved into the Assiniboine River valley. Guns and horses extended their range out onto the plain.

Joining the Cree, they fought the mighty Blackfoot Confederacy for control of the seemingly infinite grass fields. They also waged wars southward against the Sioux and the Mandan. As the Europeans pushed west, the Assiniboine had found themselves being elbowed onto the open plain. They couldn't go back; their lands had been overrun quickly; but when they pushed ahead it was against a jostling crowd of other Indians whose homeland this already was, and who also viewed the vanishing bison as their traditional foodstuff.

So it went across the swells of grassland, washing up against the burst geological lip of granite so effectively guarding the distant Pacific. Everyone was being elbowed and shoved. The resource base was collapsing. There was a thunder in the earth, but it was no longer the beat of a billion hooves upon the dried-up sea bottom, it was the rhythmic pummelling of steel hammers on steel spikes coming from the east – an entire land of steel, it seemed, advancing inexorably. Who, seeing their food vanish all around them, would not feel the pressure?

By the time Alexander Morris arrived in Fort Pitt to conclude the second stage of the Treaty Six negotiations, some four thousand Indians were camped there, with more families and bands drifting in all the time.

Impressed by the fact that chiefs Mistawasis and Ahtukukoop had accepted treaty at Fort Carlton, Sweet Grass, the principal chief of the Plains Cree, addressed himself immediately to the issue of the declining buffalo, stating flatly: "It is for that reason I give you my hand." In the face of an ecological catastrophe, mature leaders sought all the help they could get, and the priests, who had more influence among the Indians that were already trying farming, favoured a deal. At the onset, cunning old Commissioner Morris had encouraged the formation of small bands as a way of preventing the Cree – or any other Indians – from concentrating in numbers that were too large. It was classic divide-and-rule strategy, aimed primarily at Cree leaders like Big Bear, Little Pine, and Piapot, who were manoeuvring to achieve large concentrations of their people in accord with provisions of the treaty that allowed them to accept or reject a reserve site.

With the Treaty Commissioner and his small but effective army practically at their doorstep, the Karhiios could hide no longer.

Louis and Bernard were, of course, long dead. The new generation had grown up and taken over. Louis' oldest son, Michel, a gangling man, taller than most Indians, was Chief. Despite the fact that his mother had been white, he had classic Iroquois features – a hooked nose, extremely high cheekbones. With his moustache, goatee, and ponytail, he was a striking man. Since before his father's day, voyageurs had dressed in a combination of European and native clothes, and although Michel had been raised as a traditional Iroquois farmer, he had inherited his father's voyageur taste in clothes. Accordingly he stood out from the Plains Indians.

He had heard stories from his parents about conditions at Caughnawaga, and under the white man generally. He had absolutely no desire to be put back under the white man's rule. The freedom he'd enjoyed all his life was precious. He had talked the matter over with everyone, though, and nobody could see any way around the fact that they were cornered. Even if they could somehow muster the weaponry and will to pack up their bags and run one more time, they'd quickly run into Kootenay territory. Besides, the Kootenay were bound to fall under these rules soon, too. The miracle of untenanted land would not be repeated. Except for these crumbs called reserves, it was all the white man's land now, from sea to sea to sea.

There was no use fighting. Michel, his brother Baptiste, and the others had seen what had happened to the resistance movement on the prairies. They knew from the traditional stories what had happened to their great-great-great-grandparents when they did battle with the white man. Back then, the Iroquois had been a great power. One small offshoot Iroquois band, entrenched on the edge of the mountains a century later, could hardly hope to hold off the redcoats – who were now calling themselves Canadians. Knowing as much as they did about what was then happening to the Indians of the plateau on the other side of the mountains, and hearing plenty of rumours about the fate of the coast tribes, the Karhiios had long felt themselves caught in a truly gigantic pincer movement.

The Karhiios had intermarried with the neighbouring Cree, Louis's marriage to Marie Patenaude being an exception. Indeed, Cree was commonly spoken among the Karhiios. In their rush to learn to communicate with the Indi-

ans living around them, the generation after Louis and
Bernard had quickly shed their ability to speak Iroquois and
now blended in linguistically. Such, in fact, had been the
degree of intermarriage and the amount of association with
Cree in particular, that there were those among the current
Karhiio generation who thought of themselves as Cree. To be
specific, Woodland Cree.

If they spoke Cree, and identified themselves as Cree, they
had a pretty good chance of being treated as Cree. As Cree,
they would not only be able to take treaty, like the other
Indians around them, but, as a small band, they would fit in
perfectly with Commissioner Morris's administrative scheme
to break the big confederacies down into smaller units, the
smaller the better. In Morris's view, a hundred members per
band was the optimum number. The Karhiio weren't that
small, but they were small enough, compared to other entire
nations. Their objective meshed perfectly with Morris's own
political goal, even though he thought he was succeeding in
breaking a fragment of the Cree Nation loose from the rest.
Here was a band who wanted to be considered divided from
the main tribe, since it knew it was going to be conquered
anyway.

There was also another consideration. The men in the Parliament of the Dominion of Canada did not want to give anything to the half-breeds. There was a serious political reason
for this. There were too damn many half-breeds. Ottawa's
calculations were a serious personal complication for Michel
Karhiio. Son of a white French-Canadian woman and an Iroquois, he had been born on the land he lived on, but he was
faced with forces of discrimination that were in the ascen-
dancy. It was the Orangemen who were driving policy, not
Métis-lovers.

The Karhiios were in enough of a difficult situation, as
refugees who had been overtaken by the power they were
fleeing, without being identified as part of a group of political "untouchables." Thus, it was as a representative of a
"branch" of the Woodland Cree that Chief Michel Karhiio

marched up to a table under an awning on the Lac Ste. Anne
Trail just outside of Fort Edmonton on September 18, 1878.
Under the watchful eyes of the white commissioners and
their squadron of "police," he put his "x" to the Treaty Six
Adhesion – a legal mop-up operation – thereby taking treaty
and, with it, possession of 22,748 acres of land. It was desig-
nated Indian Reserve No. 132, and henceforth would be
known as the Michel Calihoo Indian Reserve. (The allotment
of land was based on a formula of 128 acres per person. There
were estimated to be 178 "Calihoo Indians." When a head-
count a year later turned up 231 "Calihoos," the size of the
reserve was accordingly revised upwards to 29,568 acres.)

Nearly every time the name *Karhiio* showed up on a document, it was spelled differently. Sometimes it was "Calis-
trois", at other times "Cailloux," "Calliot," "Callious," or
"Calahoo." For openers, no white seemed able to get his
tongue around the proper Iroquois pronunciation. To complicate matters, a French Catholic priest, also unable to say
the name, had dubbed the family "des Roches," after the rocks
to be found all over their territory. The Karhiios now had a
multiplicity of identities – none of them the true one.

For the moment, though, the "Calihoos" were in good
shape. The freedom they had so briefly enjoyed was gone, of
course. But on the plus side, they were living on a relatively
huge tract of land, compared to the reserve their distant Iroquois cousins were cooped up on back at Caughnawaga.

The winter of 1877–78 produced such a light snowfall that,
come spring, the plains were parched and dusty. What buffalo had survived thus far were inclined to graze southward.
Once they migrated across the line, Yankee hide-hunters set
grass fires behind them to make sure they wouldn't wander
back into Canada's newly claimed territories.

The spring drought finished them. Flies buzzed around
the humped bodies, and bones appeared through worn hide.
At a glance, one might see hundreds of big bison vertebrae

and pelvises and fragments of thigh that had been scattered by coyotes, lying like a dusting of early snow across the waving fields, horizon to long horizon.

By the end of that summer of 1878, Indian families across the Great Plains were eating mice and carrion as well as grass. As their bony horses and dogs fell, the Indians were forced to eat these, too. Around Fort Walsh, as many as five thousand starving Blackfoot, Cree, Bloods, and Sioux were to be found. Government relief shipments of flour, bacon, and beef were barely enough to put a dent in the hunger of thousands. Emaciated Cree broke into a storehouse in Fort Qu'Appelle. The prairies had become an open-air charnel house – not only the apparent extinction-ground of an entire major species, but the scene of an equally certain tragic ending for the several "nations" that constituted the surviving pockets of Plain Indians. They too were now an endangered species.

By 1879, nearly all the big game had vanished from the prairies. This time, it wasn't just the plains that were affected. Once the buffalo were gone, the pressure on game was so enormous that their numbers caved in even up in the woodlands beyond Fort Edmonton. The Karhiios – now the "Calihoos" – were running out of meat too. Worse, the luck that had spared them during the first great western smallpox epidemics ran out. They were hit by lack of animals to hunt and by epidemic at the same time. In the next decade, the "Calihoos" dropped in number from 231 to just 74.

The once-proud barns began to suffer neglect. The corrals began to fall apart. With two-thirds of the people dying off, the cohesion of what was, after all, a highly organized farming and ranching operation began to decay. The help was suddenly no longer available to keep up with the sundry tasks of keeping the farms running. And now, when anybody tried to pull things back together, they found their hands were tied.

In the past – at least since escaping Quebec – the Karhiios had been able to use their considerable organizational, construction, and farming skills to build as they chose, when they chose, and where they chose. They knew what seeds and equipment they needed, and, moreover, they knew how to use it. They were in a completely different position from the Plains Indians, who had to be taught how to become farmers. The Iroquois had known how to farm since long before the arrival of the Europeans. But they had never tried to farm with a white Indian Agent telling them what to do and a distant bureaucracy determining what they needed and didn't need, or what equipment they would have. As disease took its toll, the "Calihoos" – unlike the Karhiios – found it increasingly difficult to regroup and reorganize. The power to make decisions – to purchase or sell – had been taken out of their hands. They were now under the control of the Indian Affairs Department, prisoners of the Indian Act of Canada, unable to borrow or buy anything without permission. Their entrepreneurial skills were utterly blunted. It was very much as though an all-pervasive "socialist" government had grabbed hold of them, forbidding them to behave like the successful capitalists they had been up until then.

Last but not least of their suddenly compounded woes, Michel and his fellow former Karhiios found themselves being deliberately starved as part of a Canadian program to break the last resistance in the west. The moment he realized he had the Indians – all of them – in his hands, the newly appointed Commissioner of Indian Affairs for the North-West Territory, Edgar Dewdney, sought to use food rations as a tool for maintaining control of the Cree. Here, the manoeuvring of the Karhiios worked against them; recognized now as Cree, they became pawns in a larger political game, the victims of a campaign aimed at another people.

To demonstrate the boot on the neck, Dewdney gave instructions that only the aged, the sick, and the orphans could receive rations – unless they had done some work for one of the government branches. The Indians – including the "Calihoos" – had barely begun to receive any welfare in place of the work they couldn't do any longer, when already they were being handed a shovel and told to dig. Food as a weapon. The campaign to tighten the noose around the Plains Indians: Canadian action, 1879.

It was highly effective, and it marked the end of one small runaway Iroquois band's taste of freedom.

Chapter 15

The Gatling Gun and the Indian Act

BY JULY 1880, SOME CREE HAD ALREADY GONE BLIND FROM malnutrition. Outside their lodges skeletal dogs whined piteously. The wind flapped the lodgeskins. No family had been spared losses from the plagues of sickness, alcohol, drugs, ecological collapse, and now mass famine. They were all emotionally numb as well as terribly weakened physically. Their ribs stood out like the poles against the skins of a lodge in a powerful gust of wind. Still, they resisted.

In 1882, Cree chief Piapot sent his warriors to uproot forty miles of railway survey stakes just west of Moose Jaw. When that failed to stop the Iron Horse, Piapot ordered his followers to set up camp directly in the path of the railway at Maple Creek. One way or another, he was determined to get the government's attention.

This incident actually did wonders for the mythology of the Mounties. Two young redcoats, one of them a supremely self-confident corporal named William Wilde, rode into the Cree encampment and gave Piapot fifteen minutes to vacate. When no one moved, Wilde tore down the chief's lodgeskins, then marched around the camp, ripping down lodges as he went. Such was the legendary stuff. Far more often than not, the reality was something else. Under Edgar Dewdney, the all-powerful Commissioner of Indian Affairs, the Mounties repeatedly stormed Indian council meetings, trying to break them up and arrest Indian leaders on the spot.

When Chief Piapot declared he would hold a council to discuss grievances, the Mounties were ready. They had planted a man inside the reserve Piapot had chosen as a location for the council, and they arranged for him to accuse the chief of trespass when he arrived, thereby giving the Mounties an excuse to lay charges. A gang of fifty-six intrepid Mounties also sneaked into the encampment, under cover of darkness, hoping to kidnap Piapot. Intercepted and surrounded by scores of armed warriors, the Mounties did the prudent thing.

Piapot eventually got his way. He wanted a reserve in the Qu'Appelle Valley, close to the Cree on the Pasquah reserve. Fearing war, and knowing that his people would lose – as the Nez Percés, Blackfoot, and Dakota Sioux had lost – Piapot used what little manoeuvring room he had to position the scattered Cree close enough to each other so that they could unite in times of crisis. Knowing that any concentration of Cree would leave a *de facto* Cree Nation intact, the Mounties, in turn, attempted to keep them apart.

More and more raw force itself wasn't working all that well. Rather than being intimidated, the Indians simply got angry, and, faced with situations where they were bound to lose, the Mounties were as quick to back down as the Indians.

When starving Indians broke into the storehouse at the Sakemay Reserve in the Crooked Lakes area in southeastern Saskatchewan, the police, upon arrival, were surrounded and threatened with death. Only the promise of an immediate delivery of rations to the reserve got the Mounties out alive.

On another occasion, finding out that Big Bear intended to go to a dance and council at Poundmaker's reserve, Dewdney had choked off Poundmaker's rations to prevent the gathering. The hungry Indians went ahead stubbornly with the meeting.

Big Bear didn't want war any more than Piapot, yet both knew they had to try to get the treaties revised while they still had any bargaining strength at all. Once they were pinned down in scattered reserves, it would all be over. It was clear that the promises made in the early treaties were already being broken. Rather than providing all the farming tools they needed to make the transition to an agricultural society, the government was sending them inferior-quality farm tools, wagons, and equipment, providing inadequate food and clothing, so that the people remained weak from hunger and cold, and withholding many of the oxen and cattle. Nor was medical care being provided.

Back in Ottawa, the Deputy Superintendent General of Indian Affairs, Lawrence Vankoughnet, had looked at the bottom line of the costs of administering Dewdney's carrot-and-stick program of controlling the Indians through rationing. Meagre though the rations were, cheap as the wagons and farm tools were, and scaled-down as the promised livestock supply was, the cost, he concluded, was still too much. He promptly ordered across-the-board cuts in spending on Indians and fired what little staff existed to teach agriculture, as per treaty pledges.

At Michel Calihoo Indian Reserve No. 132, the effects were devastating. When they had had their own tools and had been able to make their own decisions, the Karhiios had been famous throughout the region for their industriousness. But for the Calihoos, life was now radically different. Tools could no longer be replaced. If something were needed, it took much too long to arrive to be of any use during a given season, and when it did arrive, it invariably proved to be of such inferior quality that it was practically useless anyway. Desperate pleas for adequate equipment were ignored. Complaints about lack of proper seeds went unanswered. Combined with the drastic decrease in their population and the resultant decay of their buildings and fences, this all brought about a breakdown in the band's morale. The realization that they really were not going to be allowed to run their own affairs any longer was possibly as corrosive as the damage that was being done to their physical health.

* * *

Out on the plains, the surviving Cree leaders could see that what was needed wasn't a far-flung archipelago of reserves, but a single Indian Territory, where the Cree could preserve their culture and come to each other's rescue when necessary. They did not need to be told about the British military doctrine of dividing and ruling. They knew full well what the Canadians were trying to do.

What none of the Indians realized was that Dewdney was preparing a trap-within-a-trap. What they were experiencing now was a softening-up. The real blow was yet to come.

Fully expecting the recalcitrant Indians to refuse to settle on reserves far away from each other, as he had ordered them to do, Dewdney asked the cabinet in Ottawa to pass an order-in-council, changing the Indian Act and making it a criminal offence for an Indian band to refuse to move to a reserve site selected by the Commissioner.

There had been nothing about such a "law" in the treaties, of course. But then neither had the treaties come with any booklets explaining the mechanisms for oligarchical rule that Canada had inherited from the Mother of Parliaments: mechanisms such as the nefarious order-in-council, which allows a cabal of cabinet ministers to sit behind closed doors and invent or abolish virtually any law they wish, on a moment's notice, without having to debate it in the Commons, let alone to take it before the electorate. By the very nature of Canada's flawed constitutional heritage, all treaties, it was turning out, had an enormous, unwritten "notwithstanding" clause that exempted everything. It wasn't enough to get it in writing, you had to get it written into law, and even then, at the whim of cabinet, any new regulation could be conjured away. As the fledgling nation-state of Canada set out on her own first colonial quest, the tricks of conquering and ruling were well understood. A fragment of empire was making itself larger, becoming an empire of its own.

With the Cree, Ojibwas, Assiniboine, Blackfoot, Crow,

Saulteaux, Piegan, Blood, Gros Ventre, Sarcee, and the little band of "Michel Indians" more or less corralled and forced to eat out of the government's hand, the only potential remaining indigenous resistance to the "Canadian" invasion came from the Métis.

Since as early as 1862, some of the Métis – the guerrilla leader Gabriel Dumont prominent among them – had foreseen how events at Red River were going to affect the whole west, and had acted to try to forestall the advance of the easterners by concluding an alliance between the Métis and the Cree. In his effort to find common ground, Dumont had succeeded in arranging a peace between the Cree and the Blackfoot, ancient enemies who had been fighting each other since prehistory. At this juncture, the Métis and Indians between them still controlled 580 millions acres of land, except for a sprinkling of trading posts and forts. But as the steel unfolded westward, the sprinkling of white outposts grew quickly. By 1884, some eight hundred prairie towns had been seeded between Winnipeg and Calgary.

Appalled by the rate at which immigrants were pouring in, Big Bear, Piapot, and Little Pine had almost managed by underground means to unite the Cree in a call for new treaties and the establishment of a territory. But at that very point, when they were so close to political success, Big Bear, for one, started losing control of his young men. They were flocking to Little Poplar, a warrior chief who advocated the killing of Indian Agents and government officials as the means of restoring Cree independence.

Dewdney, of course, knew through his network of spies about the radical resurgence on Big Bear's and the Battleford Assiniboine's reserves, but he wanted to wait until the order-in-council changes to the Indian Act had passed so he would be in a position to arrest all the chiefs at once. However, as an interim measure, before the changes were approved, all Indian councils were abruptly prohibited, starting with an upcoming one at Duck Lake for all Treaty Six participants. The normal allocations of guns and ammunition for hunting, as per the treaties, was cancelled, denying the Indians not only rations, but even the means to hunt for small game for their subsistence. Serious consideration was given to placing an artillery unit at Battleford.

While these preparations were going on in the background, and the militant young braves under Little Poplar were milling about in the foreground, the Métis continued to try to form a cohesive pan-prairie alliance. They were thwarted by Cree rejection of their entreaties.

At the same time, the Cree, under Little Pine, were trying to involve the Blackfoot in a joint call for treaty revisions, and having no more luck than the Métis. Blindness, apparently caused by starvation, struck Little Pine before he could pull off a diplomatic coup. Big Bear found himself being challenged for the leadership by his son Imases and one of his headmen, Wandering Spirit, both of whom wanted to line up with Little Poplar on the side of violence.

When it looked at one point as though the Cree were going to manage to pull off a council meeting, despite everything he could do, Dewdney switched strategies. He suddenly conceded that the government's failure to distribute food, equipment, and livestock was, indeed, a violation of the treaties, and pledged to implement all the stipulations of the treaties immediately. This meant a dramatic increase in the delivery of goods to the beleaguered reserves, a move calculated to placate the Indians.

If that didn't work, Dewdney's plan was to arrest all the leaders, charge them – as was now possible, thanks to the order-in-council – with incitement to insurrection, and have them locked away. This wouldn't be hard to do since, in anticipation of this moment, all Indian Department officials in the west had been appointed stipendiary magistrates, meaning that they were trial judges who could bring Indian troublemakers to "justice" promptly. In violation of every principle of British common law, Prime Minister Macdonald volunteered to communicate to the magistrates the importance of imposing long prison sentences on any Cree leader convicted of incitement.

None of this affected the Calihoo Indians immediately, since none of them were about to attempt to rise up. They were caught in a belated and vicious spiral of disease at the very time when government agents had clamped administrative handcuffs on them, making it impossible for them to do anything for themselves other than hunt or fish. They sank quickly from a state of self-reliance to one of forced dependency. When they had been masters of their own farms and ranches, it had been child's play to feed themselves and attain a considerable degree of financial independence. With government bureaucrats dictating their every move, such productivity was no longer possible. All of them were hungry. All of them were stymied. Many of them were mortally ill. And so some of them turned to drink, and others began to drift – or limp – away.

When the Riel Rebellion of 1885 erupted, the pace of technology had outstripped Métis political awakening, and this helped bring about their downfall. But it was more than that. It was more than that the CPR was on the verge of bankruptcy and its ambitious and ruthless general manager, William Van Horne, was looking for an excuse to manipulate the government into further loans. It was more than that the North-West Mounted Police were established in stockades and forts across the plains with telegraphs at their disposal. Nor was Riel's doom entirely due to the Gatling gun having been invented.

The legalistic machinery of a police state had been set in place. All the instruments of oppression and control that could be asked for were now at the disposal of Dewdney and Macdonald, courtesy of orders-in-council and backroom patronage politics. Henceforth, anything to be done against the Indians or Métis would have the veneer of legality. It was this, more than trains or guns or forts, that would undo Riel and his patriots – and leave the Calihoos permanently trapped in a bureaucratic nightmare.

Chapter 16

"A Just and Honourable Indian Policy"

UPON ACCEPTING GABRIEL DUMONT'S PLEA ON BEHALF OF THE Métis to return to the North-West Territories and lead them, the exiled Riel set out on the long journey across the rolling hills with his wife, two small children, and a handful of grim Métis, to face off against the new empire to the north. Riding to Batoche on the banks of the South Saskatchewan River, he travelled in a Red River cart, hardly the most heroic vehicle in the world. Only seventy Métis gathered in the Church of St. Anthony of Padua the day after his arrival, but their passion was enough to fire up any leader.

When the white men in Saskatchewan discovered that Riel was back and trying to stir up not only the Métis but the Indians, they set up contingency plans. The Hudson's Bay Company quietly reserved some buildings at Fort Carlton, just twenty miles from Batoche, to house extra troops. By March, Riel had formed the "Provisional Government of the Saskatchewan," and sent four hundred men into action, led by Dumont. They cut telegraph poles, set up a fortified head-quarters for the provisional council, and grabbed a couple of horsemen who proved to be Mountie spies.

It took only days before Riel's men came into collision with the first excursionary force of twenty-two Mounties, who were lying in ambush. They were sent packing when Dumont rushed the Mountie sergeant and disarmed him, forcing him to order a retreat.

When the second assault came it involved 177 men, Mounties and civilian volunteers, against what appear to be less than 30 Métis at Duck Lake. Dumont was wounded in the shooting, but his men rallied and forced the redcoats and volunteers to scramble for their lives. The appearance of Riel on horseback, leading reinforcements and brandishing a cross, was a factor in the Métis *esprit de corps* – and one much needed by then, what with Dumont on the ground bleeding from a head wound.

However, from the point of view of military leadership, whatever good he might have done, Riel quickly undid. When Dumont's brother Edouard shouted for his men to ride after the retreating Mounties and wipe them out, Riel cried: "For the love of God, kill no more of them!" It was too late to save ten white men who had fallen in the hail of Métis bullets, but it was enough to let the main force of the Mounties escape to Fort Carlton from whence they hastily pulled back to Prince Albert.

While Métis guns were blazing away at Duck Lake, the Battleford-area Cree were holding a council meeting on the Sweetgrass Reserve. Many of them by then were mere skeletons, and their ambition was no greater than to lobby for increased rations. Hoping that the uprising at Duck Lake would make the Indian Agent think twice about holding back on food, the Cree, travelling with their women and children to signify that they came in peace, marched on Battleford.

The townspeople at Battleford, most of them newly arrived from Ontario and raised on blood-curdling stories of prairie savages, panicked and crowded into the stockade, where they could be defended by two hundred policemen and three hundred home guardsmen. They abandoned their homes and storehouses. Finding everything unguarded, starving Indian women couldn't resist looting the food supplies. But as soon as they'd done this, they realized the trouble they were in. The

Indian Agent wouldn't come out of the fort to talk to them, so they decided to get out of there.

One of the Cree leaders, Red Pheasant, had died the night before they set out for Battleford, and another, Little Pine, died the day after. These were more than merely "signs." It had long been the Cree practice to leave an area where a chief had died. Accordingly, they fled to Poundmaker's reserve, hoping he could explain things to the Mounties when they came to retaliate. They arrived at about the same time as a group of Assiniboine, a few of whose young men had picked a bad time to get even with a white man accused of having murdered their sister. Poundmaker now spoke for the Battleford Cree and the Assiniboines as well as his own people.

In all, some twenty thousand Indian survivors still clung to life on the plains, despite the loss of nearly everything around them. If it came to war, the French- and English-speaking Métis between them could field no more than a thousand fighting men at the most, some of them armed with old smooth-bore hunting pieces, others with shotguns that were collector's items. Arrayed against them was an intimidating force of arms. From Winnipeg, 120 men of the 90th Rifles were already setting out for Qu'Appelle. When word came through about Duck Lake, the defence minister called for both the Regular Corps and the Reserve Corps to be sent in. In Quebec, some thousand men were mobilized from the 9th Voltigeurs, the Montreal Garrison Artillery, and the 65th Mount Royal Rifles. Ontario raised two thousand men from the Queen's Own Rifles and the 10th Royal Grenadiers. Manitoba created the 91st and Light Infantry Regiment to augment the 90th. Nova Scotia vowed to send four hundred men from the Halifax Battalion. Close to eight thousand men in all, armed with nine wobbling old cannons and two shiny new 1,200-rounds-a-minute Gatling guns marched against the Métis forces.

The Métis desperately sought an alliance with the Cree, but the chiefs, even if they had wanted to agree, probably could not have enforced any joint actions. They were losing control of their bands, who were feeling the pressure as the Métis were pushed back onto their turf. In any event, none of them were willing to joint the Métis uprising.

Instead, anger at being penned in on reserves and fury that the treaties had provided to be nearly worthless was breaking out and could not be contained. While Big Bear was away from his reserve, his rebellious son Imases and the militant Wandering Spirit decided to avenge themselves on an abusive Indian Agent and a farm instructor who had sneaked into the tents with Cree women. When the two men in question refused to open a storehouse to feed the hungry, they were killed. Then, at Frog Lake, Wandering Spirit, crazy with hatred, led the slaughter of nine whites snatched from a Catholic church. In the end, his control reasserted too late, Big Bear led his people northward through the quagmires of swamp toward the tundra, hoping to escape the advancing Canadian armies.

Edgar Dewdney, by now Lieutenant Governor of the territory as well as Indian Commissioner, had all the excuses he needed to declare a state of war. Privately, Dewdney reported to Ottawa that he saw violent incidents involving Cree at Battleford, Fort Pitt, and Frog Lake as the actions of a desperate people in the grip of starvation. They were not in any way related to the Riel Rebellion. "Things just got out of control," he would write to Macdonald on June 3, 1885 (Public Archives of Canada). In his public pronouncements, however, Dewdney claimed the Cree were definitely part of the Métis insurgency. Henceforth, any Indian who left his reserve, for whatever reason, would be considered a supporter of the rebellion, which meant, of course, that he could be shot on sight.

Dewdney quickly dispatched troops to the reserves of Piapot and the Treaty Four Cree to keep them intimidated, and likewise ordered troops to Medicine Hat and Swift Current to drive a wedge between the Blackfoot and the Cree, who had been showing signs of getting together to press for treaty revision.

At Cutknife Hill on May 2, the Canadian troops launched an assault on Poundmaker that nearly ended in utter disaster for the attackers. A force of 325 men found themselves surrounded and pinned down. They lost eight men and fourteen were wounded. The Canadians would likely have been slashed to ribbons in their retreat, if Poundmaker had not held back his warriors from pursuing them. Instead, the Cree let them depart, and the tide began to turn.

Carried from the Lakehead by train, the eight-thousand-man North-West Field Force was deployed to staging points along the newly laid tracks in time for a spring offensive. The Métis, for their part, fought a few good guerrilla battles, scoring some legendary victories. At Fish Creek, for instance, on April 24, although outnumbered five to one, Dumont's men drove back the main force of soldiers, with the loss on the Canadian side of fifty men dead or wounded, nearly ten times the Métis casualties. However, it was one victory of very few. Another occurred a couple of weeks later, when Major General Frederick Middleton, with a new appreciation for his enemy, planned an attack incorporating a flat-bottomed sternwheeler, which was bringing supplies down the South Saskatchewan. The Métis under Dumont caught the cumbersome vessel under a ferry cable, ripping off the smokestacks, mast, whistle, and loading spars, and submitting it to such withering fire that the frantic soldiers poured on the steam and fled around a bend in the river. It was a scene out of a modern Hollywood action-comedy.

When the inevitable siege of Batoche came, the Métis fought valiantly, with Riel crawling through the trenches mumbling prayers and Dumont hissing at them to spare the ammunition. The advancing militia was equipped with 70,000 Gatling-gun rounds and 1.5 million bullets for their rifles. When, after four days, one of Middleton's officers called for a bayonet charge, and led nine hundred screaming soldiers into Batoche to overcome two hundred out-of-work buffalo-hunters firing metal buttons, nails, and even pebbles, it was over swiftly. Riel's surrender three days later was almost as anticlimactic as the surrender of Poundmaker's Crees.

The only remaining military drama was the pursuit of Big Bear and those rebellious Crees who had slipped out of his control and wreaked such havoc. Big Bear was blamed for the bloodlust of Wandering Spirit. Pursued relentlessly into the swampy northland by five hundred of General Thomas Strange's men, Big Bear's two hundred remaining followers kept the army at bay until the arrival of Middleton's force of two hundred additional soldiers. The last spasm of resistance occurred at Loon Lake. After that, Big Bear's starving people gave up and struggled in to Fort Pitt to surrender. The chief himself, in a bizarre but wonderful gesture, walked a hundred miles to the east to give himself up at Fort Carlton.

In all, about eighty whites and as many Métis and Indians had been killed.

Among others, the Cree leaders, Poundmaker and Big Bear, were charged with treason-felony, even though Dewdney and his bosses in Ottawa knew that neither man had been guilty of insurrection. But these two were the main remaining agitators for treaty revisions, and it was in Ottawa's interest to lock them away. The chiefs were each given three years in the newly built Stony Mountain Penitentiary, a gothic fortress in the middle of the plains north of Winnipeg. "I would rather prefer to be hung at once than to be in that place," Poundmaker cried.

Prison life and prison guards broke the two proud chiefs: Poundmaker was so far gone physically after less than a year that he was released, only to die four months later. Big Bear lasted longer; it took a little less than two years' imprisonment to destroy him. He was released in March 1887 and died ten months later.

As for Riel, he saw at least one of his visions fulfilled. Just before crossing into Canada on his way to Batoche, he had confided to a priest: "I see a gallows on top of that hill, and I am swinging from it." He was convicted of treason and hanged on November 16, 1885.

After Riel, eighteen Métis were convicted of treason, receiving terms of up to seven years. Eight Indians, including Wandering Sprit, were hung from a common scaffold. The noose had come west with the Iron Horse. Just nine days before Riel and his death-vision became one, the last stake thus being driven through the heart of Métis resistance, the last spike itself was driven into the railway bed at Craigellachie, British Columbia, opening the Canadian Pacific line, bringing British Columbia into Confederation, and sealing the shape of the great, continent-straddling Dominion.

It had taken just fifteen years, from 1870 to 1885, to subjugate the once-mighty Cree, to banish the Blackfoot and Assiniboine and Saulteaux and Gros Ventres to internal exile, and to crush the Métis rebels. Dewdney confiscated horses and carts and arrested any Cree leaders protesting his policies. By breaking up the bands and forbidding any Indian to be off the reserve without permission, Dewdney and his successor, Halter Reed, had succeeded by 1890 in confining and subjecting the Indians of the plains to the edicts of a labyrinthine set of draconian laws.

The moves Dewdney made to control the Cree were themselves violations of the treaties, and any number of other laws. These involved political manipulation of the courts, the police, the military: sneak attacks were made on villages; men, women, and children were deliberately starved; and an environmental disaster was fostered. But perhaps the worst aspect of all was the fact that the moment Canadian authorities had the upper hand militarily, they unhesitatingly turned the North-West Territories into a prairie archipelago of what could be viewed as concentration camps, with starving prisoners watched over by soldiers and bureaucrats. This was the result of Canada's "just and honourable Indian policy."

The Indian Act – nowhere mentioned when treaties were being negotiated – had become the instrument of Ottawa's supreme rule by 1876, and it dictated virtually every detail of an Indian's life. While it allowed for elections on the reserves, the elected councils were hamstrung at every turn by their inability to make monetary decisions; true power remained in the hands of a distant white elite. And while Canada was supposed to be developing and growing as a "democracy," its growth was built squarely on the existence of hundreds of pockets of land where conquered people lived under a totalitarian thumb. The Department of Indian Affairs was from the moment of its inception an occupier's dream, a bureaucracy with absolute control over its victim's lives, from birth to death. A broken people had been scattered and locked away in camps. Canada, as the nationalists liked to say, had "become a nation."

For the Calihoos, there was an especially bitter irony: they had fled Quebec to escape the rule of Jesuits, only to find themselves under the thumbs of a secular authority no less obsessed with controlling their lives. Now, however, instead of being done in the name of God, it was done in the name of the Dominion.

PART III

Chapter 17

A Bold, Distant Pen-Stroke

WHEN THE LAST SPIKE WAS DRIVEN AT CRAIGELLACHIE, IT NOT only sealed the doom of the Plains Indians and the Métis, it also sounded the death-knell of freedom for the Indians of the Pacific Northwest.

With their backs to the mountains, the Karhiio had watched the militant white immigrant wave that was breaking across the dead sea bottom of the prairies follow them like a relentless tide out of the east. From experience, they thought of the invasion as coming from the Atlantic, whereas one had in fact been launched via the Pacific no less definitely. For more than a century, by the time Riel was hanged, European ships had been probing the west coast.

It might have seemed reasonable to Louis and Bernard Karhiio in 1820 that the Rockies were a barrier that could never be penetrated in any large-scale military way, not just because of the avalanches and rapids, but because of the powerful tribes entrenched along the way. If ever a land could be held against an invader, surely it was the mountain country between Jasper and the Great Western Sea. Guerrillas could operate there for a thousand years, one would think, sealing passes and launching attacks along canyons. And the defence would have to be mounted only during the summer months. During winter, not even a Napoleon or a Hannibal would attempt a passage.

But the coastal Indians had fallen and been swept aside, and the Indians of the Interior could mount no effective resistance either. The unbreachable wall of the Rockies had proved terrifyingly porous. How had it happened? Some of the answers everyone could guess from the fate of the Iroquois and others back east, and from the Indian experience on the prairies: disease, famine, alcohol, priests, politicians, entrepreneurs, armies, orders-in-council. Like the Plains Indians, the Coast Indians were caught entirely off guard by the federal and later the provincial "laws," kept secret from them but forced on them at gun-point.

Caught in the middle of a great power struggle over their land, the Coastal Indians, who had had the initial monopoly on trade with the Europeans, found themselves being assiduously courted by English and Spanish emissaries. So long as the outcome of the distant clash between rival empires remained in doubt, the local chiefs were treated with a degree of respect. But once surveys had made unaided navigation possible, and commercial considerations had dictated the construction of smaller ships to push deeper into the labyrinth of islands and channels and inlets, the status of the chiefs began to decline, and the invaders started to reveal their true colours.

It didn't take very long for the preliminary stage of the encounter to complete itself. The ships of the Spanish explorer Juan Jose Perez y Hernandez had been sighted at the mouth of Hesquiat Harbour, halfway along the western coast of Vancouver Island, in 1774, but luckily for the Indians there, given the Spanish record, nobody came ashore.

Four years later, the Nuu-chah-nulth became the first Indians on the west coast to discover white men when Captain James Cook's vessels worked their way into Nootka Sound. To the Nuu-chah-nulth, the ships were "houses on the water," and they decided to call the men who waved at them from the decks of *Discovery* and *Resolution Muh-mul-ni*, "floating people." When the adventurers who had gone out to the "houses on the water" reported back to their elders, the entirely reasonable conclusion was reached that the visitors were Salmon People disguised as humans.

At first, the arrival of the white men seemed like an enormous piece of luck. Nuu-chal-nulth Chief Maquinna made himself and his brother-in-law, Wickanninish, filthy rich through the trade in sea-otter furs that followed Cook. However, in order to maintain the high-volume fur trade, Maquinna had to pull people back from subsistence activities and deploy as many as four hundred men to stand by to repel rival tribes that were trying to horn in on the trade or to fend off unexpected attacks from the white men themselves, who seemed compelled to demonstrate their system of extreme punishment – usually involving cannons – at the drop of a pilfered spoon.

Between 1785 and 1825, some 450 European ships arrived on the west coast to deliver merchandise, and to pick up furs and freight them over to China, where lucrative markets waited. Trade increased to the point where it became routine for scores of huge ships to arrive from Hawaii in the spring, anchoring in Nootka or Clayoquot sounds, spending the summer trading for furs, and taking the polar route to Asia before the winter storms came howling down from the Bering Sea.

Maquinna's domination of the fur market lasted until the overhunted sea otter began to disappear. He could no longer supply the Europeans, and, in the context of the intertribal coastal social network, he promptly fell from grace. As though to add insult to injury, the white men now dared to treat him disdainfully. By heaping indignity on chiefs – thereby insulting the whole tribe – the white men guaranteed that sooner or later they would reap a whirlwind. In 1802, when an angered Maquinna launched an attack on a trading ship, killing two dozen crewmen, they did.

The near-extermination of the great herds of sea otter was the first of an interminable series of ecological disasters. At the peak of the fur frenzy, white traders were absolutely mad for sea-otter pelts. They would pay what seemed to the Indians outrageously over-inflated prices. Yet hardly anyone could argue with the Indians for directing their energies into otter-hunting on a scale no one had imagined before. The proceeds from trading a single pelt could keep an Indian family well supplied with staples and European luxuries for a year, to say nothing of helping them potlatch their clan's way to power and prestige.

Huge fleets of canoes accordingly swept the coast in search of otter, until finally the animals were so scarce that the hunt was no longer worth anyone's time. Long before the collapse of the sea-otter herds exacerbated tensions, however, skirmishes between whites and Indians had grown common. Raised on horror stories about Indians, the white men were paranoid and trigger-happy. In the very early days, if several large canoes were to approach a ship at the same time, the crew frequently would open fire with muskets and cannons. If an Indian were to steal a piece of cutlery or a metal fitting from an anchored ship, hostages – including chiefs – would often be seized and whole villages would be shelled. The Spanish commander at Yuquot shot Chief Callicum over a minor matter, and when Chief Wickanninish tried to grab a British ship to even the score, the captain retaliated by burning down the entire Clayoquot village of Opitsat – "the work of ages," as an appalled sailor, Columbia officer John Bait (quoted in Wisdom of the Elders), who had been forced to take part in the torching party, sadly put it – consisting of some two hundred beautiful longhouses, with all their totems, carvings, treasures, and heirlooms.

By the time the Europeans landed on the sandy slopes of the west coast, nearly three centuries had elapsed since they had initially struggled up on the rocks of Newfoundland. The original French interlopers on the Atlantic side had been equipped with blunderbusses, which, while spectacular, were scarcely any more effective than bows and arrows. However, by the 1790s, the British and Spanish alike were carrying much more serious armaments. In contrast, the native people had not developed a new killing tool since the double-bladed knife. Their creative energies had gone primarily into art and theatre, the problems of hunting and fishing having been solved.

From the moment that "unscrupulous traders" – as the history books like to call them, as if they were an exception rather than the rule – began handing over guns and alcohol in exchange for sea-otter furs, an arms race began among the local adversaries. A balance of power that had endured for thousands and thousands of years came crashing down virtually overnight. Warriors who had been trained in hand-to-hand combat were suddenly mowing each other down *en masse* from a distance. Although the French and English had been warring with each other for centuries – so long that they referred to each other as "the ancient enemy" – the nations of the Pacific Northwest had been pitted against each other four times as long. These were deeply rooted rivalries, complete with linguistic, cultural, political, and even mythological dimensions.

The impact of guns on the societies of the Pacific Northwest was no minor side-effect of the invasion. It collapsed everything like a deck of cards. In Europe, centuries before, an entire system of warfare had come to a thundering end thanks to the introduction of gunpowder. Its effect on very, very ancient native feuds on the west coast was to make possible an Armageddon, in which everyone was forced to go for a final solution because the other side was coming with it too. The rate of escalation was so exponential that skirmishes became full-scale "contests of mutual annihilation" overnight.

The southern Kwakiutl raided down into Puget Sound, as well as plundering northern tribes that were making their way down to Fort Victoria to trade. Armadas of armed warriors assembled to do battle with one another, the most epic contest being between the Euclataw Kwakiutl and Salish forces from the Fraser River, Puget Sound, Comox, and Victoria, which ended with the Kwakiutl making their last great push into Salish territory before the iron European boot came down on all of them.

The arrival of guns was, of course, paralleled by the arrival of disease. The first infections were among the Tlinkit, thanks to Spanish navigators in 1775. The Haida population plummeted from perhaps 8,400 in 1800 to less than a thousand a century later. Today, only two inhabited villages remain in the Queen Charlotte Islands. An early missionary estimated a population of ten thousand Tsimshian, but only some three thousand survived into the twentieth century. The Bella Coola, whose ranks when Alexander Mackenzie visited in 1793 were approximately two or three thousand, have since been reduced to scarcely three hundred living in a single village. The Nuu-chah-nulth plunged from six thousand at the end of the eighteenth century to a low point of fifteen hundred. From perhaps eight thousand in 1750, the Kwakiutl were ultimately cut down to fewer than two thousand before they began to recover, although the casualties may in fact have been much higher. Some archaeologists now suspect there may have been twenty thousand Indians living on the west coast of Vancouver Island alone, a figure previously given for the population of the Nuu-chah-nulth, southern Kwakiutl, and Nuxault combined, in which case the death-rate rises horrifyingly to nine out of ten.

In 1853, a brig arrived from San Francisco at Neah Bay and a sailor came ashore with smallpox. A trader named Samuel Hancock recorded what happened:

> It is truly shocking to witness the ravages of this disease here. . . . The natives after a time became so much alarmed that when any of their friends were attacked, all of the other occupants who lived in the house would at once leave it and the sick person with a piece of dried salmon and some water, laying all their personal effects by the sick persons, not intending to ever approach them again; sometimes the retreating ones would lie down anywhere on the beach until they died. I have, in walking along, encountered them

lying in this situation when they would beg in the most
supplicating manner for medicine or something to relieve
them, promising to serve me as slaves all their lives should
they recover, if I would contribute some way to their recovery. . . . In a few weeks from the introduction of the disease, hundreds of the natives became victims to it. The
beach for a distance of eight miles was literally strewn with
the dead bodies of these people. . . . In their distress [they]
concluded I might afford them some relief, and as soon as
they would feel the symptoms of the disease, they would
come about my house and lie down in the yard to die. They
continued this until the dead were so numerous I could
scarcely walk about around my house, and was obliged to
have holes dug where I deposited fifteen or twenty bodies
in each. Still they continued to come about me to die, in
such numbers that I finally hauled them down the beach at
a time of low tide, so they would drift away. (*Wisdom of the
Elders*, p. 226)

The worst year was 1862, when smallpox was introduced at
Fort Victoria, and within two years, one-third of the native
population of what is now British Columbia had died horri-
bly. Travelling back and forth by canoe, families would have
to stop so often to land and bury children who had died that
little "towns" of new graves sprang up along the coast.

Against this background of decimated families and shattered clans, it is astonishing that the coastal tribes stuck so
tenaciously to their collective political agendas. They had
been virtually atomized, yet they continued to trade, to war, to
dance and carve and sing, and, above all, to potlatch.

The potlatch lay at the heart of coastal civilization. It not
only consolidated everyone's position within their clans,
since they all had to pull together in a united effort to maintain the dignity and prestige of their chief, and henceforth
themselves, it was the means by which wealth could be regu-
larly redistributed. Nobody could ever be poverty-stricken,
since they were always bound to receive gifts, and nobody

could hoard wealth, since there was no prestige attached to conspicuous consumption. Quite the reverse. The potlatch meant conspicuous sharing, conspicuous giving. Indeed, during a potlatch nearly every article of furniture, every utensil, every blanket in the longhouse might be given away. In exchange, the host would have retained or acquired a certain social standing, as well as considerable long-term security, since sooner or later, all that had been given out would be given back at 100 per cent interest.

It was a kind of "pyramid scheme" in reverse, with the people at the bottom constantly receiving payoffs. A society where giving and sharing were institutionalized as the central mechanisms of power was obviously going to be at tremendous ideological odds with an empire based on taking and accumulating. Among the Coast Indians, "winner give all" was the rule.

Potlatches also served as forums at which a host chief could reiterate his precise ancestry to the assembled witnesses, thus clarifying for the community the prerogatives of his children and grandchildren in terms of crests, names, dances, songs, and stories – all the means by which their pedigree was established.

In a non-print society, such public affirmations and acknowledgements were essential to stability. These gatherings took the place of legal documents and genealogical records. Such information couldn't be stored. It had to be kept in the public domain through repetition. This was all the more essential when, as among the Southern Kwakiutl and the Nuu-chah-nulth, the personal names of people of high rank might change several times as they were given other names held in trust by the family. The origins of these names would be narrated by an orator. By the time the narration was over, everyone would know everything they ever wanted to know and more about the family giving the potlatch, the chief especially.

As white trade goods came flooding into the system, the potlatch itself was transformed from a sensible exchange of maybe a few hundred elk skins, otter skins, mink blankets, and deerskin blankets, into an extravagant orgy in which buckets, washtubs, Hudson's Bay blankets, cups, plates, bowls, barrels, boxes, sacks of food and clothing, tools, you name it, were poured out.

On the surface, it was a brief golden age of potlatching, but underneath, family groups decapitated by epidemics were desperately still struggling to avoid the social chaos that would follow if broken lineages weren't mended. It was absolutely essential that people regroup. What outsiders took to be the wastefulness of the potlatch was an overcompensation for hideous losses and a frantic scramble to build something up again.

At the same time – and for the same reasons – native carvers bent to the task of creating totem poles with such speed and additional artistic capability, thanks to superior tools, that their work was revolutionized and brought close to the point of mass production. Forests of totems arose along the coast, just as the culture that erected them was being chopped down.

All this artistic, political, and social turmoil meant that, so long as the Indians remained in their own villages, haunted and semi-abandoned as they may have become, with weeds growing up between the planks of empty neighbouring longhouses, the old ways were essentially secure. They could have put their civilization back together again, given time. But a pivotal event that reduced the chances of such a recovery occurred on the western side of the Rockies in 1824 – just a generation after the runaway Karhiio family of Iroquois had settled down in their woodland Promised Land a thousand miles to the east. Had the Karhiios realized what was happening beyond the mountains, they might have seriously reconsidered their location.

That year the Hudson's Bay Company opened its main trading post at Fort Vancouver, in what is now Oregon, and started pushing up the coast and into the interior, establishing a chain of posts. Trade between ships and coastal villages slowed. Now the Indians had to bring their furs to the trading post.

By this time, they had grown accustomed to a wide assortment of trade goods, had even developed certain dependencies, including alcohol. As the supply of sea-otter pelts began to run out, the Indians found themselves having to buy cloth and clothes to keep warm, but they had nothing to buy them with, the main trade item, the pelts, having vanished.

Moreover, the men who operated the posts didn't go away when winter came. And, soon, they were marrying native women.

In 1849, Britain issued a Royal Charter proclaiming Vancouver Island – all of it – a colony. At that time, there were 774 non-natives living on the entire island, concentrated mostly in tiny pockets at Fort Victoria and Nanaimo; 11,700 Indians occupied the rest. Nevertheless, ownership of the mighty Pacific Ocean island had unilaterally been changed by a bold distant pen-stroke, backed up, of course, by two hundred-ton navy gunships with their rows of enormous cannons. Britain's grip tightened inexorably, and the drastically weakened coastal people were in no position to resist any longer.

When businessman Gilbert Malcolm Sproat landed at the head of Alberni Inlet to set up a sawmill in 1869, he marched up to the chief and told him flatly that his people would have to move their village. This shoreline that the Indians' homes were sitting on – and had been sitting on since the last Ice Age – had just been bought by Sproat and his friends from the Queen of England. Would the chief hurry up and get everyone moving?

An old Indian man told Sproat: "We see your ships and hear things that make our hearts grow faint. They say that more King-George-men will soon be here and will take our land, our firewood, our fishing grounds. That we shall be placed on a little spot, and shall have to do everything according to the fancies of the King-George-men" (quoted in *Wisdom of the Elders*, p. 218.) Truer words . . .

By 1858, word had reached San Francisco of a gold bonanza along the Fraser Valley. Thousands of gold-miners from America, Britain, France, Italy, Germany – white-skinned men, black-skinned men, yellow-skinned men – were pouring ashore from paddlewheelers at Victoria, which had become the base camp for one of the most insane gold rushes in history. With the miners came fishermen, cooks, speculators, land agents, auctioneers, loan sharks, remittance men, and brokers. The oh-so-pleasant wooded hillsides were cleared immediately. Amid the stumps a shantytown arose, with the price of lots being flipped from $50 to $3,000 over-night. A small armada of boats was suddenly being con-structed in preparation for a major landing on the mainland across the Strait of Georgia, where the trek to the goldfields could begin. The arrival of all these rough-hewn men prompted the original British colonists to call for military assistance from the Crown. Some 160 Royal Engineers and a "hanging judge" arrived.

So ferocious was the impact of the miners that the sandbars of the Fraser River for some two hundred miles upriver were panned out within no time at all. The boom tumbled swiftly into bust and stayed that way for half a decade, until word came of a bigger find – gold by the tons! – in the western foot-hills of the Cariboo Mountains. This was what the colony at Victoria wanted to hear, since it reaped a fortune each time the miners passed through. The Cariboo rush eventually pro-duced about $100 million worth of gold, enough to draw upwards of ten thousand miners and camp followers to the diggings. Barkerville, in the interior, briefly became the big-gest town west of Chicago and north of San Francisco. Sternwheelers began to appear on the rivers of the plateau. The Cariboo Trail was rammed through – a four-hundred-mile roadway blasted out of solid rock and propped up by timber cribwork filled with rock ballast, capped by a steel cable suspension bridge across the chasm of the Thompson River. Greed, as ever, financed the work of empire-building.

And what resistance did the miners encounter as they stormed up onto the plateau – the last bastion of free Indians in the southern part of what would soon be Canada?

Some. About a hundred miles up the Fraser, a band of armed Indians intercepted a band of armed miners, and it was only because the chief was bought off by British authorities that a head-to-head shooting match was avoided. But it was very muted, the interior resistance.

For one thing, the plateau had been a peaceable kingdom as long as memory went back. The people living there – Lillooet, Thompson, Shuswap, Okanagan, Lakes, Carrier, Chilcotin, Sekani, Nicola, and Kootenay – shared resources, traded, and wintered with each other, fished together, and enjoyed a common political system. Each village was autonomous. Village chiefs were picked by a council of elders on the basis of status, knowledge, and worthiness. Sometimes, if a chief stopped making sense, everyone would simply ignore him. Chiefs were seen as managers of resources, which were held collectively. Collaborative activities like deerhunting and fishing led to a lot of interaction between the groups, which meant that the peoples of the plateau were not given to xenophobia.

However, they were at a disadvantage militarily, because they were decentralized democracies. Observing the Okanagans in the early 1800s, a fur trader noted with some amazement: "Their general maxim is, that Indians were born to be free, and that no man has natural right to the obedience of another" (quoted by Douglas Hudson in *Native Peoples*). Such individualism mitigated strongly against the mobilization of the plateau peoples into large, unified military commands.

Moreover, by the time the legions of gold-miners and claim-jumpers had clawed their way into the interior, the region had already been reduced to the status of a semi-haunted land. As early as 1782, the first smallpox epidemics had spread from the coast, carried by Indian traders. In 1800 and again in 1832, plagues had swept across the plateau, dropping thousands of men, women, and children in their tracks. A Carrier Indian band in the Ootsa Lake region was completely eliminated in 1837. Even if they had had the man-power in the first place to defend the high country between the Rockies and the Coast Range, by the time the white man started penetrating in formidable numbers, the Plateau Indi-ans were much reduced in their ability to defend themselves.

Chapter 18

One Big Claim-Jump

IN ORDER TO GET THE CROWN COLONY OF BRITISH COLUMBIA TO vote to join Canada, all the Dominion had had to do was promise to push a rail line through to the west coast, a move that would make every speculator, hustler, and developer in British Columbia wealthy beyond his wildest dreams. The terms of the union proposed by the colonists, however, made no reference to the Indians. It didn't matter that, at that time, the Indians living in the area numbered thirty thousand, compared to ten thousand whites. The Indians weren't consulted, let alone allowed to vote.

In the normal course of events, such activity by an immigrant minority would offend the people of any country, no matter how tolerant. Certainly the British themselves would never have permitted it. But even if they hadn't been ravaged by disease and divided among themselves, there was little the Indians could have done against the British. The trouble with being a coastal society, they had learned, was that nearly every village could be fired upon point-blank by gunships.

Led by an autocratic, nepotistic, "furiously violent" giant of a man, James Douglas, who had once reputedly run single-handed into an Indian village and blown a suspected murderer's brains out in front of his entire family, the British colonists used an entirely illegal tactic to give themselves everything in sight, taking it from everyone around them. To smooth over the rough edges of the impending gigantic land heist, Douglas took the "moderate" position that, while the Crown obviously had absolute title to the land, the Indians did have a few proprietary rights (such as twelve thousand years on the same spot), which ought properly to be extinguished by "deeds of conveyance" and by payment of small amounts of compensation.

While acting as chief factor for the Hudson's Bay Company, Douglas negotiated fourteen such treaties with the Coast Salish and Kwakiutl around Victoria, Nanaimo, and Fort Rupert, giving them small reserves and a few blankets in exchange for the surrender of the rest of their land "entirely and forever." Naturally they would retain their hunting and fishing rights on adjacent unoccupied "traditional" hunting grounds. In total, these treaties, negotiated between 1850 and 1854, covered only 358 square miles of Vancouver Island! The rest of the island and of what would now be called the Province of British Columbia would become part of the huge new empire the colonists and the Canadians were cobbling together hurriedly, lest the Americans swoop up from Oregon and grab the place for themselves.

Douglas's successor, contractor Joseph Trutch, was frankly contemptuous of any mollycoddling of the Indians. His view was that "Indians really have no right to the lands they claim, nor are they of any actual value or utility to them; and I cannot see why they should either retain these lands to the prejudice of the general interests of the Colony, or be allowed to make a market of them either to the government or to individuals."

Trutch's attitude reflected perfectly the views of the settlers. In the discussions that preceded Confederation, there was only a brief mention of "Indian affairs." When a motion was introduced in the legislature for the protection of Indians, it was defeated twenty to one. Another motion that attempted at least to urge the extension of Canadian Indian policy into

British Columbia after union was withdrawn. The Act of 1871, admitting British Columbia into Canada, included the following incredible provision: "The charges of the Indians and the trusteeship and management of the lands reserved for their use and benefit, shall be assumed by the Dominion Government, and a policy as liberal as that hitherto pursued by the British Columbia Government shall be continued by the Dominion Government after the union."

Grabbing everything except 358 square miles was considered "liberal"!

At midnight, July 19, 1871, white residents of Victoria gathered in the streets of their staid, Kentish-style hamlet, dominated by the "bird-cage"-like government offices of which they were so proud, to listen to the bells ringing and the cannons sounding. It was a stirring moment.

However, for all but a handful of the Indians affected by this momentous transformation, the entry of British Columbia into Confederation meant that the full force of the Indian Act would slam down around them and they would be enclosed by the bars of an invisible cage. In addition to new masters in London and Victoria, the Indians now found themselves having to contend with yet another white overlord, this one called a "prime minister," John A. Macdonald, who was also Minister of the Interior, and who had just successfully concluded one of the most far-reaching conquests in history.

The main ramification of Confederation for the natives was that the Indian Act immediately applied to everything they did. It allowed for the establishment of small reserves – permitting concentrations of no more than five hundred people – for each of some two hundred widely scattered local bands. The allocations were unilateral, involving little if any consultation, and no latitude was left for disagreement. When it came to pushing Indians around, it was hard to differentiate between these new Canadian bosses and the King-George-men of old. Perhaps these were trickier.

Witness the Indian Act! If a "Catholic Act" had been devised which prohibited Catholics from going to Mass or

Confession or having Communion or listening to Latin or reading their Catechisms, it would quickly be dubbed the "Anti-Catholic Act." The Indian Act, by the same token, should have been called the "Anti-Indian Act," and there would have been a lot less confusion. In its initial efforts to deal with the problem of the surviving inhabitants of the land which Canada had just taken at gunpoint, the lawmakers in Ottawa cooked up a legislative witches' brew of regulations that covered every imaginable contingency in an Indian's life, leaving government agents hovering over his or her every activity from birth to death, with the power to snatch children from homes, monitor movements, prohibit "undesirable" activities, seize property, deny freedom of speech, religion, and self-expression, and throw "troublemakers" into jail promptly. Indians could not vote, drink, or own any land. The occupation was complete. And that's what Canadian union was: the successfully completed occupation of a host of formerly sovereign countries.

In 1884, amendments to the Indian Act made the potlatch illegal. This was the single most damaging blow the Canadians could have delivered to the west coast Indians, since the potlatch was the all-purpose central family and political event of tribal life, especially in the wake of the epidemics. Potlatching was, among other things, the means of passing on the names and traditions and history of one's family. Without that continuity the Indians could fall into a state of rootlessness, of separation from the past and all its meaning. With more people having died recently than were now alive, the Indians needed to keep track, to stay in contact. By forbidding the potlatch, the Canadians sought to dismantle native societies from within.

At the same time, the government gave Indian Agents the power to control travel between reserves, even if they didn't always use it. Since the usual practice in a potlatch was to bring the different clans together, led by their chiefs, agents could station themselves to intercept visiting chiefs, demanding to know what they were doing away from their reserves. So far as one infamous Indian Agent, William Halliday (quoted in *Prosecution or Persecution*), was concerned, the potlatch, by causing Indians to "waste time", rendered them "generally unfit . . . for being British subjects in the proper sense of the word." However, Halliday and his superiors were perfectly aware, that "banning the potlatch" meant literally banning west coast Indian society. The Indians went underground, of course, and, as had the Christians and so many others before them, nourished the flame of their religion (and everything else) despite persecution. The Canadians locked up Kwakiutl elders who were caught secretly potlatching, forcing dignified chiefs to feed pigs in Oakalla Prison and strip-searching gentle old women.

Beyond stamping out potlatching, the deepest damage the politicians and their religious allies the missionaries could inflict was to drive a wedge between the generations. Children were whisked off to missionary schools, where they were subject to beatings if they were caught talking, even whispering, in their own languages. The "Secret Societies" of the Kwakiutl were likewise outlawed, even though their real-life function was to provide theatrical entertainment during the rainy months. As the schools did their brainwashing work and young Christian Indian couples started marrying in churches, they were instructed to move into single-family dwellings, an intentional death-blow to tribal culture.

Although gold-miners had been pouring into the Fraser Valley and pushing up into the interior since 1858, the real waves of immigrants didn't hit until Confederation and the CPR were *fait accompli*. Reduced fares on the railway and the promise of free land in British Columbia were the means the Minister of Immigration used to lure settlers. The results were predictable. Modern-day Chief Counsellor Edward Moody, quoted in *Wisdom of the Elders*, described the situation at Bella Coolla, where a whole valley leading up to the Chilcotin Plateau had belonged to the Nuxalk people until the arrival in 1912 of Norwegian colonists who had taken the Canadian government up on its kindly offer:

They didn't even let the Indian people know what was happening . . . . The population of the valley today is about eighteen hundred and we make up eight hundred of the eighteen hundred. We occupy just over three thousand acres and the others have six hundred thousand acres from the head of the valley to here. Yet (when Mackenzie arrived) we had thirty-four villages from the mouth of the river to the precipice. (p. 237)

Finally, timber leases began to be handed out to white companies. "Crown" land had now been passed from the uncalloused hands of the distant British monarch into the sweaty paws of local robber barons.

Nuu-chah-nulth elder Peter Webster recalled in his autobiography, *As Far As I Know*, also quoted in *Wisdom of the Elders*:

Fisheries officers (in the early 1900s) demanded licenses for fishing and arrested us for shooting seals. . . . The lumber people . . . seemed to own the entire forest. This made it illegal for us to get trees for canoes, cedar bark for weaving, except from our tiny reserves. When the loggers moved in, the animals we hunted and trapped disappeared. The destruction of the forests was easy to see. Our use of the woods was hardly noticeable. All these things made it easier to get into trouble with the law. I think a lot of us became "criminals" without really knowing the reason. Once, I was arrested for possession of the fur of fur seals . . . the white people took away our land and made so many rules and regulations that I sometimes wonder if it will end when we have to buy a license each time we want to sleep with our wives.

In the same book, *Wisdom of the Elders*, Clayoquot Chief Jimmy Jim observed bleakly in 1916: "We cannot sell timber or we can't cut down the timber on our own reserves. It is just like holding us as blind men."

Told years before by the provincial government that he would only be given twenty acres per family of reserve land, while white people were being given 320 acres per family just for coming here, and could buy an additional 320 acres, while the Indians could acquire nothing more, Southern Kwakiutl Chief Dawson of Mamalillikula cried out: "We can't allow the place to go that way! We never sold it. . . . What right has [the government] to sell it before I was through with it, because I was the owner of it!" (*Wisdom of the Elders*)

There is no way around the historical truth. The land had been invaded and taken over by illegal means. It was stolen from the natives: stolen, hijacked, grabbed, ripped-off, strong-armed. All of those words apply. The legal niceties of the marriage between the country of Canada and the colony of British Columbia cannot disguise the fact that British Columbia was one big claim-jump from beginning to end, and the claim-jumpers got away with it.

Chapter 19

The Empire of Canada

IN THE LATE 1960S AND EARLY 1970S A WAVE OF BOOKS AND articles appeared that took a second, harsher look at Indian history in Canada, and the sheer scale of the disaster which had taken place a century earlier began to unfold. In a sense, it had actually begun eight centuries before, when the Norsemen arrived to stake out tiny settlements in Greenland. It is ironic indeed that the Inuit, the very last of the "Canadian" native peoples to be brought under imperial control, were, in fact, the first to have encountered the Europeans.

The initial brush with Norsemen in Greenland produced no lasting effect. The Norsemen left only a few small ruins on the windswept rocks. The next Inuit experience of European adventurers came in the late 1400s with the arrival in northwestern Atlantic waters of Basque and Portuguese whalers and fishermen. In 1501, several dozen Inuit were captured by Gaspar Corte-Real and hauled back to Europe for inspection. Their survival is not recorded, so they no doubt expired in Europe's alien climate. Over the sixteenth and seventeenth centuries, fishermen and whalers, along with a few explorers, appeared in ever-increasing numbers around Greenland, Baffin Island, and Labrador, but the Inuit were spared any more contact than that until the eighteenth century, when perma-

nent European outposts first appeared, established by traders
and missionaries.

These influences were relatively benign at first, especially
compared to what the Russians were doing to the Aleuts in
the western Arctic. The Aleuts, the Pacific Yupik Eskimos,
and the Tlingit Indians fought back bravely, but they were
overwhelmed by Russian cannons once the Czar got wind of
the fortune in furs to be had. On Unimak Island, a place since
known as the Bay of Women, the Russians massacred all the
surviving Aleut males who had dared to resist them, leaving
only women in the tribe. To this day, many of the Aleuts,
descendants of Russian fathers, have red hair. The invasion
and destruction of the combined Aleut nations was an imperial action by the Russians, unresisted by any other outside
power. The spoils – the Aleutian Islands and Alaska – were
sold to the United States after the animals of the area – as well
as the Indians and Eskimos – had been rendered just about
extinct.

Then, during the eighteenth and nineteenth centuries,
white men brought smallpox, measles, and mumps to the
Arctic. Measles caused horrendous depletion of populations,
and in 1902, the inhabitants of Southhampton Island in Hudson Bay were killed off completely by typhus. In 1826, when
John Franklin explored the coast between the Alaskan border
and Cape Bathurst, 2,000 Eskimos lived there: by 1929, there
were less than 800, most of them refugees and immigrants
from the Alaska area. The Canadian Eskimo population had
been estimated at 22,500; by 1929 it had reached a low of
8,000.

In 1915, an unusual combination of snow and rain, freezing
and thawing – a small climatic variation – left the snow-cover
so ice-hard that caribou couldn't break through to their food
supplies underneath; they died in massive numbers. This
signalled the beginning of the decade-long Great Famine,
and the Inuit, already devastated by sickness, were ill-
prepared for it. Equipped with rifles by the traders, encouraged to buy European goods with the profits from the sale of

hides, Inuit hunters had gone after the slow-moving musk-oxen, which could be easily tracked and killed. By 1900, the muskoxen had all but gone. When faced with a scarcity of caribou such as that in 1915, the Inuit would normally simply have switched to hunting and eating the muskoxen, which could handle such environmental disruptions. But there were no muskoxen; overkill had done in this alternative source of nutrition. Reduced to eating their dogs and boiling their parkas, five Caribou Inuit tribes saw an average of two out of three of the survivors of the plagues die from hunger. A sixth tribe, the Tahiuyarmiut, were reduced to a mere handful and eventually disappeared into another tribe with which they took shelter. It was technical extinction. By 1925, only about five hundred Caribou Inuit survived.

Still worse was to come. The Inuit had been visited by influenza, tuberculosis, and infantile paralysis all at once. Unable to hunt, starving, they were on the verge of extinction. In the 1950s, writers like Peter Freuchen and Farley Mowat began to make the Canadian public aware of the Inuits' situation, and the federal government decided to act – at least up to the point of spending some money on the dying Eskimos. While they were at it, why should they not realize an administrative dream? It was decided to move the Caribou Inuit, whose eco-system had been destroyed, into five "administrative centres," and to make them complete wards of the state. Mixed up there with survivors of the Netsilik and Aivilik people, the remnants of the Caribou Inuit were subjected by teachers, missionaries, administrators, and mandarins to the final assault on their independence and self-sufficiency.

As disease, weapons, and famine, introduced or caused by the white man, were striking at the mainly coastal Inuit, the tribes of the Mackenzie and Yukon river basins were experiencing the same disasters. Mainly woodland peoples, the Sekani, Beaver, Chipewyan, Slave, Dogrib, Nahani, Kutchin, Hare, and Yellowknife were spread thinly over the largest remaining "unoccupied" terrain in the world, so there was never any hope of them uniting in time to meet the threat. They were knocked off one by one.

The Sekani, the People of the Rocks ("rocks" meaning the northern Rockies), controlled the valley of the Peace River, having been stopped from moving any further south by the Carrier and Shuswap Indians. They were an extremely loose-knit group, barely what you could call a tribe, but they had a common language and a common culture and there was plenty of intermarrying. Several independent bands were under the guidance of a leader with no official powers. Polygamy was permitted, with marriage between brothers and sisters common.

In 1805, a trading post went up at Fort McLeod in what is now the Northwest Territories, and alcohol and disease were passed on immediately to the natives. Demoralized and stricken, the Sekani watched helplessly as white trappers tramped across their hunting grounds and white miners began tearing up the earth wherever they choose. Game began to vanish, and the sickened natives started perishing from hunger, as well. There were more than 1,000 Sekani before the traders arrived: by 1923, there were 160 left.

Next to fall were the Beaver Indians. The Beavers were a deeply religious, nomadic band, equally as independent as the Sekani. They deposited their dead in trees and the families threw away the belongings of the deceased. Youths fasted to acquire guardian spirits. Leadership was by example and dedication; there was no formalized authority. Their first experience of the influence of the white man was second-hand: in 1760, bands of Cree, armed with rifles by fur traders, crossed the Mackenzie Basin and forced the Beaver from the Athabasca Valley into the Peace Basin. Fur-trading posts followed, and then the alcohol and disease and hunger. Suddenly there were too many dead for the living to leave in trees; they had to lie where they fell. When they became christianized, they began burying them in coffins in the ground. By 1924, at the end of the long cycle of epidemics, there were about six hundred Beavers left in communities scattered along the Peace River. About a hundred years earlier there had been at least fifteen hundred by even the most conservative estimates.

The Chipewyans inhabited a huge expanse of mosquito-haunted land projecting westward in a blunt wedge from near the mouth of the Winnipeg River. Well-equipped with firearms by the Hudson's Bay Company, the Chipewyans had made good use of their control of the land around the Hudson's Bay Company post that had been established in 1717. They made the Yellowknife and Dogrib pay a fee to trade their furs, and they drove the coastal Eskimos northward. Battles were fought with armed Cree who had driven the Beavers to the west, until a peace was concluded in 1760 – just in time for the arrival of smallpox. According to explorer Samuel Hearne, some "nine-tenths" of the Chipewyans were stricken.

A trading post was built at Lake Athabasca in 1788, which lured the survivors in from the woodlands. Shaken to their roots and weakened in every respect, they gradually became more and more dependent on the post. New diseases appeared, including influenza, so that they were wracked intermittently by epidemics, but were no longer able to flee. At one point, their population plunged from probably 3,500 – they were the most populous of the sub-Arctic Indians – down to a tenth of that number.

Surrounded on all sides by other tribes, the Yellowknife people, never a very big tribe, perhaps some 430 strong in the late eighteenth century, ranged around the area northeast of Great Slave Lake. They saw traditional political boundaries around them collapse as a result of the introduction of guns. Harassed in the east by armed Chipewyan, the Yellowknife had nowhere to go. They fought back against the Chipewyan, and became engaged in skirmishes with their Slave, Dogrib, and Hare neighbours, who were also feeling pressure from the disruptions caused by drastic arms-instigated change in the balance of power. They were eventually defeated by the Dogribs, and forced to retreat to the northeast corner of Great

Slave Lake, where they amalgamated with the Chipewyans. Today, they tend to consider themselves Chipewyans, although some 150 Yellowknife descendants can be traced. As a people, they vanished into a crack created by the re-arranging of the political landscape that occurred almost overnight. Another technical extinction.

The Slave Indians lived in the forests on the edges of the barren grounds, protected by their reputation for witch-craft from attack by other tribes – at least until the Cree, equipped with rifles, sent them packing down the Mackenzie River to the mouth of the Laird. They were known for the most part as peaceful people, although, when pushed, they turned around and pushed the people next to them, in this case the Nahani who were forced out of the Upper Laird into the mountains. Although the Slaves attributed sickness and death to sorcery, they never abandoned any of their sick or aged, no matter how rough the going got, and they believed in an afterlife. Today they number 800. The pre-European population was around 1,250.

The Nahani, whom the Slaves displaced from the Upper Laird, remained about as isolated from the white world as you could get, which could account for the fact that there are half as many of them today as the estimated fifteen hundred of pre-European times – an unusually large percentage. There were several tribes among them, two of which – the Pelly and Ross River Indians – were obliterated when a displaced, heavily armed neighbour crossed the mountains and stormed into their valley. The invader was probably a tribe fleeing the Slaves or Dogribs, who were in retreat before the Yel-lowknifes, who were in turn being harassed by the Chipe-wyans, who had been armed by the fur traders. This is what it kept coming back to: the rifles brought chaos to a long-stable land. The other fatal afflictions arrived only after the chaos had been generated. Disruption, dislocation, and war strike directly at the health of a people, softening them up for disease.

Trapped between Great Bear and Great Slave lakes and the

Mackenzie River, with the Yellowknifes raiding from the north, the Dogribs, flanked by the Chipewyans and Slaves, could have suffered a fate similar to the Pelly and Ross River Indians, except that two things happened. First, the smallpox plagues opened up an escape route for them in the southeast, where the Chipewyans and Cree were so badly decimated that the survivors pulled back from valleys they had occupied. And secondly, the Dogribs rallied and decisively routed the Yellowknifes. Their position as one of the very last tribes to be run to ground, as it were, by the traders, or by others wielding the traders' weapons, meant that the Dogribs survived the interregnum relatively well. There are some 750 of them today, compared to 1,250 in the days before gunfire began to echo across the tundra.

Caught in a fastness between the Tlingit on the other side of the mountains in the Pacific Northwest, with whom they traded, and the Eskimos to the north, with whom they both traded and fought, the Kutchin created a flash of rainbow colours amid their more dourly attired neighbours. They wore brightly decorated garments and were passionate games-players, singers, and dancers. Descent was counted on the female side. Their chiefs, like others in the region, were appointed during emergencies on the basis of merit, and discarded as authorities when emergencies were over. The spirit of egalitarianism reigned in the basin of the Yukon until the beginning of the twentieth century, despite the steady decline in population caused in part by conflict with the Russians on the coast. However, inland "remoteness" proved utterly useless as a defence against the diseases of the white man. They weren't actually conquered until the RCMP arrived in their midst quite a while later, but their death rate was appalling. Where three thousand Kutchin used to live, only seven hundred live now. When the silence fell, it left huge, empty, domed sweat-houses, and not even an echo of the singing.

By the time the ripple effect of imported arms, alcohol, and germs reached the 750-odd Hare Indians, living north and west of Great Bear Lake, it seemed somehow more cruel and pitiless because it was being visited upon a timid people who lived almost totally on rabbits, who hid their camps under fallen trees, and who fled from strangers on sight. They were afraid of the Eskimos, afraid of neighbouring Indians, and showed sensible fearfulness when approached by white men. The Hares had been chased by Yellowknifes equipped with guns. Later, they were stricken by all the epidemics that were ravaging the other tribes along the Mackenzie River. There was no place to burrow, no place left to hide. In fact, by then, there was no place left in all of North America where the Indian people had not been physically overrun, surrounded, and cordoned off.

Political repression of the kind still experienced in the Canadian North today, as opposed to mere economic and cultural imperialism, began as a side effect of Confederation. With the transfer of Rupert's Land to the new Dominion in 1870, all native people north of the 60th Parallel, whether they knew it or not, were placed by a stroke of a pen under Canadian administration.

Since headlong free-enterprise development was a phe-nomenon in the southern parts of the new nation-state, there had been no move to do anything more about this last great territorial acquisition until 1880, when the Arctic islands were handed over by the Crown and incorporated into the North-West Territories. In 1898, the Yukon was broken off as a separate administrative parcel to satisfy the greed of gold prospectors in the Klondike, and Treaty Eight was signed. In 1900, the area south of Great Slave Lake was included in Treaty Eight, to clear the way for more mining activity. The Indians were told they could no longer move beyond their new reserve limits. When oil was discovered at Fort Norman in 1920, and a decision was quickly reached to clear the decks of any Indian claims, as had been done on every previous occasion when valuable resources were found, a new and brilliant manoeuvre was tried.

Since the North-West Territories, unlike the southern "Fertile Belt," wasn't going to be used by immigrants for farming, there was no pressure to isolate the natives from the land itself. The only pressure was to isolate them from any control of the resources in the land. Thus, a new treaty – Treaty Eleven – was written, allowing them to roam freely. It sounded reasonable, because it did not involve any limitations on freedom of movement. The only limitations were that the Indians would be subject to ever-more-ubiquitous conservation regulations dictated by Ottawa, and they would not share in the awesome profits to be gained from mines or oil wells. Their needs would come second to the "national interest" every time resources were allocated for exploitation, and the taxation prerogatives on all these natural treasures would be vested, in the name of "all Canadians," in mandarins living far in the south.

In short, Treaty Eleven was to effect a complete alienation of the Indians and Eskimos from the land, except to the extent that they could walk where they wanted and sniff the air – at least until somebody started polluting it. Likewise, they could pause to drink where they would, until the water was contaminated by discharge from mines or rigs whose construction they could not oppose. And they could hunt as they wished – until white sportsmen and industrialists combined to reduce the traditional game source in the same way that the buffalo had been eradicated.

The neo-colonial Canadian Empire had reached its apogee, which meant that all the people whose lands it had been had reached their nadir. Opposition had been crushed so thoroughly that only a fraction of the original populations had survived, and they had lost very close to absolutely everything. Only Newfoundland – where, in fact, the conquest had begun – was left to bring into the Canadian net.

Chapter 20

The Beginning of the Holocaust

IN THE FOUR-HUNDRED-PLUS YEARS BETWEEN THE ORIGINAL European probe of Newfoundland and the final conquest of the North-West Territories, a holocaust befell the Indians of Canada. What the Karhiio family had seen of the fall of the Prairies to the invaders, what they had heard about the fate of the Indians in British Columbia, what they remembered of the days of Iroquois servitude in Caughnawaga, and what they knew about their own bitter experience, was enough to leave them without any illusions whatsoever about which side they were on. For them, the founding of the great white nation on top of the scattered rubble of Indian land was a long-drawn-out nightmare.

However, the collapse of resistance west and north of the Lakehead was a relatively swift thing, an acceleration of the process that had begun nearly simultaneously with Columbus's arrival in the Caribbean.

It was from the Beothuks of Newfoundland, rather than from the Indians further south along the Atlantic coast, in fact, that the term *Red Indian* came.

The Beothuks painted themselves and their canoes with red ochre, or powdered hematite, a mineral, a foreshadowing, as it turned out, of blood spilled on a terrible scale. The last

Beothuk, a captive woman named Shawnandithit, died of tuberculosis in 1829 at the age of twenty-three. The time between her ancestors' first sighting of ships from afar about 1500 and her death had been more than enough time for a people to be exterminated.

It has been estimated that there were at the very least two thousand Beothuks when the Europeans landed. During the seventeenth century, northeastern Indian populations in New England suffered a catastrophic 80 per cent decline, due to epidemics – this was apart from war or starvation – and if these figures are applied to Newfoundland, it would mean that there were only about four hundred surviving Beothuks on the entire island by the turn of the century.

In the Caribbean, the men who followed Columbus had wiped out entire island populations by working them to death, replacing them as soon as they dropped with new slaves from Africa. In Tasmania, the aboriginals were simply snuffed out. Being trapped on an island in the path of the Europeans, with no hinterland to fall back into, made you a marked people. Yet in the case of the Beothuks, no slavers or farmers came, and so at least two of the usual reasons for mass murder did not apply. The Beothuks were "little prone to warfare if their enemies do not search them out," as one European observed. They were sensible, unaggressive people. An account written in 1500 in Lisbon, where no less than fifty-seven captive Beothuks had been dragged, describes them as having long, curly hair, greenish eyes, "and when they look at each other, this gives an air of great boldness to their whole countenance. Their speech is unintelligible, but nevertheless is not harsh but rather human. Their manners and gestures are most gentle; they laugh considerably and manifest the greatest pleasure. . . . The women have small breasts and beautiful bodies and rather pleasant faces." (Quoted by Upton in *Out of the Background*)

The Beothuks also seemed to have good instincts. No sooner had a few dozen of their people been kidnapped, several villages pillaged, and a few retaliatory raids stopped in their tracks by overwhelming firepower, than the Beothuks decided to do a quick fade. Having got the picture, they opted to disappear into the woods and try to stay out of the way until this gang of marauders left.

The strategy made sense in view of the fact that the strangers were fishermen who didn't try to stay year-round. They swarmed ashore in summer, then vanished back across the sea. Inland, the Beothuk had a network of deer fences to control caribou movements. They also had storehouses filled with preserved food. They could forfeit much of the seafood component of their diet in exchange for peace and still not go hungry.

The Beothuks remained out of sight for the rest of their history – until the very end. All we have are a few glimpses of them through the accounts of the white men who stalked them: men and women fleeing for their lives with their children through snowy woods, pursued by men whose very breath could mean doom for them all. But if they were smitten by epidemics at this time, which in all likelihood they were, there was no way of telling, because the Beothuks were doing such a terrific job of staying invisible.

This standoff might have lasted forever. By the middle of the eighteenth century, some twelve thousand cod fishermen were making the trans-Atlantic crossing every year, lured by the bonanza on the Grand Banks, but British policy was to maintain the island as a fisheries base, not a colony. Accordingly, no development was allowed. This held off the usual course of events. It wasn't until 1785 that the balance shifted, and summer residents became a minority surrounded by people who, for one reason or another, had chosen to stay year-round.

To supplement their meagre incomes, the new residents started poking into the bush, curious about what they might find to exploit. At that stage, they weren't even sure if the mysterious Beothuks were still alive or not. Soon enough, they were slaughtering the birds at Funk Island for their feathers. When the Indians made their annual trek by canoe to the familiar wildfowl hunting grounds to collect eggs and secure meat for winter, it was to discover a swath of death and destruction, uneaten sea birds strewn all over the place, their feathers plucked; when the Beothuks filed down quietly beside the Exploits River to catch salmon, it was to find that the white men had been there ahead of them, and there were far fewer salmon than usual. Worst of all, the immigrants had decided to start trapping fur, laying trap-lines across the deer runs. As they fanned out through the woods, the white men quickly discovered the network of trails the Beothuks had created over the years. And as they penetrated everywhere, the whites started ransacking Indian encampments when they stumbled across them, destroying the storehouses, sacking fur depots.

Sticking to their strategy, the Beothuk guerrillas remained on the move, falling back, living off the land as they went, dodging, weaving, pilfering sails and nets when they could. They resisted slightly by uprooting steel traps and occasionally firing arrows from ambush, but mainly they tried to blend in with the landscape.

However, the Beothuks were running out of manoeuvring room, and the clashes began inevitably to intensify. In 1782, a white man named Rousell was killed and beheaded. Eight whites plunged into the bush to seek revenge. Eventually, finding an Indian encampment, they put it to the torch, ate all the food, and destroyed the weapons, tools, nets, and canoes, leaving the Beothuks, virtually naked, facing months of winter with no supplies or shelter. In another raid, they shot a Beothuk man who emerged from a tent carrying a child, and left both of them to die. Another group opened fire on an encampment in a surprise attack. When a wounded Indian was found inside one of the tents, his head was bashed in with a steel trap.

As early as 1766, the British governor of Newfoundland, Hugh Palliser, had decided that enough was enough. In a memo quoted in L. F. S. Upton's *Extermination of the Beothuks*, he complained that he didn't like the "barbarous system of killing [which] prevails amongst our People towards the native Indians . . . whom our People always kill." Innocently, Palliser came up with an idea for getting in contact with these elusive Indians. He would offer a reward for one brought in alive. Plied with food and gifts and sent back to his tribe, this Beothuk would be sure to urge the rest of them to come out in the open and greet their generous white brothers and maybe start trading. That this someone would have to be forcibly abducted in order to establish a friendly relationship wasn't seen as a problem by the good governor. The fur-traders, at any rate, weren't interested in seeing the Indians brought back as players in the industry; they would just complicate business practices.

In the end, one live Beothuk was brought in, so the reward could be collected. This was a small boy whose mother had been shot in order that he could be captured, and he wasn't of any use as a linguistic resource to Governor Palliser, since he was in a state of shock.

Even more bizarre was the capture and attempted release of a Beothuk woman named Demasduit, whose camp was surprised. When her husband tried to save her, he was shot, and she was taken to Twillingate to be trained as an interpreter. It was from her that white men first heard the name "Beothuk," after all that time and all those deaths. The governor, to his credit, was overcome with guilt at her kidnapping and the murder of her gallant husband; she should be returned to her surviving family forthwith, he ordered. Alas, it took nearly a year for an expedition to be organized to return her to her people, and in the meantime Demasduit took sick and died.

Here, the plot takes a strange twist. Rather than merely bury her, the Englishmen decided to make a magnanimous gesture. A squad of fifty men set out with Demasduit's body in an ornate red coffin. As they crunched through the bush, there were signs everywhere of hasty departures by Beothuks. Tramping onward to the spot where Demasduit had been seized, they left the coffin mounted above the ground in a tent with presents and a Union Jack and marched smartly away. Just how Demasduit's family interpreted this gesture when they eventually crept out of the woods to peer inside the tent and open the coffin is nowhere recorded.

The end came when three Beothuk women were dragged into St. John's. The youngest, Shawnandithit, was fated to be the last of her race to survive. This was a new era. The courts had got around to saying that Indian-killing amounted to murder, and had started laying charges. The liberalized atmosphere had come too late to save the Beothuks, but at least it guaranteed that the three female kidnap victims would be repatriated.

After a two-week stay in town, they were escorted back to the frontier area where they had been captured. A cabin was built for them, and presents provided, in the hope that Beothuk relatives would show up to retrieve the women before the gruesome tragedy of Demasduit was replayed. But no one emerged from the bush to rescue them, and the two older women died waiting. Shawnandithit was eventually taken into a white household, where it was learned from her that the last time she had seen her family, there were only fifteen alive. With the three women kidnapped and three other family members believed to have died, it might well be that there were only nine Beothuks left alive out there in the winter of 1824. After that, there is no record at all.

The next grotesque chapter in the history of the expansion of the Europeans across the upper half of North America concerned the Micmacs.

The first written account we have of a Micmac is of a Grand Chief, or *sagamore*, who ruled all the Micmac people at the end of the seventeenth century: a "tall, majestic" man with a beard, named Membertou. He was described as being truly exceptional, a combined warrior, political leader, and shaman. To him fell the ultimate responsibility of summoning all the lower chiefs and their advisers to a Grand Council, should the fate of the Micmac people be in doubt.

They had lived a rather blessed existence in the eastern Maritimes, some 90 per cent of their food coming from the sea. Inland, wildlife was abundant. The Micmacs had lived so long in this lush homeland that they knew its secrets by heart, knew where the moose were, when the eels were running, on what days the enormous flocks of birds would arrive and depart. In winter they pulled back from the Atlantic storms and took refuge in the woods, where they picked up their bows and arrows and set out with their superbly trained hunting dogs to seek a different kind of diet.

Their lives followed an elegant, stately rhythm, in harmony with the seasons. When the snow piled up and big animals like moose floundered, the Micmac moved easily over the drifts on snowshoes. For variety, they went after seals and ate dead whales, took eggs from seabirds' nests. In mid-summer, there were cranberries and blueberries. Sometimes they drank seal-oil straight from a moose bladder. It was also used as a body ointment and a hair grease, very necessary if one is going to spend a lot of time exposed to salt air.

Micmac territory was divided into seven districts, each run by a chief. Each chief had local chiefs beneath him, and each of these included at least thirty or forty people, counting slaves. The presence of slaves was an indication of how abundant the land was, that it could support such luxuries, since slaves did not actually produce any food. They just did menial chores, and ate.

The Micmacs enjoyed large families; there was enough food to permit this luxury. Solid taboos against incest kept the gene pool healthy and vibrant. Adultery was rare. Even more than a warrior, a man was admired if he was a good hunter and family man. A chief could have more than one wife, in fact, he needed several just to keep up with the catering chores involved in hosting the endless meetings that a chief must chair. Those wives, we may guess, valued each other's help.

It was possible, in Micmac society, for a common woman to acquire respect in the community of men for demonstrating some skill or achievement. Legends and tribal history were preserved through the teaching of story-telling techniques to children.

The Micmacs believed in the Great Spirit, and also in Glooscap, a lesser deity, who may or may not have created the animals, but who was definitely credited with teaching the Micmacs how to make weapons and tools. Before departing from the earth, he prophesied the coming of the Europeans. The Micmacs were highly religious people. Among them, the shamans ranked second only to chiefs. The Micmacs used sweat lodges, rolled in the snow afterwards, had herbal remedies for most ailments, and employed a free-enterprise medical system, in which the shamans were paid handsomely if they intervened successfully when medicine had failed. A really good shaman never had to go hunting for himself.

All this explains why Grand Chief Membertou was such a splendid fellow. He represented perhaps one of the best-adjusted, healthiest, well-fed societies in the world. Alas, when a top-notch shaman failed to cure Membertou of dysentery, and French priests succeeded, Membertou, knowing nothing of the scientific method, jumped to conclusions and allowed himself and his followers to be baptized. For the Micmacs, this was the symbolic end of their Golden Age, although its actual collapse was well-advanced by the time Membertou died.

The Micmacs had been so eager to trade that they would strip the furs off their very backs in exchange for axes, knives, and kettles. This was all very exciting, but there was a catch. The trading ships from Europe could only hang around in the open offshore waters in summer, which meant that in order to trade, the Micmacs had to give up their summer hunting and fishing. This meant that, come winter, they didn't have their usual stockpiles of food.

Now, taking a fatal step deeper into the trap, they started buying European dried vegetables and hardtack to replace the smoked fish, dried berries, and ground nuts they usually ate. It was only the hardtack that lasted through the long winter, and then just barely. For the first time in memory, the Micmacs experienced hunger before the arrival of spring.

And of course there was alcohol from the ships. The Micmac males turned so violent during drinking bouts that the women would go and drink off in the woods somewhere on their own, to avoid trouble. Inebriated, with their men off brawling drunkenly somewhere in the night, the women were easy prey for sailors sneaking ashore.

The change in diet had an immediate side-effect on Micmac health, which had been so superb. Partially because they were starving, their resistance to disease weakened. At the same time, because they weren't getting enough vitamins and proteins, they started coming down with disorders of the gut and chest. Their life expectancy suddenly plunged. Children were dying.

There is no written record of Micmac population prior to 1600, but contemporary French accounts, quoted in a chapter in *Native Peoples* by Virginia Miller, say that Membertou, who died in 1710, could remember when his people were "as thickly planted [along the shore] as the hairs upon his head." Thus, before the record even begins, the Micmacs had been seriously depleted. According to Trigger, in *Natives and Newcomers*, there may once, indeed, have been as many as fifty thousand. However, they went into immediate decline upon contact with the white man, the population falling dizzyingly during the two and a half centuries after contact until it had shrunk down to a mere three thousand.

The French were the first Europeans to ship in permanent settlers and build forts, and they stirred up trouble between the Micmacs and the British, who were grabbing for an Acadian foothold too. By 1722, the Micmacs were unwisely harassing English vessels and daring to attack a garrison at Port Royal. This provoked the English to launch a campaign of genocide that was to carry on for fifty years. At a feast in 1712, the English served poison food to their guests. In 1745, they deliberately traded contaminated cloth to some Micmacs, triggering an epidemic that eventually caused the deaths of several hundred Indians. Groups of English soldiers roamed the Nova Scotia countryside, murdering any Indians they happened upon, including women and children. Wherever they found Indian camps, they destroyed them. They even brought in companies of Mohawks and Algonquins, traditional enemies of the Micmac, to track them down and kill them.

Faced with mass murder at the hands of the English, many Micmacs had already taken refuge around the French fortress at Louisbourg when a severe smallpox epidemic broke out in the early 1730s. In 1746, the dozen remnants of a mighty sixty-five-ship French fleet reached Halifax harbour. Two thousand men of the fleet had died of typhus. The moment the first French sailor staggered ashore, the fever leapt along the dock to where the Indians were crowded, waiting to trade. As many as four thousand Micmacs may have died just that year.

Their genocide policy still in full gear, the English stalked the surviving Micmacs relentlessly. Not surprisingly, some fought back. When five white woodcutters were shot, Colonel Edward Cornwallis, the head of the Halifax settlement, promptly called for all Englishmen to "annoy, distress and destroy the Indians everywhere." A ten-guinea bounty was slapped on every Micmac head. Taking yet further losses, the Micmacs backed away, hauling their dead with them, hiding in the forest.

Several Micmacs tried in 1752 to work out a peace treaty with the bloodthirsty English. Four such treaties were signed, but each was violated. The English, in any event, maintained their search-and-destroy operations. From 1744 to 1761, the English allowed death squads to prowl the countryside where Micmacs had not long ago hunted with their dogs. The Micmacs found themselves fallen so far that they themselves had become the prey. The following is from an account of a "routine" massacre of Micmacs by volunteer Englishmen in Nova Scotia in 1759 (quoted by Virginia Miller in *Native Peoples*):

Major Rogers . . . went to reconnoitre the village by moon-
light. . . . He surveyed the Indian settlement of wigwams
with its rude inhabitants now engaged in festive entertainment, wholly unaware of the presence, almost in their
midst, of a British soldier preparing for battle. After all was
quiet, Rogers, joined by his men, attacked the sleeping
settlement, killing the chief on the spot. Thus surprised
and having no effective weapons of defence the Indians
fled in disorder before the disciplined pursuers, who followed them along the shore . . . here, most of them were
slain, some being shot on the bank while others plunged
into the waters and were drowned.

On top of this came the United Empire Loyalists, displaced
from the rebel American colonies. The influx of armed white
men meant that moose began to disappear quickly. A progres-
sive environmental bill was actually proposed in the Nova
Scotia legislature to prevent the destruction of moose, beaver,
and muskrat, but it was defeated. White poachers in Cape
Breton went ahead and slaughtered nine thousand moose
and caribou in a single winter. Wildlife, right down to the
small game like rabbits and birds, was so scarce by 1793 that
starving Micmacs crawled out of the woods to white settlements and begged for food.

Pushed this way and that by fear of epidemic, hunted and
massacred, their food chain overwhelmed and torn apart
around them, their diets deficient and their intestines rid-
dled with worms, their lungs fatally wounded by tuberculosis, great numbers of Micmacs starved to death.

In 1800, a pittance was voted by the Nova Scotia government to be set aside for the relief of the dying Indians. More
hungry people always showed up at the depots than the supplies could feed. The vast majority, some of them "entirely
naked," were turned away, still starving.

It went on like that, more or less, for sixty-seven more awful
years.

New waves of immigrants poured in, each bringing new

epidemics, and smallpox or infectious hepatitis or measles or whooping cough inevitably rippled out into the regions around the spots where they landed. In exhausted terror, the Micmacs limped back into the forest, hoping to escape contact with the new plagues that kept coming. But their withdrawal only spread disease more quickly among their own people, and because they were afraid to go near the settlements to collect relief supplies, even more of them starved or came down with tuberculosis.

The long nightmare of the Micmacs was made up of a combination of disease, mass murder, and starvation. The killing went on for centuries.

About 1840, for some mysterious combination of reasons, the Micmac population stopped going downhill. It bottomed out at about three thousand people, who were spread out across Nova Scotia, New Brunswick, and Prince Edward Island; then it began to rise. The Micmac had survived the crushing blow of European invasion, survived a deliberate extermination program, survived germ warfare, survived generations of famine – but just barely.

Chapter 21

The Soul-Hunters

RUMOURS AND HORROR STORIES PRECEEDED THE EASTWARD advance of the Europeans after their initial encounters with the peoples of the East Coast. From the beginning, the Huron experience of white men was clouded with foreboding. Reports had filtered through the woodlands to the south about "floating islands" appearing off the Florida coast, people being taken aboard and carried off to the realms of the dead. From the Micmac, with whom they traded, the Hurons would have heard how the legendary figure of "White Rabbit Man-being" had appeared aboard one of the floating islands. When missionaries wearing white robes appeared, the initial Huron reaction was dread, along with a thrill of prophecy come true.

The Hurons were particularly noted for their spirituality. They considered everything from a cosmic point of view. For them, the white man was a perturbation at the edge of the mystical realm long before he jostled onto the stage of their history. And then, when he did, the world was hit by cataclysm. In Virginia, white men passing through Indian villages had left so many dying in their wake, literally dropping in their tracks, that the whites were regarded as spirits of the dead. The reaction of the Huron shamans to news of approaching white men was one of professional rivalry, which became genuine nationalist alarm when the priests, the Black Robes, started pushing their way into Indian life.

It was to obtain metal and glass that the Huron chiefs had swept aside the advice of their shamans and opened up trade with the European ships in the first place. Bits of tin, brass, copper, silver, anything that they could fashion into ornaments that allowed them to tap into occult powers, was valuable. Its presumed magic properties had a definite effect on personal status.

As furs began to flow toward the Europeans, and a trickle of fish-hooks, knives, glass beads, and metal objects passed back along the rivers from the sea to the inland people, there was a ripple effect. More and more Indians were being drawn into the vortexes of exchange that were forming. What began as a trade in metaphysical power objects soon changed into a more pragmatic intercourse, furs were exchanged for cutting tools, pots, kettles, and cloth – that is, until fur-bearing animals began to die off from massive overexploitation.

Jacques Cartier had barely hand-signed hello to Donnacona's group of St. Lawrence Iroquois and distracted them with a display of allegedly magical objects, when he hauled two of the chief's sons away with him to France. Having been raised in a society where children were treated in a civilized manner, the boys could not adjust to the physical punishment that was meted out for even minor infractions of the rules of the oppressively hierarchical European society. By the time Cartier returned them to their home, their hostility towards him was beginning to get on his nerves. This was but one of his early diplomatic blunders.

He made another classic error upon his return, in establishing a winter camp next to the Iroquois village of Stadacona, near present-day Quebec City, without asking the Indians if they minded neighbours. He marched across the Stadaconans' front yard as though he owned it, and later invited himself to Donnacona's lodge at Hochelaga, now Montreal. He didn't trust the Indians even at first, when he could have.

His every action was based on perceptions of the Indians that were wildly out of line and motivated by an increasingly cynical opportunism. Then, grabbing a total of ten people, including Donnacona and, again, his sons, Cartier whisked them off to France to help persuade the king to increase his investments in the New World. All but one of Cartier's victims, including Donnacona, died before being delivered back to their homes, as promised, and the one survivor was kept away so word wouldn't get out about the deaths. But the kidnapping, and then non-return of a hostage chief and his entourage, including his two sons, was too serious a crime to hide. When Cartier landed with several hundred colonists at Cap Rouge, near Stadacona, he was no sooner set up than he found himself besieged by Indians – not only outraged Stadaconans, but other previously friendly Iroquois, who had heard about the French kidnappings and suspected homicides.

Cartier's colony was driven out by spring, but when the Indians fell back, another colony run by someone else was quickly established in its place. The 150 new colonists seem to have been on slightly better terms with the surrounding Indians than Cartier had been, but it wasn't enough to stop corn meal from being stolen by hungry whites. In return, the Indians allowed a third of the Frenchmen to die of scurvy rather than reveal the cure – as they had done for the ungrateful Cartier. When the second colony filed back on board their ships in 1543, it meant the end of French attempts at colonization until the next century. The Indians' attitude, understandably, was: "Good riddance!" However, this did not slow the establishment of beachheads in the Maritimes and along the eastern seaboard by the Spaniards, Dutch, Swedes, English, and the tenacious French.

In the vacuum left by the retreat of the main body of French colonists, a half-century breathing space opened. Yet, rather than recovering, the Iroquois who had had the most to do with Cartier, suffered some kind of cumulative after-effect, a disastrous shockwave for which no one was prepared.

By the time Samuel de Champlain arrived in 1603, the Hochelagan and Stadaconan Iroquois had vanished, a mystery that has never been fully explained. Epidemics, bad winters, displacement from eastern fishing grounds, and ultimately a Mohawk invasion of the St. Lawrence Valley – all were factors. It added up to complete and, by historical standards, nearly overnight, dispersal.

With the French gone, the southern Iroquois, deciding to acquire European goods through warfare rather than trade, had poured in, armed with metal arrowheads and steel axes. There was general warfare between the Algonquins and the Montagnais on the north side of the St. Lawrence and the Mohawks on the south, and the unfortunate Hochelagans and Stadaconans had gotten caught in the middle of a wider war. Control of the valley meant control of the fur trade, which continued between the Indians and the European colonies perched on the ocean's edge. Whoever controlled the middleman role controlled the distribution of wealth both ways. Among the Indians, the prizes went directly back to the home band, where trade items would be given away in exchange for prestige. A successful trader was worth his weight in almost any merchandise if he brought back power objects and later weapons that would enhance the standing of his chief.

It was against this background – a valley of ghosts where Frenchmen and Indians alike had come briefly into contact and had both disappeared – that the French came back in force, this time motivated by a fur-trade monopoly granted by the French king. Establishing trade relations with the Montagnais of Tadoussac, the French were quick to notice that Mohawk raids in the St. Lawrence Valley interfered tremendously with any trade in the west. It only made commercial sense for the French to side with the Montagnais, which they did by first handing out hatchets and knives to upgrade Montagnais armaments, a proxy form of involvement in the local wars. It wasn't enough, however. The Montagnais needed more help than that.

They got it in the form of armed French guardsmen living

in their midst by 1608, which escalated into the inclusion of Frenchmen in allied war parties. The war parties included one particular Petite Nation chief whose cousin, as it turned out, was a Huron. The chief invited his cousin to join the expedition against the Mohawks. Thus, the French first marched shoulder to shoulder with the Hurons, and the fate of the French in North America was sealed.

Three Frenchmen with muskets were sufficient extra strength to allow a force of sixty Hurons, Algonquin, and Montagnais to defeat some two hundred normally irresistible Mohawk warriors. In the first battle, fifty Mohawks died. In the second only fifteen out of one hundred were taken alive.

In the stand-off that followed, the Mohawks analysed their situation and decided it was inherently unstable, even though, as part of the Five Nations confederacy, a federated nation-state, they were bound politically and militarily to the Cayugas, Senecas, Oneidas, and Onondagas. Together these Iroquois tribes traded with the Dutch in the south and fought the French in the north. Yet they knew perfectly well that if the Dutch ever got a chance to trade directly with the northern tribes, in competition with the French, they'd do it immediately. Northern pelts were of better quality than anything the Mohawks and their fellow Iroquois could offer. Therefore, it was in Mohawk interests to keep the potential partners at a healthy distance.

For their part, the French had no interest in peace. If the fighting with the Iroquois stopped, France's Algonquin and Huron trading partners might decide to do business with the Dutch directly, and there would go the very best furs.

The Mohawks did finally conclude a northern peace agreement with the French, Montagnais, and Algonquins, but just long enough to free themselves to open a second front against the unfortunate Mahican Indians, who stood between the Mohawks and the Dutch. Driving the Mahicans out, the Mohawks gained complete control of the land around the new Dutch trading post at Fort Orange on the Hudson. The French ended up trading with the Algonquins, Montagnais, and Hurons, the Dutch with the Mohawks. Any other arrangement would have threatened French and Mohawk hegemony alike.

Into this powderkeg of regional conflict stepped the first missionaries, courtesy of Samuel de Champlain. Under Champlain's patronage, the Franciscan Récollets arrived in 1615 and moved quickly to establish themselves among the Hurons and Montagnais.

The time had long since passed when the white men were viewed as magicians. Champlain had been made to look like a fool repeatedly by sly Montagnais chiefs. Behind his back the Indians laughed at him. There is no sign that the Indians felt threatened intellectually, culturally, or spiritually – until the appearance of the white shamans at Champlain's side.

The Récollet missionaries only bothered to learn enough Montagnais and Huron words to demand that the Indians learn to speak French. It would have been impossible for the Indians to fail to observe that the plans of the priests, although couched in occult terms, overlapped with the plans of Champlain. Just as he wanted the Indians to move in around his outposts, so did the missionaries. France was then in fact a theocracy. As far as the priests were concerned, converting the natives to Christianity was something to be done automatically, and Champlain looked with contempt upon the Indians, wanting to change their "uncivilized ways."

With the re-establishment of a French trading monopoly in 1613, the price of European goods was jacked up. This led to considerable unhappiness. When Frenchmen were killed by the Indians, Champlain – supported by the priests – rejected the traditional reparation gifts and tried to have the offenders executed. The French traders were aghast. Without their support Champlain was powerless to carry through on his threat, and had to back down. To top things off, he meddled ferociously in internal native politics, at one point in 1629 going to the length of appointing an alcoholic sycophant over all the other Montagnais and Algonquin chiefs, many dignified and courageous gentlemen among them.

Outraged Montagnais, hoping to bring back free trade, helped a fleet of British ships to take Quebec that July, driving the despotic Champlain out of the country. As he fell, Algonquin and Montagnais settlements at Trois-Rivières also fell. The Iroquois were pushing into the vacuum left by the retreating French. In the three-year interregnum while the English held sway, trade soared, then collapsed, as Iroquois raids made travel too risky.

More belligerent than ever by the time he returned in triumph in 1633, Champlain wanted to either grab the Dutch and English colonies to the south, or destroy the Iroquois. He was ready to take 120 men and thousands of Indian allies and go on a rampage; it was what his Grand Design for New France demanded.

Plotting in the background, the Récollets saw Champlain's ambitious settlement plans as the prerequisite to converting the heathens. Only when Indians could understand French, for one thing, would they be able to see the Light. For another, until they learned European habits, they would be tempted to cling to their traditional pagan ideas. There had to be a total dissolving of Indianness: a new language, new lifestyle, new costume, new mind. The old would have to be shed – and not simply shed. Any traces of it had to be washed away in the baptismal waters.

Few if any of the Indians who originally submitted to baptism could have suspected they were being asked to shelve all their elegantly articulated cosmologies concerning the relationship of Man to Nature and adopt this foreign cult instead. For the most part, they thought they were seeking a cure or at least an antidote to plague, or that they were involved in a ritual signifying a political alliance.

In 1625, three Jesuits had arrived to help the stumbling Récollets, among them Father Jean de Brébeuf. Focusing on the Huron as the likeliest target group for conversion, Brébeuf lived among them in the Georgian Bay area for three years, learning to speak Huron and displaying a knack for rain-making, before having to flee before the English. By the time Champlain retook Quebec, the Jesuits had acquired exclusive rights to do missionary work. The Récollets were out.

Brébeuf understood that missionaries would only be allowed among the Indians so long as the trade with France flourished. Accordingly, he ingratiated himself with the traders, trying to grease the skids as much as possible for them. Trade and mission work went hand in hand. At the same time, the Jesuits tightened control over the loose network of interpreters the Récollets had planted among the Indians. The priests also viewed the Frenchmen who were already living happily with Indian wives as sinners, interfering with the sacred mission. The Jesuits and traders, for their own reasons, agreed on keeping the Indians separate from the French. The traders wanted the Indians out there hunting and trapping, never mind learning about farming. Nobody wanted to trade for vegetables! The traders were happy to let the priests have the heathen's soul as long as they could have his furs. A compact was formed.

Champlain introduced a twist to trade arrangements. If the Hurons wished to maintain their trade and military alliance with France, they would have to adopt Christianity. Huron boys would have to be handed over to Jesuit educators and taken away to residential schools.

As the Black Robes reappeared among the Huron, the first recorded epidemics struck. Ships from France arrived at Trois-Rivières in June 1634, bringing either smallpox, measles, or influenza. Whatever it was, by July, Montagnais and Algonquins were dying by the score. Hurons picked the disease up from them. Other traders took it into the Ottawa Valley. By autumn, it had spread through most of the Huron villages. Fields and fish-nets were left untended, since there was no one able to work. While plenty were stricken for prolonged periods by impaired vision and diarrhoea, most of them recovered. The unlucky Hurons were those who weren't contaminated until nearly spring, when, weakened by food shortages, they died in large numbers. The French sickened too, but they inevitably recovered within a matter of days, further proof of what the Indians all knew in their hearts right from the beginning: the pestilence was caused by witchcraft. And the witchcraft was easy to see. It was practised openly. Little bits of human flesh called communion wafers were eaten in cannibalistic rituals. The drinking of "symbolic" blood was somehow involved. As the epidemics intensified, Huron fear of the Jesuits turned to pure terror.

Among the Hurons, it was believed that the strange image and pictures the priests worshipped seemed to have something to do with ghosts. Behind closed doors, on their knees, the sorcerers cast their spells, sometimes using a disease-causing cloth, sometimes making hexes, sometimes killing by removing names from the baptismal record. Throughout Huronia, people had dreams in which apparitions appeared and warned them that unless the Jesuits were driven out, the Hurons would perish.

The next plague, in 1636, was definitely identified as influenza. It spread from the St. Lawrence Valley to Huron country in about a month. There was no village that remained unscathed. The disease spread and abated and started up again fitfully all through the winter. This time, no Frenchmen got sick at all. The Black Robes prowled unperturbed through the snow, their skins so pale as to be almost ethereal, spreading their maledictions.

In 1637, it was probably scarlet fever that rolled through Huron country, killing more people than the previous two plagues combined. In 1639, it was definitely smallpox, brought up from New England by the Algonquins, so many of whom were dying that the dead were left unburied. When the Huron traders took the infection home with them, the epidemic that followed, persisting all through the winter, caused casualties worse than those of the previous three afflictions added together.

Still the Black Robes stalked and muttered their shamanistic incantations, performing their arcane baptismal rituals whenever they could. Despite the fact that many people thought they were gaining immunity from the sorcerers' spells by joining the cult, so many died who had been touched by the Holy Water that baptism came to be fixed for the most part in the Huron mind with death and witchcraft. Meanwhile, although they did not have the priests among them, the Iroquois were being decimated by plague just as badly as the Hurons. Since no one has been able to calculate the population of North America at the time of the European invasions, no over-all figure for the death rate among the natives is possible. Figures for the total number of Indians in 1500 range from below 3.5 million to as many as 9.8 million. The larger the number, the more catastrophic the decline. Little has been said about the scale of the holocaust until fairly recently, because estimates of pre-contact populations had been so low. Judging roughly from what the populations were by the time the pandemics of mumps, chicken pox, rubella, measles, smallpox, influenza, and possibly bubonic plague had run their terrible courses, and comparing it to new estimates of how many Indians there were before Columbus, we begin to see that something about as awful as any catastrophe in human history took place on this continent.

Over the first five generations of contact with the white man, it appears that 90 per cent of the Indians were wiped out. By the middle of the eighteenth century, there were probably only eight thousand Hurons and Iroquois left alive. The survivors found themselves living in villages that were largely uninhabited. There were more canoes than they needed. Lodges that had been full of laughter were full of echoes. Weeds had grown up in intended gardens. For the Hurons, picking themselves up out of the ashes, the obliteration was far worse than for the Iroquois.

At the moment of Huron near-extinction, it was the cowled figures of the Jesuits who stood out. The surviving Hurons were faced with the realities of severely diminished power. Because so many children had died, there would be fewer warriors to defend the tribe in years to come, and because so many of the old had died, invaluable accumulated skills and lore were lost, to say nothing of plain wisdom. Ironically and bitterly, the Hurons were thrown into a deeper dependency on the French than ever. Tremendously weakened, they needed supplies and protection from the very men who had brought them pestilence. Nobody could afford the luxury of retribution just yet. Survival was what counted.

But the Jesuits couldn't let up. They concocted a new scheme to capture Huron souls. Christian Hurons would be given better deals and extra presents when they came to trade at Trois-Rivières or Quebec. They would be fêted by officials and included in negotiations. Non-Christian Hurons would be segregated, charged more, and dealt with less graciously. The baptism ritual quickly became the ticket to entry in the traders' club. Sitting for instruction from the Jesuits again became something large numbers of Hurons were man-oeuvred into. Many Hurons may have ached to avenge them-selves on the priests, yet had to submit to their indoctrination sessions for the sake of survival.

In 1641, the Jesuits unveiled their master stroke on behalf of the Prince of Peace. When the French began selling guns to the Indians, they arranged that the guns would be sold to Christians only. This had a dramatic effect on requests for baptism among adult male Indians. The Jesuits were soon doing a brisk business. Huron traders were converting and picking up their guns at the rate of a hundred per year, which was as fast as they could be processed.

This was just the first wedge driven into the political heart of post-epidemic Huronia. Christians could not, of course, take part in pagan public events, including the rituals and ceremonies by which power and wealth were distributed throughout native society. Thus cut off from the ebb and flow of internal politics, the Christians came to form a distinct minority outside the mainstream. Manipulated shamelessly by the Jesuits, some Christians even refused to fight alongside traditional warriors. This division within the house of Huro-nia was something new and fatal. Until then, the Huron sense of identity, however much crippled by disease, had remained intact.

Now, Christian turncoats who had traded their souls for guns were seated in the very midst of Huron councils, refusing to go along with non-Christian decisions. Since the process was based on consensus, the system ground to a halt the moment a power bloc was introduced. To the traditional Hurons, it was clear what was happening. The Jesuits had successfully cast spells on the converts, taking them over as puppets. Moreover, the mesmerized Huron Christians were soon staging public feasts, luring other Indians, rallying and evangelizing. This was getting down to a very serious struggle between a fanatical foreign-controlled religious faction and the remnants of the Huron old guard – and it could not be coming at a worse time. With Huronia's fighting strength sapped, the Iroquois were probing along their southern flank.

The Iroquois had obtained rifles initially from English traders, but once they had them, the Dutch gave in immediately and began an arms trade of their own. Whereas until now the French had been able to scare off Mohawks with a wave of the flag because of their reputation as gunmen, the Mohawks were now firing back, and could no longer be chased from their positions along the St. Lawrence.

In the face of armed Iroquois, the French were ready to start arming their Indian allies. But even in the midst of a national emergency, the Jesuits clung to their insistence that baptism had to come first, thus leaving the Hurons decisively outgunned by the Iroquois. They need not have been; it was simply one final crippling blow from behind by the Jesuits.

As Huron losses mounted, and Iroquois marauders roamed the countryside, it looked as though the Huron confederacy was being overrun. Yet when a grand council was called to deal with the challenge, a faction that blamed the priests for the collapse of Huronia and wanted to oust or kill them was defeated. The French were the Huron's only remaining hope against the Iroquois, and the price of a French alliance was *carte blanche* for the Jesuits.

The capture of seven hundred Hurons in a single attack by the Iroquois left the besieged survivors on the verge of panic. Great holes were being torn in the confederacy, and no one seemed able to organize resistance.

In the midst of the fall of Huronia, the unrepentant Jesuits were still making mischief. They boldly tried to stage a coup. When Christians became a majority for the first time at the Huron village of Taenhatentaron, the Jesuits instructed them to demand that a priest be named as headman. That way, a Jesuit would usurp the hereditary rule of the chiefs. Council would be used to rubber-stamp his instructions. Audacious and transparent as the manoeuvre was, the priests might well have gotten away with it had the Iroquois not come storming out of the forest, capturing or killing all but ten out of four hundred people at the town of Taenhatentaron.

It seemed that were no defences any longer, although Huronia was not in fact ready to be completely overwhelmed. One group of Christian Hurons fought so valiantly, even though they had been decimated by disease, that the Iroquois attackers pulled back, not wanting to risk those kinds of losses in further adventures.

Then, on a foray to burn down hamlets and villages near Taenhatentaron, the unstoppable Iroquois caught up with Fathers Brébeuf and Lalemant, took them captive, and turned them over to the Huron prisoners back at their base camp.

What happened to Brébeuf and Lalemant wasn't torture: it was an exorcism. The fallen Hurons, forcibly adopted by the Iroquois, were well-treated by their conquerors, as long as they didn't get out of line. But they had lost their own nation, had seen their people slain *en masse* by these Jesuit sorcerers, and had been dragged from their own country, Huronia, into slavery – as a result, they believed, of the spells and machinations of these foreign shamans.

The Huron prisoners of war had much reason to hate the Iroquois, but they had many more reasons to hate the two Jesuit monsters. With the Iroquois, what you saw was what you got, even if it was more likely than not a war-club in the

face. The Jesuits, on the other hand, were to them the personi-
fication of manipulation. If two mass murderers who had
been responsible for the death of half your race were to be tied
to stakes in front of you, what would you be very tempted to
do? And if the means these agents of evil had used to kill your
family and friends and fellow warriors was a grotesque ritual
called "baptism," which was supposed to cleanse your soul
for God, but which was really a means of breaking your spirit
so that a distant demon might kidnap you to the Land of the
Dead, where white men tortured Indians for all eternity,
would you be angry enough to pour boiling water over his
naked scalp? And supposing their allies had used hallucino-
gens to drive your brother mad and had taken advantage of
sisters who had never been taught to say no and who then
came down with syphillis? What would you do?

The Jesuits had been caught at night secretly dabbing
"holy water" on the foreheads of sick boys who became sicker
and died of diarrhoea and feverish convulsions within days.
This was a fact. Worse than ghouls, these Black Robes. Where
they strode, Death followed.

Chapter 22

The Collapse of the Five Nations

THE ARMING OF THE IROQUOIS BY THE ENGLISH AND DUTCH AND
the perverse refusal of the Jesuits to let the French build up
corresponding Huron military strength, even after having
started the trouble by using gunpowder against the Iroquois,
was demonstrably the single biggest factor in the sudden
collapse of the Huron Confederacy. It has been estimated that
by 1648 the Hurons had only 120 rifles, whereas the Iroquois
had more than 500. It was this military imbalance that led to
the catastrophe.

And, when the damage was done, the Jesuits, who had
been erecting stone bastions at Saint-Marie and who had
stockpiled a good harvest, were loath to give their Huron
"children," who came to them as refugees, any real help in
their hour of extreme need. Knowing that the Iroquois would
not give them the chance to regrow their own crops, the
Hurons could see that their position was untenable. Grimly,
the Hurons burned their villages to keep them from being
used by the enemy and split up into local clans to seek refuge
where they could. Only one Huron tribe, the Tahontaenrats,
stayed together as a unit.

Many others found shelter with the Algonquins or Neutrals, and a few marched off into the remote bush to live off the

land until they could start over again as horticultural people. But a large number of Hurons accepted the advice of relatives who had been captured earlier by the Iroquois and surrendered to their rivals. Whole families were accepted into Iroquois villages. Individuals were adopted into Iroquois families. Their children were fully integrated as part of the Iroquois community.

For their part, fearing that, with the Hurons overrun, the Iroquois would come after them next, the Jesuits retreated to what is now called Christian Island in Georgian Bay, built a European-style palisade, and allowed Huron refugees to clear the woods around it so they could start planting crops. Only Christian Hurons were allowed, of course. Those who arrived unbaptized quickly submitted to the ritual in order to stay. The crops, planted too late, were inadequate. The Jesuits had food, but not enough to go around. With ghoulish consistency, they doled out rations that did not amount to subsistence level to those they deemed "most worthy." Thus, to get food, the starving Indians had to get down on their knees and pray by the hour every day.

In the meantime, the Jesuits and the rest of the French made sure they did not go hungry in the least themselves. The Jesuits rationalized this by citing the need to stay healthy in order to administer to the needs of the dying Indians. In the winter of 1649–50, so many Hurons were dying of hunger on Christian Island that some in desperation turned to eating the dead, despite their deep loathing for the practice. In the spring, many fled back to the mainland to try to find food. There they were frequently intercepted by Iroquois and either captured or killed.

The Jesuits decided to retreat again, this time to Quebec, taking about three hundred of the "most devout" Hurons with them. There, they built a fortified mission on Ile d'Orléans. As a sanctuary, it was useless. Eventually the Iroquois came and killed or captured seventy Hurons. The French did nothing to try to rescue the prisoners.

The conquering Iroquois spread out across central and

northern Ontario, chasing Hurons and Algonquins where they could find them, attacking the Nipissings, and destroying the Neutral town of Teotongniation. Most Neutrals fled west and south. Those who submitted to the Iroquois were absorbed, with the net effect that the Neutrals became extinct as an identifiable people by about 1650, victims, as much as the Beothuks, of a chain of events that had been set in motion by the European invasion. The Tahontaenrat Hurons ended the war by asking to join the Seneca Iroquois, who displayed great statesmanship by allowing them to settle on Seneca territory, to build their own town, and to retain their customs and language. The two peoples lived in peace for several generations before the Tahontaenrats became indistinguishable from their hosts.

The last of the Iroquoian cousins to be dealt with by the Five Nations Iroquois were the Eries. In 1654, some fifteen hundred western Iroquois launched an assault, driving the Eries south to Chesapeake Bay. Eventually, some five hundred of them surrendered to the Iroquois. But this was a mop-up operation. Essentially, by the early 1650s, the Iroquois had shattered New France's laboriously built-up trade network, driven their neighbours out of their traditional tribal territories, and turned all of central Ontario into a vast Iroquois hunting-ground from which they could obtain beaver pelts to trade with the Dutch and English. By pushing the Hurons out of the St. Lawrence Valley, the Mohawks had cut the French off from the help of experienced guerrilla fighters. As for the Hurons who had fled into Quebec and who wanted to mount a counter-attack against the Iroquois to rescue relatives who had been taken captive, there was no hope. The French continued to hold back on the guns that would have made the difference.

Continued internal threats to Iroquois security led to the adoption of harsher methods of repression. The Iroquois, having offered the defeated Huron what they considered to be generous adoption terms, with a chance for upward mobility and full citizenship, were angered by initial Huron intransigence. After a few years under the new regime, however, life settled down. One Huron became an Iroquois chief. Iroquois men found they liked marrying captive Huron women because they didn't have to put in time working for the bride's family to pay for her. Many of these men and women, we can be sure, in a land where only a fraction of the entire people had survived a string of holocausts, sought consolation in each other and fell in love.

Except for the distant ringing of Frenchmen's axes to the northeast and the same sound coming from the Dutch, English, and now the Swedes to the southeast, the forests around the Great Lakes were unusually silent, so much of their wildlife having been decimated in the race to trade pelts for power.

Whether power came out of the barrel of a gun or from magic, it was all the same to the Indians. Rather than being passive victims of an overwhelming wave of superior technology, the Indians – particularly the Iroquois – went after power from the moment they realized they were up against something new. Their "awe" of the shamans and the blunderbusses was a short-lived thing. They had their own economic and social reasons for wanting bits of bright metal, all of which came down to local power structures. No sooner were the new weapons deployed than Indians began guerrilla operations to obtain such arms for themselves. Early Iroquois action to obtain weapons from the Europeans, based on quick reflexes, is what saved them and, moreover, allowed them to carve out a larger empire than ever.

For the first time, the Iroquois could bargain from strength. So tenuous was the French grip by 1653 that the governor, Jean de Lauson, signed a bilateral peace agreement with the Iroquois, throwing France's allies among the Algonquins, Montagnais, and refugee Hurons to the wolves. The wolves came, to be sure. But it wasn't to kill so much as to build up depleted Iroquois ranks through forced assimilation, while keeping the free Hurons from aiding the French.

The tireless Jesuits then concocted a scheme to penetrate the Iroquois. They urged the refugee Hurons huddled around them to surrender to the Iroquois – with the provision that missionaries be allowed to come along to administer to the needs of the captives. This was a new variation of the gambit they had used to grab control of the Huron villages before the fall of Huronia.

If the Hurons who got to avenge their families and nation on Brébeuf and Lalemant had hoped to get rid of the machinations of the Jesuits, they were to be disappointed. In 1657, the Jesuits inflicted yet another major betrayal on the Hurons. Having talked some four hundred Hurons into going into voluntary captivity, a Jesuit father named Ragueneau, supported by French soldiers, accompanied one group of Arendahronon Hurons when they turned themselves over to the Onondaga Iroquois. As they were being escorted to their new village, all but one of the Huron males was murdered in retaliation for a sneak attack by the Hurons on Iroquois several years before. Rather than attempt to rescue the unarmed Hurons in his protective custody, Father Ragueneau let the Iroquois have their way, ordering his soldiers to hold their fire, ignoring the screams of the dying Hurons and their watching families. No Huron afterwards could forgive the priests.

But the Jesuits were pleased. They got what they wanted: the Onondagas accepted a Jesuit settlement in their midst. Horrified that Frenchmen had penetrated Iroquois defences, the Mohawks planned to drive them out the moment cooperation could be assured with a majority of Onondagas, many of whom were appalled to find the dreaded Black Robes on their doorstep, no matter what kind of secret blood pacts had been made between the Onondaga chiefs and the priests.

Meanwhile, as the Black Robes were worming their way into Five Nations territory, the French traders back in Quebec were forging new alliances, this time with the Ottawas, who soon took over any of the trading duties that the Hurons had performed. In their role as middlemen, the Ottawas made it possible for French goods to be delivered to the Indians who had been driven into the area around the upper Great Lakes.

With the revival of the fur trade, the beleaguered colony of New France came back to life. This time, the French, under a more militarily astute governor, Louis d'Ailleboust de Coulonge, dispensed guns to their trading partners. When the Seneca and Onondaga Iroquois attacked the Algonquin, Montagnais, Petun, and Ottawa fur-traders using the Ottawa River, it was to discover that the superiority in weapons that had allowed them to destroy Huronia was gone.

The fur trade had recovered and was growing again. That was the good news for the French. The bad news was that it had not reached anything like the volume needed to sustain the ambitious colonization plans first visualized by Champlain. And the reason it was failing to live up to hopes was the continuing Iroquois presence in central Ontario. Unless the Five Nations could be defeated, New France was going to cave in as an economically viable proposition.

In 1663, Jean-Baptiste Colbert took charge as governor, with the goal of getting the stagnant colony rolling. The solution, Colbert quickly saw, was immigration. Outnumber the Indians. Overwhelm them with human waves. Take over the land. Start growing and eliminate them as the middlemen. If Frenchmen became the middlemen themselves, then they would have the control over what was now the biggest economic game on the continent, a prize over which the Hurons had lost their civilization: the fur trade. The wealth it generated so outstripped any redistribution system that had gone before it among the Indians that it distorted everything around it, from boundaries to marriage patterns.

With the appearance of Colbert, the French outposts became bustling armed camps. In 1665, a twelve-hundred-man militia regiment clanked ashore.

The Iroquois Confederacy was divided by then. Here was the weakness of a democratic federal jurisdiction in the face of a dictatorship. Seeing the build-up of troops at Quebec and Trois-Rivières, the autonomous states of the Oneidas, Cayugas, Seneca, and Onondagas decided to make peace with the French. There was a peace faction within the Mohawks too, but the war chiefs had worked diligently to sabotage any diplomatic overtures. Standing alone, the Mohawks fended off the first major French assault in 1666, counter-attacked, took prisoners, and then sent a delegation to talk peace. The French commander, Alexandre de Prouville de Tracy, ignored this gesture and came for the prisoners, burning five Mohawk villages and destroying the entire winter supply of food.

It was the mighty Mohawks' turn to run. After taking refuge with Five Nations kin who had already sued for peace, they decided it was time for the peace chiefs to do the talking. A pro-French faction among the Mohawks even invited the Jesuits into their settlements.

When the Jesuits set up a mission at Caughnawaga, Christian Mohawks began to gather there. Some eighteen years of peace followed, before war broke out again, this time over the fur trade much further west, where the Iroquois and the French had been pursuing their independent policies. The Iroquois pushed into the Ohio and eventually the Mississippi valleys, where they clashed with the Illinois Indians. Passing along the upper Great Lakes, French *coureurs de bois* had also advanced as far as the Mississippi Valley, establishing trade with the same Illinois. When the Iroquois not only rejected French instructions to stop trading with the Illinois, but started attacking French cargo canoes loaded with furs, the French decided to build a series of forts that would seal the Iroquois off from the west and north.

In 1687, accompanied by unenthusiastic Huron and Ottawa allies, seventeen hundred French soldiers swept across Seneca country, burning cornfields and towns, killing pigs, and desecrating graves. At one point, thirty-six Iroquois were captured and sent off to the Mediterranean to serve as galley slaves in the royal fleet.

The Iroquois held out against Frontenac's offer of peace in 1690, thereby suffering a loss of three hundred men, women, and children who were captured three years later, and, a few years after that, sustaining casualties in the order of two hun-

dred warriors killed in a single spring. The result was that, in
1701, the Iroquois agreed to a peace not just with the French,
but with the thirteen western tribes. They also agreed to let
northern tribes pass through their territory to trade with the
British at Albany. Declining power meant the Iroquois had
little recourse but neutrality. What they did have still was
their independence.

This suited both the French and English for the moment,
since so long as the Five Nations lay between the competing
European colonies, a buffer remained that continued to curb
the territorial ambitions of the other.

Among the Iroquois, for every passionate Jesuit-hater, there
was a pragmatist who saw the Jesuits as allies among the
French. Yet others welcomed the Jesuits as potential hostages
in an emergency. Their influence was minimal for a long time
among the Mohawks who remained on the New York side of
the St. Lawrence, but it waxed – or seemed to wax – among
those Mohawks who decided to move in next door to the
French at Montreal. They settled in around the colony, shuffling from here to there, until they finally put down their roots
at Caughnawaga. Members of all the tribes of the Iroquois
Confederacy gathered there – Cayugas, Senecas, Oneidas,
and Onondagas, but mainly Mohawks.

Their adoption of Christianity didn't prevent them from
developing a thriving and lucrative bootleg traffic in furs
between Montreal and Albany.

Chapter 23

The Great Gift of the Iroquois

IT WAS AT CAUGHNAWAGA THAT THE KARHIIO FAMILY OF Mohawks adapted their skills in canoemanship to the needs of the northwestward fur trade, becoming voyageurs. It was from there that they set out in the late eighteenth century in the wake of Alexander Mackenzie. It was at Caughnawaga, as boys, that Louis and Bernard Karhiio had grown restless under the tyrannical rule of the Jesuits and the meddling of French bureaucrats, never dreaming that, no matter how far they fled, they would be pursued by waves of foreigners.

By that time, the French conquest seemed complete, although even in "Christian" Caughnawaga there was always a longhouse; the Longhouse People were never wholly eliminated. In fact, their religion staged a come-back when a prophet named Handsome Lake appeared and reconciled the Iroquois to the terrible reversals of fortune they had experienced. But the Iroquois were down. No doubt about it.

Ironically, it was about this time that their influence began to make itself felt on a global basis, setting in motion a chain of events in political thought that would ultimately shape the geopolitical face of the twentieth century.

The Iroquois had been fatally weakened by disease and overwhelmed militarily, but in their fall they had "contaminated" the victors with ideas that would eventually shatter the European dictatorships as thoroughly as pestilence and cannons had shattered the Indians. Although the Europeans were far too ethnocentric at the time to suspect it for a moment, even as they struggled to thrust the natives aside, they were being exposed to seditious ideas. In the end, the Old World would be transformed almost as much as the New World – in some ways, more.

At first, the white men had taken no notice whatsoever of Indian political practices. If the Indians had felt superstitious awe at the beginning of the relationship, the Europeans suffered from quite the reverse. Even the most enlightened among them saw only "savages." Yet what the Europeans encountered and swept aside was nothing less than an interlocking network of federated democracies. Among the Indians, no free man stood above another. They were equal. They believed in liberty. They bowed to no one. To what do we compare this?

In Europe, at that time, everyone bowed. Everyone stood above or below someone else. In England, liberty was an idea that had not been extended much beyond the inclusion of the landed gentry in the king's power bloc on the signing of the Magna Charta. All that had really happened as a result of that particular document was that an absolute monarchy had become an oligarchy. For the common people, life was as brutish and short as ever. And on the Continent, it was arguably worse.

At the time that Columbus sailed, there was nothing in the kingdoms and empires he left behind him remotely to compare to the egalitarianism of the loose confederacies that lay ahead. Even into the sixteenth century, Europe was a collection of miserable, poverty-stricken, downtrodden, disease-wracked, fear-ridden peoples, oppressed from above by tyrannies that could be run by madmen and perverts, and from all around by a class structure built on selfishness and intolerance. There were no old-age pensions, no disability benefits or unemployment insurance. Crippled beggars squatted in filthy streets, while lords and ladies gambolled by in ornate carriages.

The power of life or death was in the hands of corrupt officials. Unscrupulous religious bigots wandered the corridors of power, whispering in the ears of the aristocrats. Even when the word *freedom* was used in ancient Mediterranean literature, it meant freedom from domination, rather than implying any kind of personal liberty. It was freedom from slavery or bondage or foreign rule. It could justifiably be said that a political Dark Age had been upon the European continent since the fall of Greece, which at best had liberated only an elite. When the "Age of Exploration" began, its main effect was to export the political darkness.

So swiftly did the Spanish move to decapitate the native societies they encountered, clamping the Crown, Catholicism, and the Spanish language on cultures along the way, that nobody back in Europe had a chance to find out much about the Indians of what are now South and Central America before they were gone or irrevocably changed. It was the Indian societies to the north, which had the relative good luck to fall into the hands of the French or British, who provided the image of native society that filtered back to Europe via letters and first-hand reports. The incredible notion that technologically inferior people might be living under superior political conditions, free from kings and class bondage, unencumbered by magistrates or police, with poverty eradicated, surely this was something to think about!

It was the letters of Amerigo Vespucci that first aroused intellectual curiosity. His descriptions of Indian hospitality and charity and his explanation of the Indian concept of collective ownership of property influenced Thomas More as he was writing *Utopia*, published in 1516. More put forward for the first time a vision of a perfect society, where no man could be dispossessed of the land upon which he subsisted, the divine right of kings no longer existed, and government was by the consent of the governed. It was an idea that lit up the European darkness. More's work was translated into every language on the Continent.

For Francisco Vitoria, a teacher of moral theology, these

same reports from the other side of the ocean showed that one could build an international legal order based on reason and mutual accommodation. Influenced by Vitoria, Hugo Grotius, the man who invented the Law of the Sea, the prototype of all modern international agreements, was no less profoundly influenced by what he had heard about the Indian system of government. When it came time to champion the right of revolution, philosophers John Locke and Thomas Hobbes were quick to find proof of the proposition that it was possible to live without European-style government by looking to the American Indians.

By the late 1600s, the French ethnographer Baron de Lahontan had written several books based on his experience among the Hurons. These were avidly read back in France. In one of them, he quoted a Huron as saying: "We are born free and united brothers, each as much a great lord as the other, while you are all slaves of one sole man. I am the master of my body, I dispose of myself, I do what I wish, I am the first and the last of my Nation."

One of Lahontan's books was adapted for the stage by playwright Delisle de la Drevetière, who chose as his protagonist an American Indian visiting Paris. Titled *Arlequin Sauvage*, the play was a hit. It ended up with the heroine falling in love with the Indian and escaping to America and freedom from money and property. The play deeply influenced a young man named Jean Jacques Rousseau, who later wrote an operetta in which Christopher Columbus sang "Lose Your Liberty!" to the Indians while waving his sword at them. Later yet, Rousseau wrote his *Discourse on the Origins of Inequality*, one of the key books that excited the French imagination in the years leading up to the 1789 revolution. The "Liberty, Equality, and Fraternity" for which the French howled at the barricades was a concept refracted back to Europe from the New World. In the revolt of the Spanish Colonies and the American Revolution itself, a lust for liberty inspired by the American Indians burst upon the international scene, changing everything.

In England, Indian societies became the focus for theorists interested in natural rights and alternatives to private property. In France, it was to be Rousseau's concept of the "Noble Savage," an idealized natural man who could be held up to the downtrodden European masses as a shining example of what they could become. For the great social and political reform movements that were taking shape in the darkness, the Indian had shown the way.

The Indians remained indifferent to the political furor that the news of their existence and unique lifestyle had stirred up in Europe. For a while, they were trooped over in droves to tour European castles and to provide entertainment at parties. One stage production after another either extolled or satirized the carefree life of the liberated North American Indian, and as the hoopla piled up, gross distortions and exaggerated expectations set in.

Yet, for all the satire and gimmickry, the terrible, wonderful, unavoidable truth was that the Indians did possess a political system that was the bipolar extreme of any systems then in place in Europe. The Indians, objectively speaking, were far more advanced in terms of the development of personal liberty than Europeans, and had been for a long time.

The Iroquois, as an example, had been part of a federal union since somewhere between 1000 and 1100 A.D. There had been thirty-three previous holders of the office of presiding chief of the union before Jacques Cartier appeared. The holder of the office, the *Atotarho*, performed the job for life, unless he violated the Great Law of Peace, in which case he could be impeached.

At whatever specific date it was formed, the League of the Iroquois came into existence out of the need to end several generations of warfare that had raged among all five Iroquois tribes. It was a multilateral peace agreement that led to the formation of a confederacy. A Huron peacemaker named Deganwidah devised the plan, but because he stuttered and was a non-Iroquois, he was unable to convince anyone of his vision. An enlightened Iroquois took up his idea and communicated it to the Iroquois, who became the benefactor of a Huron's dream. After long negotiations among the Five Nations, an Iroquois constitution was hammered out, based on the Great Law of Peace.

The league headquarters was at the centre of the confederacy, on Onondaga Nation land at the present site of Syracuse, New York. There, a white pine, called the Tree of the Great Peace, was planted. According to the text of the Great Peace, as set down in wampum belts at the time, "any man or any nation outside the Five Nations [who] shall obey the laws of the Great Peace" could be adopted into the tribes, regardless of race or nationality. Dual citizenship was also allowed. The power of each nation was balanced against the others by a complex set of checks. No actions could be taken by the Council of the League without the permission of all five nations, and each of them would have to debate the matter at home.

> The council of the Mohawks shall be divided into three parties . . . the first party shall listen only to the discussion of the second and third parties and if an error is made, or the proceeding irregular, they are to call attention to it, and when the case is right and properly decided by the two parties, they shall confirm the decision and refer the case to the Seneca statesmen for their decision. When the Seneca statesmen have decided in accord with the Mohawk statesmen, the case or question shall be referred to the Cayuga and the Oneida statesmen on the opposite side of the house.

After these four tribes had thus reviewed an issue, their recommendations would be passed on to the Onondagas for their decision, which had to be unanimous among all the Onondaga statesmen and their deputies before it could be passed into law. If there was a tie between the "elder brother" Mohawks and Senecas and the "younger brother" Cayugas and Oneidas, the Onondagas would break it.

Essentially, they acted as an executive with a veto over a two-house congress.

In the Great Law, there was provision for amendments. Chiefs were appointed by the women, who held the rights to chieftainships, although they didn't hold the office. They could fire the chief if need be. Individuals of special ability could be appointed to the council. Upon becoming chiefs, these special individuals weren't subject to impeachment by the women, but if they lost the confidence of the people, everyone was instructed to "be deaf to his voice and his advice." A single war chief from each of the Five Nations also sat on council. In peacetime, his function was to report back to the people, a kind of combined journalist and general. He was also responsible for bringing petitions from the people before the council. In wartime, it fell to him to raise an army. Since there was no draft and there were no press gangs, it was up to him to muster the troops purely on the basis of charisma. Successful war chiefs tended therefore to be eloquent men.

Factionalism within the confederacy was reduced by building in a system of clan kinships that transcended the borders of different tribes. Thus, the clans of the Hawk, Turtle, Wild Potatoes, Great Bear, or Deer Pigeon would have had members among the Mohawks, Seneca, Onondagas, Oneidas, and Cayuga alike, and these individuals would view each other as members of the same family. In other segments, the Great Law wampum belt – a message in beading – referred to a "united nations," gave the people the right through their war chiefs to seek redress from the Grand Council itself, guaranteed religious freedom, and make a person's home legally safe from forcible entry by anybody.

In 1727, Cadwallader Colden, who rose to be a governor general of the colony of New York, quoted in Johansen, *Forgotten Founders*, wrote:

The Five Nations have such absolute Notions of Liberty that . . . each nation is an absolute Republick by itself, govern'd in all Publick affairs of War and Peace by the Sachems of Old Men, whose Authority and Power is gained by and consists wholly in the opinions of the rest of the Nation in their Wisdom and Integrity. They never execute their Resolutions by Compulsion or Force Upon any of their People. Honour and Esteem are their principal Rewards, as Shame and being Despised are their Punishments.

The war chiefs, he added:

obtain their Authority . . . by the General Opinion of their Courage and Conduct, and lose it by a Failure of those Vertues. . . . Their Great Men and captains are generally poorer than the common people, for they affect to give away and distribute all the Presents or Plunder they get in their Treaties or War, so as to leave nothing for themselves. If they should be once suspected of selfishness, they would grow mean in the opinion of their Country-men, and would consequently lose their Authority.

It was Colden's opinion that, politically, "our Indians have outdone the Romans." In any event, they had definitely arranged for public opinion to play a central role in democratic society. So long as the war chiefs continued to report back to the people, the Council couldn't get too far out of line without the folks back home finding out and pulling their support, if necessary.

As Thomas Jefferson observed about the Iroquois, in a statement quoted in *Forgotten Founders*, "every man, with them, is perfectly free to follow his own inclinations. But if, in doing this, he violates the rights of another, if the case be slight, he is punished by the disesteem of society or, as we say, public opinion; if serious, he is tomahawked as a serious enemy." From this, slightly modified, followed Jefferson's First Amendment, allowing freedom until it violates another person's rights.

One early observer of the Iroquois was astounded to discover that "Women are treated in a much more respectful manner than in England & they possess a very superior power."

Another, even more astute eventual student of the Iroquois was a Boston printer named Benjamin Franklin, who was so fascinated by what he read in accounts of treaty council meetings that he began publishing them in 1736, hoping to draw the attention of his fellow colonists to some quite radical ideas. In 1744, an account reached Franklin of a diplomatic meeting at which an Iroquois chief named Canassatego had stood up and told the white colonial commissioners that what they ought to do was organize themselves into a federal union, just as the Iroquois had done.

That was an amazing thought. It had never occurred to Franklin quite that way, nor to any of his friends. After that, Franklin began noticing other astounding concepts being put forward by Indian orators at these meetings. He could see the outlines of something wonderful the Indians had found: a way to outlaw tyranny. They had liberated themselves, become free men.

He was particularly fond of the way they ran their Council meetings:

> Having frequent Occasion to hold public Councils, they have acquired great Order and Decency in conducting them. . . . The women . . . are the Records of the Council . . . who take exact notices of what passes and imprint it in their Memories, to communicate to their Children. . . . They preserve traditions of Stipulations in Treaties 100 Years back; which, when we compare with our writings, we always find exact. (Quoted in *Forgotten Founders*)

There were even more wondrous discoveries: "All their Government is by Counsel of the Sages; there is no Force, there are no Prisons, no officers to compel Obedience, or inflict Punishment."

Little surprise, then, that so many colonists over the years had run off to live with the Indians. They were usually described as having been taken captive, but most of them were volunteers. When discussions were held between the Iroquois and Pennsylvania colonists to examine the possibility of an alliance against the French, the main hesitancy on the part of the Iroquois was caused by the lack of coordination among the colonists. Each colony was conducting its own diplomatic relations with the Confederacy. The Iroquois could see what was going to happen if they went into battle with such rabble alongside, artillery notwithstanding. It was this concern that prompted Canassatego to tell the assembly of colonial commissioners at Lancaster:

Our wise forefathers established union and amity between the Five Nations. This has made us formidable. This has given us great weight and authority with our neighbouring Nations. We are a powerful Confederacy and by your observing the same methods our wise forefathers have taken you will acquire much strength and power; therefore, whatever befalls you, do not fall out with one another. (Quoted in *Forgotten Founders*)

Shortly after reading the report of Canassatego's words, Franklin launched his fervent campaign for the colonies to form themselves into an Iroquois-style confederacy wherein each colony would become a state with control over internal affairs, and a federal council would emerge charged with responsibilities for external matters. Common defence under a federal government would be possible.

The Albany Congress of 1754 was called to confirm the alliance against the French and at the same time to ratify an agreement to form a union among the colonies. During the debate, Franklin referred to "the strength of the League which has bound our Friends the Iroquois together in a common tie which no crisis, however grave, since its foundation has managed to disrupt." Thus, he proposed a federation of British

American colonies under one legislature, with a president general to be appointed by the Crown. The ultimate sovereignty of the states would be guaranteed by each of them being given a veto over any federal decision. Unanimity would be the prerequisite of federal actions. The system, Franklin urged, should be unicameral – a one-house legislature such as the Iroquois used. The proposed Colonial Grand Council would have had forty-eight representatives, compared to forty on the Iroquois Council. That particular plan, too radical for its time, eventually died. Certainly, the British were none too pleased when they saw what the Albany Congress was proposing. What was all this talk about internal control and vetoes and unanimous decisions? Twenty years passed before Franklin got to repackage his Albany scheme as the Articles of Confederation.

When the War of Independence came, it was fought by former colonists who raised an all-volunteer militia in the proper Iroquois fashion and adopted Iroquois guerrilla tactics in their battle with the British. The British shouted "Unfair!" United, thanks to a Constitution that was based on the Iroquois's own egalitarian Great Law of Peace, the colonists fought as successfully as their Indian mentors had told them they would. It was thus all the more bitter a pill for the Iroquois to swallow when the dust settled at war's end to reveal that Britain and the newly emerged United States of America had sawed the Iroquois Confederacy in two, throwing half to the British in Canada and half to the Americans.

Somebody had not quite understood what the Great Law of Peace was intended to mean, and this was not to be the only case of the Iroquois model of society being borrowed and twisted into something else. The process, in fact, had only begun.

By the dawn of the nineteenth century, the Indians were permanent fixtures in European thought, even though, in the wake of the idealized versions of Indian life, had come a string of attacks on "primitivism," launched by the likes of Voltaire and Immanuel Kant. It was against this background of jaundiced viewpoints that a book entitled *Ancient Society*, by an adopted Mohawk named Henry Morgan, was published in England. Morgan was read by important anthropologists. About that time, two unsung political heavyweights, Karl Marx and Friedrich Engels, were poring through the works of important anthropologists of the day, looking for something factual on which they could hang their case against industrial capitalism and class stratification. They found it, sure enough, in Morgan's account of the Iroquois system of communal ownership of property.

As he read about it, Marx scribbled ninety-eight pages of notes. The notes closely followed the text. What caught Marx's intense interest was the way in which the economic system and the method of democratic political organization were intermeshed. The Iroquois had found a way to accomplish a levelling of society, making all men equal, without using coercion. In 1891, as a "bequest to Marx," Engels used the notes as the basis for the book, *The Origin of the Family, Private Property, and the State.* In it he wrote that the Iroquois Confederacy "substantiated the view that classless communist societies had existed among primitive peoples." Iroquoian society "knows no state."

Wrote Engels, albeit somewhat idealistically:

Everything runs smoothly without soldiers, gendarmes, or police, without nobles, kings, governors, prefects or judges; without prisons, without trials. All quarrels and disputes are settled by the whole body of those concerned. . . . The household is run communistically by a number of families; the land is tribal property, only the small gardens being temporarily assigned to the households – still, not a bit of our extensive and complicated machinery of administration is required. . . . There are no poor and needy. The communistic household . . . know their responsibility toward the aged, the sick and the disabled at war. All are free and equal – including the women.

The American Revolution had spread around the world. So too would the revolution being triggered by Marx and Engels.

What is most fascinating in the historical perspective is the way the political structure of the Iroquois came to be adopted by two mutually antagonistic world powers. In one version of the Iroquois way, communism evolved. In another, democracy. Both processes were half-true to their roots, but only half-true. The half-truths at the heart of both systems distorted them equally, with poverty festering in one, freedom squelched in the other, and militarism running amok in them both.

Whatever the outcome, both political tidal waves had been set in motion by the discovery of new forms of political organization in America. The weary imaginations of Old World thinkers were stimulated to start imagining utopias again. And from the new utopias came theories of socialism, communism, and anarchy.

It was thanks to Rousseau, who got it from a playwright, who got it from a travel writer, who got it from the Hurons, that Michael Bakunin was eventually able to dream up the idea of an anarchist collective. Building on that, Peter Kropotkin dreamed dreams of anarchist communism, which became wildly popular and subversive in Spain. Another version, pacifist anarchism, inspired thinkers as diverse as Leo Tolstoy and Henry David Thoreau, who in turn inspired Gandhi . . .

Even as they rattle their missiles at one another, the Soviets, Americans, and Chinese have something in common: a joint political heritage. Their ideologies all begin with the same on-paper revolutionary belief in the equality of men. Nobody, but nobody, favours the divine right of kings any more. "They" – the foreigners – have all "gone Indian" one way or another, communists and democrats alike.

So who really won?

Ideologically, the Iroquois.

PART IV

Chapter 24

The Death of Nelson Small Legs, Jr.

AMONG THE PRISONS, THE STREETS, THE BOYS' SCHOOL, THE foster home, the reserve, and his original life with Mama, Robert Royer had picked up several identities: Bob Calihoo, Robert Royer (en français), his nickname Rob Roy, a joke about his "Scottish" blood, then Rob Royer – or just Royer – and finally plain Bob Royer.

Each name suggested a style of self-presentation. He could be a polite, grown-up version of Little Lord Fauntleroy, Catholic, obedient. He could be the student of *realpolitick*. He could also be so flawlessly correct and logical and rational that it drove some people nuts. He could be the straightshooter who wouldn't rat on anybody, a guy who fought back and laughed a lot. A guy who used to carry a knife all the time, had no respect for authority and not a whole lot for property, and found cops a bad joke. Prone to flaring up and threatening if pushed. Mouthy little son-of-a-bitch. Watch a guy like him. You just can never tell. Nobody gets through the prisons without being battered around, especially a kid with a "radical" background. And now Royer was going to push back.

His hair was neatly shoulder-length by the time he stepped out of the Drumheller Penitentiary in 1968. He favoured billowy-sleeved purple shirts, open-necked with the collar turned up – James Dean, Métis style, mixed with a modern hippie influence. Somehow, despite what he had been through, he was almost always "on" – bright, ready, listening. "Well, let's go, man!" Sure, his head had been hammered against the wall, and there were moments when he would pause, ever so faintly, as though momentarily dazed.

He did believe, as he stepped out into the sun and Mary's waiting arms, that he had actually not been damaged by prison so much as he had been simply hardened. You could say that hardening was an awful thing to happen to a human being, he argued, but it could also be good training for a hard world, especially if you intended to spend the rest of your life fighting the government.

Royer had a kind of certainty by then that would have been envied by many men – men who had not spent all those nights in a cell finding out whether they would flip out in the crunch or not. Self-pity was the killer, Bob knew. Once you started feeling sorry for yourself, you were in deep trouble. The one sure way to avoid that was to fill up with rage and defy the bastards at every turn. But he was out now. He could take a breath.

There was a lot to learn. A very intense, uptight, twenty-three-year-old, Bob stepped out of a feudal age of inquisition into the world of paisley shirts and flared jeans and Black Power and Joan Baez and protest and the Beatles singing about revolution. Mary was waiting with a borrowed car. She cried in his arms. God, she hoped this was the last time. He promised her, very softly, that it was. During the time he was in prison, she had left her parents' home and was now working as a waitress in a donut shop. She wrote nearly every day. The letters had been Bob's anchor to the outside world during the months and years of his incarceration, a world to which he otherwise felt virtually no attachment at all. The first step on his road to rehabilitation – or, as he preferred to see it, to rehabilitating the world around him – was to propose to Mary.

Consider this as a Canadian Moment: a young half-white, half-Indian man standing in the dust, holding his woman, with the grim outlines of a stone prison in the background and centuries of defeat and subjugation – a full diaspora – behind him. The prison: where the original purpose of a wall had been turned right around. It had been the first defensive weapon, a barrier to keep the enemy out. Here, rising up out of the waving golden fields of wheat, it kept the "enemy" in. Emerging, Bob knew damn well he was considered the enemy, and that, moreover, he sure was now.

He perceived himself first and foremost as a political prisoner. He had not read as much of Canadian history as he would over the next few years as a student, so he had not yet been able to put what had happened to his father and grandfather, poor Albert and poor Sam, and therefore what had happened to him, into a full political context. But he knew enough to know that the way he had ended up in prison was wrong.

He had become a status Indian by now, "Chief" of the General Indians, following his struggle with the Alberta government. There is a big difference between being half-breed and being status: status had land; half-breed is on his own hook. Royer could jump the systems now. One of the definite benefits of being status was that education, including university, was paid for. For him, a door had opened that could lead from poverty to the great Canadian middle-class dream of a home in the suburbs, two cars, umpteen TVs and hi-fis, and a barbeque.

Bob had always been quick to learn. He didn't feel at all daunted when he applied to enter the University of Calgary as an adult student. His goal was to become a social worker, and while he had not been inside a classroom for several years, he had certainly been learning about human nature, society, and law. He took to his studies hungrily, eager to dig out the reasons for the way things were, even if the answers the authors and teachers gave were, for the most part, grounded in a white, liberal tradition. The great – and to Bob

wonderful – exception was Saul Alinsky, the American activist who practically wrote the book on modern non-violent
protest. Alinsky combined audacious media stunts with
hardball politics.

Studying, of course, wasn't enough for Bob. He soon found
himself being drawn into political circles on campus, becoming a member of the Advisory Committee to the Indian Student University Program. At last he could lift his voice – and,
to however small a degree, he was listened to. He had the
beginnings of power in his hands, and he thrived on it, eventually becoming president of the committee. Just like that, he
had become an "activist."

In prison, Royer had met Roy Little Chief, an angry young
Blackfoot who wanted change so badly he could taste it. Once
out of prison, Roy introduced him to other young militants
like Devalon Small Legs and his brother, Nelson Small Legs,
Jr., and another Blackfoot activist named Urban Calling Last.
Four years after Royer got out of prison, in 1972, they decided
between them to form the Calgary Urban Treaty Indian Alliance (CUTIA). Their idea was to help the six to seven thousand
Indians drifting in and out of Calgary from surrounding
Peigan, Blackfoot, Cree, and Blood reserves, where conditions, with a few exceptions, remained abysmal.

As recently as 1967, while Canadians were celebrating
their centennial, the RCMP, prodded by social workers, had
conducted door-to-door surveys, confirming reports that
most reserve households were virtually without food – no
game or other meat, often only tea and flour. Migrating to the
city, Indians headed to the Indian Affairs office, where they
were either provided with assistance or arbitrarily sent back
to the reserve. With luck, they might be referred to Manpower,
various government agencies, or the Calgary Friendship
Centre.

On the basis of their own experiences, Roy Little Chief and
the others knew perfectly well what happened to migrant

Indians seeking a better chance in the city. The pattern was well-established. It was all very well for bureaucrats to ordain that an Indian should go back to the reserve, but the fact was, by then, that populations on the reserves were growing, especially in Saskatchewan. It was from there that most Cree-speaking migrants came. All were unemployed, all were poor, and many, if not most, were struggling with alcohol problems as a direct result of the poverty and unemployment. If they were turned down for support by Indian Affairs, the alternatives were bleak. The Friendship Centre was strictly limited in what it could provide, and, of course, in the government agencies, including Indian Affairs, nobody was likely to speak any of the Indian languages. An unemployed, under-educated Cree who didn't speak English or French might as well have arrived from the moon so far as opportunities went.

And, so far as the staff at Indian Affairs was concerned, such a person should have stayed on the moon. Documented examples of discrimination and insensitivity at the district office included a staff member who complained, "Whenever I speak to Indians, I have to speak very slowly and loudly." When asked where native women should go for emergency shelter when funds were cut back in Calgary, an ex-probation officer snapped: "Let them hustle." A secretary was seen washing off a phone after it had been used by an Indian client. Indians were not allowed to use the staff toilet, although white visitors were. This was on top of the usual frustrating situations caused by bureaucracies, such as being kept waiting for hours and having confidential financial situations discussed in loud voices by staff in front of other people.

With initial backing from Indian Affairs, CUTIA plunged into its appointed task by counselling, providing legal advocacy, forming an urban Indian parent-school committee, establishing referral services, finding homes, setting up emergency services for the destitute, organizing cultural activities, making hospital and home visits, and supplying transportation for the elderly, sick, and dispossessed. If they

weren't exactly changing the world overnight, Roy Little
Chief and his friends were at least making a slight dent. The
big difference between CUTIA and other department-
sponsored initiatives was that, although it had white supporters, its director, co-ordinator, board members, and staff
were all Indians.

Soon enough, the innovative, successful Indian self-help
organization made the ultimate mistake: it was doing its job
so well that there was an outside chance some staff hours
would have to be cut over at Indian Affairs: the department
could no longer even pretend to be doing some of the various
jobs that CUTIA had taken up. There were fears about a precedent being set for the funding of off-reserve programs, and of
course the constitutional issue of responsibility for Indians
reared its head. Despite the sympathy of well-intentioned
individual white Indian Affairs staff members in the field,
memos began flying back and forth in Ottawa concerning this
upstart program being run in distant Calgary by city Indians
themselves.

The big danger, one senior civil servant sagely noted, was
that if this program proved to be viable over an extended
period, word would go out on the moccasin telegraph – that
mysterious means by which Indians had learned to communicate through kinship networks and various affiliated
groups without waiting to hear from Indian Affairs. Then, the
next thing the bureaucrats would know, there would be Indians applying in all the Canadian cities to set up similar programs to run themselves. "We should reflect on our decision
to ensure that we are not placing ourselves in a most awkward
position," wrote the Director of Finance and Management for
Indian and Eskimo Affairs, E. T. Parker. Any final decision
about supporting CUTIA, it seemed, should be based not on
the validity of the work it was doing, but on the chance of a
dangerous precedent being set that would allow power to slip
through the fingers of the bureaucrats into the hands of Indians. When applications went to the Treasury Board in Ottawa
for on-going funding of CUTIA, then-Indian Affairs Minister

Jean Chrétien turned it down cold on the grounds that "once Indian people move from their reserve to non-reserve communities, they should be regarded as citizens of the Province in the foremost sense. This is not to say that my Department would not continue to assist, but in a secondary role."

After a year of doing good work, Roy Little Chief was told that, in fact, he shouldn't have gotten any money from Indian Affairs to begin with, because such funding was constitutionally illegal, and that, if it turned out the province was not providing adequate assistance to Indians coming in from the reserves, Indian Affairs was there to help "avoid hardships." In other words, Indian Affairs would have to cut off funding to Indians trying to help Indians, since it was unconstitutional, but the department would maintain its own white staff to be available in the event that the province didn't live up to its responsibility, which everyone concerned knew it wasn't living up to, otherwise the Indians wouldn't have had to help themselves in the first place. It was classic federal-provincial buckpassing.

There was one further catch, according to the minister: no welfare-delivery-system agreement had ever been made between the Province of Alberta and the federal government. What Chrétien was saying was major news to all concerned, since Ottawa was being displaced as the primary provider of assistance to the Indians, as set out in the treaties, with the job being fobbed off on the provinces. Pinning Chrétien down on his amazing new interpretation of history proved impossible. When Roy Little Chief called the minister's office, he was told that Chrétien had changed his mind about federal-provincial jurisdiction and would provide interim funding, but when the cheque did not arrive and Little Chief persisted, it was to learn that Chrétien had moved on to the post of President of the Treasury Board. A man named Judd Buchanan had become the new Indian Affairs minister. He'd heard nothing about funding any such project. And so it went.

In the meantime, Little Chief and the others had been forced onto welfare themselves. The predictable result among the Indians was despair and a sense of betrayal. Roy Little Chief and Urban Calling Last turned to their friends at the University of Calgary, one of whom was Bob Royer.

The first step, it was decided, would be a "mini sit-in" at the Indian Affairs office to protest the cut-off of funds for CUTIA. Word was leaked to the media early, which meant that the civil servants knew what was coming. An administrator was taken to task later for not locking the office before the Indians got in. His excuse was that he'd heard the protest was scheduled for 2:00 P.M., and "everyone knows that Indians are always late." In fact, the protesters arrived at 1:00 P.M., sat down on the floor, and began pounding on drums. They left after twenty minutes, hoping they had made their point.

It wasn't to be that easy.

Feeling threatened, mandarins of the Ottawa Indian Affairs Department made several moves designed to defeat the protesters. What native staff the department had was cut, delivery of welfare services at the local level was subjected to more stringent regulation, and the Chrétien-inspired notion that Indians in the city were a provincial responsibility was pushed aggressively. To eliminate their influence, liberal staff members were systematically rotated out of Calgary, some under the guise of promotions to Ottawa, while disinterested and unsympathetic middle-level bureaucrats were brought in to clamp a lid on all this activism. The Indian Affairs department mastermind was a retired British Army major, John McGilp, who had helped frame the 1969 White Paper in which the government had called for the abolition of the status of Indian altogether, final dismemberment of the reserves, and the total assimilation of natives into white society. McGilp was so loathed by Indian bands across the country that many of them refused to deal with him at all, and some had called for his firing. Instead, he had been consistently promoted.

In marked contrast, when a district superintendent of social-services, Nels Gutnick, found a way to approve social-assistance grants to the now-destitute CUTIA staff members, he was investigated from above and told to either transfer out of Calgary or be fired. In the end, he resigned. He was the last liberal in the department, Royer believed, and it reverted to the old pattern.

What had happened was, in fact, not uncommon. Rather, it seemed to an angry Bob Royer, it was perfectly in line with department policy over the years. Economic and educational programs contained built-in mechanisms for failure. He felt it was obvious that it was anathema for Indian Affairs to allow Indians to succeed. Accordingly, any program that started to become viable – like CUTIA – had to be knee-capped. Either it was cut off, or a competing program was deliberately set up to deflect it into the grey area of federal-provincial responsibility, where it would bog down. Anybody who suggested this wasn't the case only earned Royer's disdain. To draw attention to this issue, the CUTIA people and their supporters decided to occupy the Indian Affairs offices in Calgary.

For Royer, there was considerable risk involved. If he joined the occupation, he would be in violation of the terms of his release from prison, which required that he not break the peace for seven years. At this point, it had been only six years since he walked out of prison. He was finishing his bachelor of arts degree program. Soon, he would be in a position to take up the struggle as he had envisioned it back behind bars. This was slightly premature. In addition, there was another, deeply personal reason to think twice before throwing everything he had earned to the winds. In August of 1973, Mary had given birth to their first son, Robbie. Bob was no longer responsible merely for himself. But there was no serious question in his mind of staying on the sidelines. It wasn't his style.

At 8:30 A.M., Thursday, November 28, 1974, Royer filed into the Calgary district office along with thirty Indian men, women, and children, including Ed Burnstick of the American Indian Movement. Roy Little Chief advised the staff to leave, promising that nothing would be destroyed and no file would be touched. The acting administrator was so unnerved by the situation that he fled to a nearby hotel, calling on the RCMP to provide his family with protection – even though no threats had been made. He even hired a guard dog. He refused repeatedly to go anywhere near the office so long as the Indians were there.

A report that the Indians were armed got out, and when it was all over, a Winchester rifle was indeed found. Since no one involved in the demonstration had brought it, protesters concluded that it had been planted to discredit them.

Calgary Mayor Rod Sykes quickly got into the act, accusing the Indians of terrorism and demanding that the police evict them immediately. The police, to their credit, refused, although officers were planted on buildings all around, and unmarked cars took up positions. The new Indian Affairs minister, Judd Buchanan, refused to talk to the occupiers, even though he happened to be in town, and when white CUTIA supporters tried to approach the minister at a Liberal cocktail party, they were hustled outside by plainclothes police before they could get anywhere near him. Buchanan's only contribution to the affair was to personally lay charges of public mischief against Little Chief and Burnstick, which was intriguing for the simple reason that this was the only one of a recent spate of similar occupations and blockades that had been unarmed. Angry Indians in Ottawa, Cache Creek, Acinawabe, Vancouver, and Nanaimo had been armed, but the minister did not act. Only in Calgary, for some obscure reason, were charges laid.

The occupation was over within thirty-eight hours. Except for a couple of chairs, nothing was trashed. One person who was negatively affected as a result of his involvement in the occupation was Nelson Small Legs, Jr., who was suspended from Lethbridge Community College after Indian Affairs told college officials they were cutting off his education allowance. He had obviously learned too much.

In the wake of the protest, a defence-fund committee was set up, Roy Little Chief, Ed Burnstick, and Nelson Small Legs, Jr., were placed under surveillance by the Mounties. Phones were tapped. Undercover operatives began to tag along behind the various activists. Indian Affairs demanded that the president of the University of Calgary launch an investigation into any students, such as Royer, who had been involved.

Former CUTIA staff found themselves having to return to their reserves, the bright hope of pulling themselves up by their own bootstraps shattered. Charges against the leaders were eventually dropped – after lawyers had threatened to subpoena senior Indians Affairs mandarins and their files.

Royer's first taste of battle against the entrenched bureaucracy left him with a flat taste in his mouth. In the long run all that happened was that the hard-line administrators ended up with their power enhanced, and the Indians who had tried to replace the bureaucrats controlling their fate in the local offices ended up out on the street – where they had started. It was not the stuff of happy endings.

But it soon became more than simply a political setback. The entire affair grew into a source of bitterness and misery when Nelson Small Legs, Jr., decided to express his sense of defeat in the most powerful way he could. Retreating to his home on the Peigan reserve, the twenty-two-year-old activist dressed himself in full ritual regalia, lay down on the floor, and shot himself through the heart. He left a note that said:

I give up my life in protest to the present conditions concerning Indian people of southern Alberta.

I also give up my life in the hopes of a full-scale investigation into the dept. of Indian Affairs corruption and also the resigning of Judd Buchanan and divide and conquer tactics present on each reservation.

For 100 years Indians have suffered. Must they suffer another 100 years. My suicide should open the eyes of non-Indians into how much we've suffered.

The Canadian government promised an investigation into why Nelson Small Legs, Jr., was driven to kill himself to draw attention to the mess around him. Of course, such an investigation was never carried out.

For a while, after he learned that his friend was dead, Bob Royer wanted to pick up a gun too, but he wanted to aim it at someone other than himself. It took a long time for the anger to ease off enough for him to get himself back on track. Steady. Get that degree. Infiltrate. Bore from within. Don't blow up. In a very real sense, Nelson had merely done what Bob felt Ottawa wanted all Indians to do – to cease existing.

The following year, Indian Affairs Minister Buchanan scheduled a visit to Alberta, but refused to deal with the CUTIA issue. Travelling – appropriately enough – by army helicopter, he hopped from one reserve to another, five in two days, dressed in slacks and a turtle-necked sweater, while chiefs appeared in the traditional hides and headdresses required for state occasions. Apart from demonstrating that he knew virtually nothing about actual Indian affairs, the minister went so far as to throw out any guests to his hotel suite who brought up the CUTIA matter. Having alienated everyone in sight, he flew back to Ottawa and was not seen again.

Chapter 25

In the Belly of the Beast

BOB ROYER'S ROLE IN THE OCCUPATION OF THE CALGARY OFFICE had not gone entirely unnoticed. He had been spotted and photographed slipping in and out of the office wearing a suit, in the weeks before anything happened. He was obviously part of the team that documented the discrimination. An instigator, as always. However, unlike Nelson Small Legs, Jr., at Lethbridge Community College, Royer was shielded from dismissal from university by the fact that the University of Calgary refused to heed the vengeful bureaucrats at Indian Affairs.

The Regional Director General of Indian Affairs had not been happy with the behaviour of the Calgary police during the occupation. He reportedly felt that the police should have swooped right away and cleared everyone out. That way there "wouldn't have been $15,000 worth of damage to the offices." (In fact, only a couple of chairs had been broken.)

He could have turned Royer over to the parole people for violating the terms of his recognisance, but instead he summoned the wary but excited young activist to his office a few months after things had settled down, and said: "You seem to be fairly knowledgeable about these problems at the grass-roots level. Finish your social-work degree, and then you should try to help us to solve the problems. You can do a lot more from the inside that you can from the outside."

Royer was suspicious. "Yeah, but under some conditions. I'm nobody's nigger. Don't get the idea you're gonna go bury me off in some corner of the province in some social-services role, and you'll never hear from me again. That's not what I want."

"If you're really serious about wanting some input, especially at the senior management level, this is the route to go," replied the director.

It occurred to Royer's street-smart mind that when one of the senior managers at Indian Affairs takes a rising young Indian social worker up to the top of the mountain and shows him the kingdoms of the world spread at his feet, and promises everything, it behooves the young Indian social worker to keep his back to something. At best, he sensed, he was being invited to play a game with a master. At worst, he was being taken in and gagged, thrown a few crumbs of authority, while the machine ground on in its usual way.

Nevertheless, the offer was concrete. Despite the risks of co-option, he really had no choice but to accept. Thus, Bob Royer, former juvenile delinquent and prison trouble-maker, found himself being appointed as commissioner on the 1977 Métis and Non-Status Indian Crime and Justice Commission. It was his job to deliver a series of what proved to be devastating reports, pointing to the heart of darkness (that he knew so well) at the centre of the Canadian system of soft apartheid that had evolved in the wake of the defeat of the northern native nations.

Royer thought he was ready to play the game, but he had underestimated the colossal size, weight, and inertia of the Department of Indian Affairs. It was like a glacier. Even if the order was given to close it down tomorrow, he thought, it would probably crunch on for another century before its momentum was spent. For years he had been regarding it as Canada's KGB, but he soon began to realize that it was worse than that. The KGB at least didn't call itself the Ministry of Love. Indian Affairs meant "Indian Controls," but pretended to be the servant of the native people. This made it trickier to deal with. You could go past row after row of desks in brightly lit Indian Affairs offices across the country and find nothing but pleasant white workers, quietly going about their business of taking care of Indians, with never a whiff of a thought in the air that this might be the bureaucratic end of a huge network of interlocked concentration camps. Nice people these, the actual nine-to-four white-collar bearer of the white man's burden.

But they would have to go.

Royer had arrived at a political position about all this. The only hope the Indians or Métis or General Indians had of wresting back any significant degree of control over their own lives was to take over Indian Affairs. Where would it start? For Bob Royer there was not a microsecond of doubt. The mountain he had to climb was Indian Affairs; the fortress he had to storm was Indian Affairs; and the doctrine he had to defeat was the doctrine of Indian Affairs, which held that the native people could be defined racially by legislation, although it was illegal so to designate anyone else. Thus defined, natives could be told what to do in new and perversely specific ways.

The government of Canada couldn't be overthrown, that was for sure. So, he thought, any of the rhetoric coming from the black radicals in the States at this time had to be taken for what it was worth: as some kind of wild fantasy of Afro-Maoist revenge. In Canada, the one reasonable hope for natives was to gain control of the Indian Affairs bureaucracy, and to run their own show the way Indian Affairs now ran things to suit its own needs.

The Indian Act, which made all of the above possible, was passed in 1876, initially to promote a two-fold policy. First, land had to be purchased to clear the way for settlement. The premise of the British occupation, in fact, was that absolute title to the land was vested in the Crown. Whenever Indian title was surrendered or otherwise extinguished, the Crown had full power to dispose of the property at will. The Crown had it at the beginning, the Crown could get rid of it in the end. Indian tenure was considered by law, from very early, to be a "mere burden" upon the Crown's "proprietary estate." Royal proclamations and treaties eventually took care of that.

The second part of the policy was the "civilizing" of the Indians. A much more complicated business, as it turned out.

It seemed simple enough at the time. In the process of acquiring land from the Indians, Canada had created a fledgling bureaucracy that was familiar with at least a few things about Indians – the location of their lands, if nothing else. It was easy and logical to set these Old Boys to work enforcing the other aspects of the Indian Act, and to hire people they knew to help them.

Seldom did anyone in the department know anything about the "clients." Federal bureaucrats squabbled with provincial bureaucrats. There was confusion in the ranks. Decisions made in Ottawa seldom made any sense at all on distant reserves.

Arguably, the Indians had been better off when they were still considered the responsibility of the British military. Even when they were passed over to the Colonial Office, they retained a fair amount of self-government. The Colonial Office wasn't really very interested in them. The Act of Union didn't affect them much either, since it made no provision for a department to deal with them and certainly included no budget. While the British North America Act left the Indians to federal jurisdiction, Confederation clarified very little. Indian matters were left in the hands of the Secretary of State until 1873, when they were transferred to the Department of the Interior, but individual Indians continued to be more or less ignored unless they made trouble. The Indian Act was passed in 1876, but wasn't until 1880 that a separate Indian department was set up, and even then it was under the Minister of the Interior, who happened to be John A. Macdonald. His only concern was that the Indians stayed the hell out of the way of his national obsession.

The importance – or lack of importance – the government attached to Indian Affairs can be easily seen by the way it has been shuffled from one department to another over the years. In 1936, it was tagged on to Mines and Resources. In 1949, it was tossed over to Citizenship and Immigration. From there it was pushed over to Northern Affairs and Resources, which became the Department of Indian Affairs and Northern Development. It was not until 1966 that a cabinet minister was made responsible for the department. Until then, no minister had ever been solely responsible for Indians. The power of the Indian Affairs bureaucracy, which should have been watched more closely than any other, since it had absolute control over a vanquished people's lives, was thus more unfettered than almost any other bureaucracy.

On top of this, Royer noted, there were at least fourteen other federal departments that impinged on Indian programs, plus whatever provincial departments were involved, and on top of that, some provinces had native-affairs secretariats, which were little departments unto themselves. It has been said that Canadians are among the most over-governed people in the world. Their degree of over-governance is lightweight, however, compared to the additional restrictions placed upon Canadian Indians.

The political world into which Royer had stepped as a social worker – moreover, that very rare bird, a status Indian social worker – was by now in a state of ferment. Things had begun to change in the locked-in relationship between natives and Canadians after the Second World War, when homecoming Indian veterans started demanding to know why they were considered fit to die for their country, but not to vote. The process was considerably stimulated in 1966 by the publication of the Hawthorne Report, which discovered widespread poverty, disease, and underemployment, leading to alcoholism and suicide. This was treated by the media as a big surprise, although a quick trip to nearly any reserve would have told even the most obstinately uninquisitive reporter that something was fundamentally wrong.

The atmosphere had heated up in 1969, when the government published its White Paper on Indian Policy, calling for the abolition of the Indian Affairs Department, the repeal of the Indian Act, the transfer of all responsibility for Indians to provinces, the end of all treaties, and a rejection of aboriginal rights. Up until that point, with Pierre Trudeau in power and talking constantly about a Just Society, Indians had begun to think that a positive change was in the air. But Trudeau and his minister, Chrétien, had something else in mind. They proposed tearing up even the little pieces of land the Indians had left by abolishing the reserves.

It was not as though the results of destroying reserves wasn't known. In the United States, some sixty reservations had been eliminated between 1953 and 1960. The results had been so uniformly disastrous that the program was halted.

What happened to the Klamath Indians of Oregon was often cited as the best – or worst – example. When it was terminated in 1958, the reservation had been thriving. Annual family income was $6,000, placing the Klamaths in the top 19 per cent of American income-earners. The moment the reservation was sold off, however, the Klamaths tumbled. Families fell apart, community cohesion dissolved, crime rates rose astronomically. By 1960, nearly a third of the Klamaths were on welfare, in prison, or in mental institutions scattered around Oregon.

What happened to the Calihoos in Canada was the result of the same process, the difference being that life on that reserve had been a social disaster even before termination. If people who were in good shape could crash so rapidly once their social world was ripped apart, how much more thorough would be the shattering of people already in a terrible, nearly comatose, state?

It had been only nine years since Indians had been given the federal vote. Likewise, it had been only nine years since

Indian Agents had been pulled from the reserve. However, that didn't mean the white presence was gone, and it didn't mean that the Indians were left by default to run their own show, as they had expected they would be able to do. The most powerful positions on the reserves were all occupied by white Canadians: missionaries, teachers, federal employees, RCMP officers, postal workers, store owners. It was not just that all the land around the reserves had been occupied, the reserves themselves had been clamped under stringent state control. In all, by 1971, there were 7,000 non-natives living in the 550 reserves and occupying all the key positions.

The facts of Indian life, by the time Bob Royer felt himself ready to try and do something about it, were bleak, bleak, bleak. Life expectancy among natives in Canada was still ten years less than for the national population. At least 50 to 60 per cent of native illnesses and deaths were alcohol-related, with some estimates attributing 30 per cent of deaths to misuse of alcohol. For young men, suicide accounted for one "accidental" death in four, compared with one in ten among the general Indian population – which was itself three times higher than the national rate. Between 1964 and 1978, the percentage of the population receiving social assistance increased from 36 to between 50 and 70 per cent. Less than half the Indian homes were properly serviced, with one in three families living in overcrowded conditions.

The degree to which natives remained isolated from the surrounding society can be seen in a single statistic: to this day, 93.6 per cent of their marriages take place within their own ethnic group. Of all the ethnic groups in multicultural Canada, this is the highest rate by far. It says a lot about the continuing enormity of the gap between Indian and Canadian societies.

As late as 1973, nearly half of all Indian reserves and settlements were accessible only by water. Only a third of them had road access, and only 18 per cent could be reached by rail. Only half the Indian homes had running water, less than half had sewage disposal, less than a third had fire-protection equipment, and infant mortality was twice as high as the national average.

Although Indians comprised only 1.2 per cent of the Canadian population, they made up 9 per cent of the population of federal penitentiaries, the proportion in western provincial jails being much higher. In Manitoba it reached more than 50 per cent. The proportion of female Indian inmates in prison was likewise considerably higher. In terms of sentencing, even though natives weren't usually involved in serious crimes like murder or armed robbery, they were still being sentenced to life imprisonment as often as non-natives, on different grounds.

According to a 1966 study, fewer than 10 per cent of Indian students were staying in school for the full twelve- or thirteen-year program, and the number of drop-outs was increasing. In general, 90 per cent of Indian kids were not finishing high school. Less than 1 per cent of Indians made it to university, compared to 7 per cent in the general population. And of that 1 per cent, only 6 per cent graduated! Having no control over curriculum, and remembering their own days in school, the parents tended strongly to dismiss schooling as that well-known white man's way of brainwashing young Indians, turning them against their parents and their old ways. It was hardly to be encouraged.

None of this was surprising to Royer – although some of the figures did take his breath away momentarily.

Chapter 26

The Bureau of Indian Control

ON THE EXTERIOR, OUT IN THE STREETS, IN THE BARS, ON TV, IN the papers, Canada seemed a free country. All you had to do, however, was step through the glass doors into the Indian Affairs offices in Calgary, and you entered another political zone entirely. It was a bit like a beehive, rigidly hierarchical. If you were an Indian, you were the slave of that beehive. It controlled your life. And it was so clean, so tidy, so *tranquil*. Yet, in Royer's oft-stated view, Indian Affairs was the euphemistic name for a Bureau of Indian Control. It was there to enforce a separate set of laws severely restricting the freedom of the defeated people. In legal terms, from before Confederation, Canada was a vehicle for an apartheid program. On this the early French and English agreed. The native should be kept apart as much as possible. The dictatorship-within-a-democracy that evolved from these attitudes was in place from the start, Royer thought. He thought about this a lot. It was quite amazing. White Canadians really did not seem to appreciate that in the middle of their liberal democracy there was a dark region, a compartment of totalitarianism. And this wasn't just rhetoric!

If he understood dictatorships, they employed plenty of restrictions and freedoms were minimal. People's lives were in the hands of uncaring, capricious officials, who could call in the police on a whim. There was no right to vote. There were travel restrictions, a limited range of career options, restrictions of civil rights, restrictions on property, restrictions on local languages. Cultural activities were banned. Ownership of property was forbidden. Children were taken away to state-run schools where they were brainwashed.

These, indeed, were the conditions that Canadian Indians had been living under for the past hundred years. The appearance of Indian Agents on the reserves had been as much a turning point for the Indians as the arrival of the Black Robes had been centuries before. The big difference was that an Indian Agent didn't need to learn anybody's language, not even long enough to tell them to start speaking French or English. He needed no ability to charm or impress anybody. He was the arm of the law. Mounties were just his muscle. He was prosecutor and judge, legal guardian, absolute despot. He was God.

The powers of the Indian Agents were so extensive that, for a number of decades, prairie Indians could not leave their reserves without passes from them. For many decades they weren't allowed to wear a "native costume" off the reserve without permission to "perform." One presumes there were good agents, but with vast, arbitrary authority at their disposal, many succumbed to the corruptions of power. Some of the rules they enforced had been dreamed up by Ottawa, and others had been patched together over the years on an *ad hoc* basis, but many others were rules the agents had invented on the spot. If they were ever challenged, all they needed to do was get one of their bosses in Ottawa to make sure it got passed into law by order-in-council.

Accordingly, prairie Indians were prohibited from selling produce grown on their own reserves unless they had permission from the Indian Agent. If an Indian Agent felt that an Indian was going into the pool hall too often, he could be banned entry for a year on that reason alone. From 1886, it was an offence for an Indian to gamble. If caught, he was fined ten dollars, half the take going to the informer. Indians were forbidden to drink on or off the reserve, and if they refused to say where they had obtained liquor, they could be charged with withholding information and sent to jail. A status Indian still cannot make a will, unless it is approved by the department. After all, technically status Indians don't own any property. For a long time, Indian Agents personally distributed food, perhaps cutting off a piece of bacon in front of the Indians' eyes, and if people weren't "good Indians," that piece would be smaller next time around. There wouldn't be any ration at all for those who made political trouble. Later, food vouchers were issued. The vouchers, it should be noted, didn't allow the Indians to choose their own groceries. They listed exactly what could be picked up.

From 1886 until the 1930s, the completely illegal "pass system" was in force in Saskatchewan and Alberta, especially in the areas of Treaties Four, Six, and Seven. Indian Agents were handed books of passes. Police were told to pick up any Indian who didn't have a pass. If caught without a pass, an Indian could have his rations cut off, which could mean death by starvation. This was no minor threat. The only way an Indian could obtain a pass was to get a letter of recommendation from his farm instructor, the first of which began appearing in the late 1880s – and the only way to get this was to do every bit of farm work the instructor assigned, no matter how ridiculous his instructions might be. So now there were two gods over the Indians – the farm instructor as well as the Indian Agent.

The more Bob Royer studied, the more he became convinced that the aspect of the Canadian master plan for the solution of the Indian problem that laid the heaviest hand over the reserves in the long run, was the policy of turning Indians into farmers. The economic effects were in fact similar to what happened to land-holding peasants once their land was collectivized in Russia. Forced to farm according to the dictates of distant masters, the Canadian native farming program was a spectacular failure from the start. Even by the time Royer reached university, only about 15 per cent of the land's agricultural potential was being used, and most of that was being farmed by non-natives. Seen as a social-control mechanism, farming made terrific sense. It kept everyone pinned down on the farm. But economically, it was a joke. Less than a million hectares of reserve lands were even potentially arable. Only about half of that was good for either grazing or crops. At most, only an estimated four thousand farms could survive, and they would feed just 10 per cent of the reserve populations. As Indian populations rose, the acreage per Indian shrank dramatically. More land, of course, could not be bought without permission of the Minister of Indian Affairs himself. In a classic paradox, the Farm Credit Act, set up to help native farmers, only allowed the native long-term credit if he took out a mortgage on his farm. Alas, all native land that might be turned into a farm was owned by the Crown. Nobody can get mortgages on Crown property. Catch 22.

But this one was Bob Royer's favourite: most bands weren't allowed to control the money they were granted by treaty. If they by chance managed to increase their per capita income through free enterprise, the money was grabbed by Ottawa and placed in a "trust fund." Rather than being re-invested in the reserve or spent on something the band wanted, it was invested in government bonds. By 1970, department-controlled band trust funds amounted to $30 million of Indian earnings – which Indians couldn't touch. Between 1968 and 1972, the $2.5-million trust fund of one band mysteriously shrank to $500,000. Requests for a loan or a grant could take up to five years to process, with the terms being changed by the bureaucrats before acceptance. Never quite enough was handed out to finance a complete developmental scheme. The average grant in 1965 had been $100.

Jean Chrétien, the Indian Affairs minister whose thinly disguised 1969 grab for the last of the Indians' lands inadvertently succeeded in uniting native organizations across the nation, captured in an interview the essence of the bureaucratic maze the Indians faced if they wanted government help:

> First the band council decides that they want to do something constructive and reasonable with a piece of their land, as many of them do. They pass a council resolution which they hand over to the Department's agency office. It is sent from there to the regional office. The regional people, anticipating that their superiors in Ottawa will ask questions, ask questions themselves. Back it goes to the agency and back to the band. The band gets another meeting organized. They answer the questions and put the proposal back into the mill. It goes to the agency, to the region, and it finally reaches the head office where the lawyers get at it. They ask more questions that the region had not thought of. Back it goes. Eventually all the questions are answered and it comes back to me. (Quoted in Cardinal, *Unjust Society*)

But worse, by far, than the farm policy, was the schools policy. While epidemics can ultimately be written off as the Red Man's bad luck, the destruction caused by guns and alcohol be attributed to Machievellianism, and famines seen as an extension of total war being practised on civilian native populations, the schools policy passed beyond even these evils.

It began innocently enough. There was one thing the Indians all agreed they wanted: education. Promises were made about schools and teachers. The federal government could have funded day schools on the reserves or established boarding schools near the reserves, both of which might have stood a chance of working. Instead, it built three token "industrial schools," scattered at distant points from each other across the prairies, and otherwise tossed grant money into the laps of whichever churches wanted to take on responsibility for the education of Indian children. The fastest way to civilize the Indians, the priests and politicians agreed, was to remove the Indian kids from "the surroundings which tend to keep them in a state of degradation."

Since it was widely assumed in the 1920s by the white man that the Indian didn't have the "physical, mental or moral get up to enable him to compete," as one Indian Commissioner phrased it in a report to Ottawa, the only thing to do was to teach him a trade. Taking their grant money, the priests quickly set up residential schools – as far as possible from the bad influences of home, family, and friends. Indian children shared the common trauma of being dragged away from their homes and cast into strange places, where they were beaten if they got caught speaking their own languages. How much trade skill anyone learned while studying the Bible or Catechism is a moot point. Since the residential schools were all denominational, Christian indoctrination was the main focus: learning a trade came a poor second.

Not surprisingly, children ran away from the residential schools in droves. So many escaped that the RCMP were used to chase them down and haul them back into classes. The "problem" of escaping children got to the point where the government passed a law stating that Indian parents had no authority over their children while the kids were in residential school. Not only had all their children been kidnapped, but the kidnappers had become the legal custodians of the children while they were gone. This was done so that runaways could be returned to the schools.

The situation would have been enough of a nightmare for parents, grandparents, aunts, uncles, and children alike, even if it hadn't turned out that the white men had built such substandard buildings into which to herd a captive generation of young Indians that many of the children sickened and died.

In 1914, Duncan Campbell Scott, poet and former Deputy Superintendent General of Indian Affairs confessed:

the system was open to criticism. Insufficient care was exercised in the admission of children to the schools. The well-known predisposition of Indians to tuberculosis resulted in a very large percentage of deaths among the pupils. They were housed in buildings not carefully designed for school purposes, and these buildings became infected and dangerous to the inmates. It is quite within the mark to say that fifty per cent of the children who passed through these schools did not live to benefit from the education which they had received therein.

Fifty per cent! Half the Indian kids sent into those Canadian schools died! How does one express the rage of parents whose children first are taken by police to schools where they are punished if they speak anything other than a harsh foreign tongue, and then are subjected to conditions that turn out to be so dank and cold that half of them die from TB?

Royer would never forget the afternoon he had run across that reference to the 50-per-cent casualty rate among the residential school children. He was in a library in Calgary, still a student, thumbing through an obscure old book called *Canada and Its Provinces*, trying to find something else, when he came across Scott's comment. He'd had to stop and look out the window for a long while, fighting for control. He didn't know whether he wanted to cry or scream. It sat there, that knowledge, like a patch of numbness where something has struck so hard it can't be felt. And then, suddenly, he was dizzy.

He knew from his own experience about being in that type of priest-run school, just like he knew about prisons. There was a legacy for you! He had never suspected, though, that half those kids had died. It was a chapter seldom mentioned in the story of the creation of Canada, "glorious and free."

After that there was a part of Bob Royer that wondered whether he could ever truly forgive Canada, no matter how hard he tried.

Many Indians couldn't forgive and the will to resist had never abated. Most Canadians seem to think that there were no

Indian organizations until the late sixties, when groups such as the Calgary Urban Treaty Indian Alliance sprang up. In fact, native protests were taking shape well before the turn of the century, as the harsh reality of the political situation that was facing natives sank in. The trouble was, early Indian organizations had to go underground, as they worked on their struggle for equality.

For one thing, it was illegal to leave one's reserve without permission from the Indian Agent. If an Indian was found anywhere off the reserve without a pass, especially in a town or city, he could be hustled off to jail. Even if a travel permit was granted, it was seldom for more than two weeks. Transportation was by horse and wagon. It could be sixty miles to the nearest reserve, which meant that the chances of getting to more than one reserve on a trip were slim indeed, especially considering the condition of the roads. This was the beauty of having dispersed the tribes. Boxed off like this, with no modern communications systems – for a long time without even postal service – the Indians were very nearly powerless to organize resistance.

Under these conditions, brave men still managed to sneak across the countryside to meet and plan, eluding the white men. They had to conspire in the open spaces, hidden only by the vastness of the landscape. If it rained, they plotted under a wind-battered, dripping tent.

Bands were forbidden by the Indian Act to contribute more than twenty-five cents to any unauthorized Indian organization, which meant that any petitions or lobbying efforts had to be financed out of the organizers' own pockets. Few of them had any money. What capital they had was to be measured in livestock. Some families went so far in their determination to organize that they sold their entire herds of horses and cattle and sheep. It was not as though they were taking their fate lying down.

Resistance to Indian organizations never ended. When, in the late sixties, natives in Saskatoon independently organized the Indian and Métis Development Society, it was swiftly broken up by Indian Affairs. When Harold Cardinal, leader of the Indian Association of Alberta, said things that the department didn't want to hear, Indian Affairs cut off his organization's funding – funding that had only just been granted. When Cardinal stepped aside, the department king-pins resumed allocations. It was dirty and cruel. Indian Affairs claimed Cardinal's group had failed to account for half its expenditures. In the end, the group proved that it could account for everything, but the smear job had been done, and the IAA was barred from appearing before the standing committee on Indian Affairs to clear themselves.

With the coming of federal funding in 1968, native organizers found themselves up their knees in a new kind of gumbo. For a change, they had some money, but, like everything else the white men offered, it was boobytrapped.

Once the funding came, the government was soon "spending" $1 million a year on native organizations. But what did this money really allow the natives to do? It allowed them to send proposals to Ottawa, so that the bureaucrats could see what they had in mind, but the actual decisions about funding still required government approval, and when it came to the nitty-gritty of spending priorities, the feds almost never saw eye-to-eye with native organizations. As federal long-range plans continually shifted, senior bureaucrats played musical chairs, delaying some allotments and pushing others ahead, even though everybody could see at a local level that a given Ottawa-inspired program was totally out of whack with anyone's needs. Once the decision was made, no matter how ill-conceived the idea, money could not be diverted into other desperately needed services. It was the nature of bureaucracies.

The repression of native organizations not only failed, however, it backfired. The late 1960s was a time of anger. By then, bridges were being blocked by Indians at Cornwall in Ontario. A highway was sealed at Cache Creek, British Columbia. Demonstrations in Kenora led to a month-long armed occupation of Anicinabe Park by the Ojibwa Warrior Society. The Native People's Caravan travelled from

Vancouver to Ottawa to present demands on the opening day of Parliament. Insisting that "hereditary and treaty rights of all Native People in Canada including Indian, Métis, Non-Status and Inuit must be recognized and respected in the constitution of Canada," the Indians arrived on Parliament Hill to find it barricaded, as though this was much too radical a favour they were asking. The Mounties saw their presence as an excuse to try out their brand-new tactical squad, which worked very nicely. It cleared the caravan from the hill in record time.

Between the 1950s and the 1960s, the number of native organizations had gone from one national and nine provincial to four national, one regional, and thirty-three provincial. The Native Council of Canada, the Inuit Tapirisat of Canada, and the National Indian Brotherhood had all come into being. With constitutional talks on the horizon, the moment of breakthrough for natives looked like it just might be at hand.

On the crest of these rising expectations, Bob Royer found himself working as a Local Government Advisor for the Department of Indian Affairs in High Prairie, Alberta, the first Indian in the department. In this job he flew from one isolated community to another, trying to identify the problems of the local people, seeing if there was some way, under the department's mandate, that he could help them. One community was much the same as another, and most weren't too different from Michel Calihoo Reserve No. 132, as he remembered it. The basic problems were the same, the legacy of defeat, mass starvation, epidemics, and generations of enforced underemployment. Politicians and administrators had meddled so relentlessly in the early days of the reserves that it was amazing anybody had survived at all. Royer did what he could to improve medical conditions and educational conditions, but all the problems could finally be traced back to the basic political condition, and there was nothing he could do about that. He had a mounting feeling that every time he remedied something in the functioning of the system, the better it worked at its essential task, which was pacification. But never mind. Bore from within. Get in there. Climb the ladder.

On January 4, 1976, six months after moving to High River from Calgary, Mary delivered their second son, Jamie.

Meanwhile, Bob continued to fill in his reports and wore his suit to the formal staff meetings and flew ten thousand trips and talked and talked and talked. He sat on committees, he chaired committees, he reported to committees, he transcribed his field notes, he wrote reports, he submitted recommendations. He did everything he could to influence policy from within. It took only a few years for this diligence to pay off. By 1978, he had been promoted to Ottawa as Chief of the Indian-Inuit Employment Section, in charge of all native employment across the land. His explicit mandate was to implement an affirmative-action hiring program to bring natives into the civil service.

Stepping into the department offices in Ottawa, Royer had a feeling similar to the one he'd experienced back at Fort Saskatchewan when he had seen the riot squad waiting in the foyer. This was formidable. There were five thousand of them. He searched in vain for an Indian face. No. The Indians were the . . . clients. It was such a delicate word, *client*. So appropriate. Here, gathered like administering angels, were scores of clerks and secretaries and file-keepers and librarians and researchers and social workers and doctors and nurses and teachers and middle managers and senior managers and executives and deputy ministers and aides and janitors and elevator operators and waitresses and cashiers and accountants, to say nothing of all the police and army units that supported them. It was galling to realize that 43 per cent of the department's mammoth budget was used to pay the salaries of these people.

To the extent that he could ever reasonably hope to have his hand on the levers of power, this was the moment. Not bad for a guy who just ten years before had been getting out of the pen, blinking his eyes in the sunlight.

Chapter 27

The Disappearance of a Reserve

OVER THE YEARS, NO MATTER WHAT HE MIGHT BE INVOLVED IN AT the moment, Bob Royer had kept up a running investigation of what had happened to Michel Calihoo Indian Band No. 132. In Ottawa, with the facilities of the Indian Affairs Department at his disposal, he began to close in on the truth. He knew enough of Canadian history to have the general picture, but it was only after studying Treaty Six and digging through department files that he started to really understand what had happened to his family.

He knew that once the treaty was in place, the Calihoos had become subject to the Indian Act. None of the Calihoos had known, when Michel Calihoo signed his "X," that two years before, in Ottawa, the Indian Act had been invented. But sure enough, an Indian Agent showed up one day, probably in the spring of 1879, to announce that, henceforth, any purchases or sales would have to be approved by him, and that all orders for seeds, feed, tools, animals, or equipment would have to be referred to him, and that, if people wished to leave the reserve for any reason, they would have to get his permission. Michel Calihoo had bargained for none of this. Little wonder that by 1885, seven short years after the treaty had been signed, some fifty Calihoos pulled out of the reserve, spreading themselves

among the Métis and their cousins on the Cree side who had
likewise fled their reserves, trying to lose themselves in such
places as Banff.

One thing Royer learned, shortly after arriving in Ottawa,
was the amazing scale of an entire sub-department within the
Department of Indian Affairs dealing with land claims – that
Indian activists had been objecting to since its inception.
They pointed out that having Indian land claims reviewed by
the department was like putting the foxes in charge of the
hens. Nevertheless, the sub-department was there. It had
been put together by bureaucrats in anticipation of any "problems" that might arise in the future. One day, nosing around,
pretending to be searching for something else, Royer uncovered a file on the Calihoo Reserve, stamped PRELIMINARY
REPORT FOR DISCUSSION ONLY.

From the paylists contained in annual reports, Royer could
see how the Calihoo population had been affected by the
epidemics. He wondered how many other bands had these
sort of records. The diseases had come late to the Calihoos,
seeming almost an aftermath of taking treaty. In 1879, there
had been 231 of them. Two years later, the population was
down to 155, and by 1889 it had plunged to 75. There was
more: copies of the documents recording the dissecting and
parcelling out of the reserve, starting with a copy of Treaty
Six.

It had been done in stages. In the initial Adhesion to Treaty
Six, dated September 18, 1878, 22,784 acres were allocated,
based on a figure of 128 acres per band member, with a population of 178 listed. By the following year, after another head
count, the population was recalculated at 231, and the
acreage of the reserve went up to 29,568.

Then, as the population began to fall off because of disease,
acreage was calmly subtracted by Indian Affairs officials.
Nothing had been said about reserve size being tied to population at any given time, but the white men were going ahead
and doing this anyway. So, on top of the misery of seeing their
family and friends killed off all around them, the Calihoos

were left to discover for themselves the chilling fact that, each time someone died, the Canadians were shaving another 128 acres from the reserve. It was like a knife whittling away behind them.

Hamstrung at every turn by the Indian Agent, short of manpower because of the plagues, unable to direct their own farming or ranching operations because management had been taken out of their hands, with starvation setting in – thanks to the incompetence or malice of the Indian Agent – the Calihoos who stayed on the reserve grew increasingly desperate.

They could not farm. Their old system, which had worked so well, had collapsed during the rounds of sickness, and could not be rebuilt, thanks to the new rules brought by the Indian Agent. There had to be a psychological dimension to this. When pride goes, what's left? Without the freedom to make decisions about one's own life, there's nothing to be proud about. Once the Indian Act had taken hold, the Indian was legally powerless to manage his own affairs.

Unable to function, their hands tied behind their backs by the new regime, no money coming in, and the game decimated, the Calihoos did what they had to do: they offered up land for sale in order to scrape together a few dollars to buy some basic equipment. It was certain that if they waited for the department to act, they'd starve. The fact that they had no right to do so was not mentioned by the government.

Accordingly, in 1903, it was duly recorded in an Ottawa Report of the Committee of the Honorable the Privy Council, approved by His Excellency, the Governor General:

KNOW ALL MEN BY THESE PRESENTS, THAT WE, the undersigned Chief and Principal men of MICHEL'S BAND OF INDIANS resident on our Reserve in the District of Alberta in the North West Territories in the dominion of Canada, for and acting on behalf of the whole people of our said Band in Council assembled, do hereby release, remise, surrender, quit claim and yield up unto OUR SOVEREIGN LORD THE KING, his Heirs and Successors, forever, ALL SAID AND SINGULAR, that certain parcel or tract of land and premises, situate, lying and being in the Michel Indian Reserve in the North West Territories containing by admeasurement Seven Thousand eight hundred acres.

The document itself, signed by John J. McGee, Clerk of the Privy Council, ended:

the said surrender having been given in order to permit of the land covered thereby being sold on such terms as may be considered by the Superintendent General best in the interests of the Indians concerned.

That was the first big chunk of land gone, apart from what had been arbitrarily chopped out by the downward revision of population figures after the epidemics. This was more the British way – all very businesslike, all very legal, with an official record. What the documents said nothing about were the mounting pressures that were forcing the Calihoo to sign away so much of their precious heritage. Nor do the documents say anything about the roles played by the various Indian Agents involved, who, some suggested, were selected in the first place because they understood what their jobs were about.

Still, what they did, Royer concluded, was criminal in every respect.

Once the paperwork was through at the Privy Council level, the agents were required by law to advertise the sale. They proceeded to place ads in the smallest, most remote newspapers they could find, where the chances of reaching anybody interested in buying land were just about totally negligible. The ads also did not make clear just how outrageously low a price was being asked. After months had gone by and nobody had responded, the land would somehow fall into the hands of a relative of the Indian Agent or a friendly speculator.

In the 1903 deal, in exchange for its 7,800 acres, the Band was supposed to get $13,000 with which to buy modern farm machinery, implements, and horses and heifers. Only one-fifth of the land was actually ever sold, and a year after the poorly advertised sale, only $900 had been received. Two years later, a grand total of $2,641.27 had come in. Royer's reading of the file led him to believe that the land had been purchased by someone acting secretly on behalf of a junior Indian Affairs official with access to the appropriate material, who therefore knew the amounts of the tenders being submitted.

In 1906, the Band was forced to make yet another desperate sale of land to raise money to buy equipment, the last effort having failed so abysmally to generate the necessary cash flow. This time, the governor general approved a memorandum "submitting a surrender, in duplicate, made by Michel's Band of Indians, of 2,400 acres of land . . . with a view to the land covered thereby being sold for the benefit of the band." There went another 2,400 acres, on top of the 7,800 acres already surrendered – with so little to show for it!

How did the Calihoos do the second time out in the market? Consider the story of one of their customers: unable to keep up with his payments, Christopher Farmly of Manitoba managed to sell his newly acquired-on-paper property to J. J. Anderson, the son-in-law of the Minister of Indian Affairs, with another tract of land going to Frank Oliver, MP for Edmonton and Minister of the Interior.

In the 1906 sell-off, the 2,400 acres involved represented the best timber land on the reserve. It went for $9.65 an acre, with the remainder of the freed-up 1903 lands being auctioned off. Almost none of the buyers were to pay their instalments on time, as required by the Indian Act. Four years after the 1906 land sale, the Band had collected another $900 on what should have been a total payment of $48,000, with no interest ever being paid on any of these delinquent claims.

One of the band members, Solomon Calihoo, went to the inspector of the Indian agencies to complain that the Michel

Indians could never get a straight answer from their Indian
Agent, a Mr. Verreau. "No matter what we inquire about, all
he does is give us a mocking laugh, and I can tell you that's
not very pleasant when we know that it is his duty to inform
us about whatever we want to know," Solomon dictated to a
letter-writer.

When the band sought legal advice, strongly suspecting
that the agent had lied to them repeatedly, the lawyers
involved advised Ottawa: "We do not suppose that the Indian
Agent really made any representations or statements of an
improper nature, but presume that their statements arise from
the usual suspicions in an Indian's mind."

In 1911, another glitch in the treaty process emerged. Precisely 40.92 acres had to be transferred out of the reserve,
according to a certified copy of a Report to the Privy Council,
because a "quarter section has been settled upon by one Jan-
vier L'Hyrondelle previous to the survey of the boundary lines
of the Michel Calihoo Indian Reserve, No. 132."

In 1918, another report was soon whisking through the
Privy Council:

> . . . submitting herewith a surrender, in duplicate, made
> on the 29th day of April, 1918, by the Michel's band of
> Indians of all that portion of land lying along the south
> limit of the unsurrendered part of the Michel Indian
> Reserve No. 132, containing, exclusive of road allowance,
> one hundred and eighty-two acres, more or less . . . the
> said surrender having been given in order that the area
> covered thereby may be sold for the benefit of the band.

Two years later, in 1920, new legislative teeth were added to
bite into the Michel reserve:

> WHEREAS application has been made to the Department of
> Indian Affairs by the Department of Public Works of the
> Province of Alberta for the following described parcel of
> land for roadway on the Michel Indian Reserve No. 132 in

the Province of Alberta, and for the regular road allowance
referred to . . . containing ten acres and eighty-five hun-
dredth of an acre, more or less . . . at the rate of $25.00 per
acre.

As he stared at what he'd found in the files, Bob Royer could
only shake his head. They never gave up, those bastards. By
1928, yet another wrinkle had been added. The Treasury
Board was advised on May 15 that ten members of the Michel
Calihoo band of Indians had applied for enfranchisement
under the provisions of Section 110 of the Indian Act, Revised
Statutes of Canada, 1927. In all, six sections were set aside for
them as their *pro rata* share of the reserve.

On September 15, 1937, His Excellency the Governor General in Council was told that the 1903 sale of 7,800 acres had
officially gone through. In 1958, the last word in Privy Council about a band that was about to be obliterated on paper:
"WHEREAS the committee . . . expressed the opinion that the
Michel Band of Indian is capable of managing its own affairs
as a municipality or part of a municipality and advising that
it is desirable that the Band should be enfranchised." With
that, the reserve ceased to exist.

Full circle, thought Bob Royer. That was where he had
come into the picture, one of the very last of the Calihoos.

When his superiors found out he was poking into the Calihoo files, he was called into the office of the Deputy Minister
and told that he was "creating a problem for the Department."
Since he was a relative of the people mentioned in the files, it
was a violation of "departmental confidentiality." He was to
stop snooping. If he didn't stop snooping, he'd be out.

He found out from supporters in the department that,
under lock and key, there were seventeen cardboard boxes
with material relating to the erosion of the Calihoo Reserve
lands – seventeen boxes containing letters and deeds of land
and duplicates of transactions, bank statements, cheques,
notices, reports, ledgers, copies of ads, tax assessments, bills
of lading, correspondence, court orders, Reports to Privy

Council. But he couldn't look at it because he was a relative, because of his Oath of Allegiance, because of his conflict of interest.

He had reached at least one of the antechambers of the corridors of power – so far as Indians under the Indian Act in Canada were concerned – within shouting distance of the Deputy Minister and with access, via the Deputy Minister, albeit rarely, to the President of the Treasury Board. But what did it all add up to? Not much, when he couldn't even look into the file on his own family.

He did manage a glimpse one day, by sneaking into the file room. In the old days, that wouldn't have bothered him. But, by now, he was intensely aware that he was jeopardizing a relatively lush middle-class lifestyle. While life in Ottawa in many ways was stifling, it was also – compared to the tiny communities of northern Alberta – richly textured, with amenities and distractions that went beyond anything his family had experienced until then. Also, here he was somebody. He did not stick around the file room for long, just long enough to borrow – and then return – a few choice specimens of the documentation. He did see the cartons of files, and what got him was that the same word had been stencilled on all of them, a word that made him as angry as he'd been when he found out about the death rate among the residential school kids in the old days.

The word was: EXTINCT.

That's what it said on the boxes marked MICHEL CALIHOO INDIAN RESERVE NO. 132. *Extinct!* That was somehow the deepest wound of all.

His initial reaction was not rational, but highly emotional. He could pinch himself. He was real. He knew all his family and relatives, scattered as they were, and their kids, everybody with kids coming along. He thought of Mary and his own boys. Were the boys also extinct?

So now, like the Beothuks, they were technically known as a "vanished people." It had been outrageous enough to have had this personal Indian identity snatched when he was a kid, but this was taking it away from everybody at once, kids included, breaking them off from their own history, denying their inherent worth. Dead. Buried by bureaucrats. Buried in legal-size cardboard boxes, locked away in Ottawa. Worse, swallowed by bureaucrats – Canadian bureaucrats. The Calihoos. The dead, extinct, lost band of Calihoos.

The ultimate rejection . . .

In prison, Royer had been angry, and then indignant. Once he began to realize that what was happening to him wasn't a personal thing, but was happening for political reasons, he could pour his energy into a political struggle. His struggle to survive became tied in, for the first time, with the long struggle of "his people." He understood how and why they had been stacked up on the garbage heap by the time he met them. It had been a deliberate policy for over a century to hamstring and hobble them, to keep them bound in legal shackles, to starve them, drive wedges through their families, eradicate their language, break up their attempts to pull themselves back together after their military defeats, and subject them to rule by despots. It had been a relentless, pitiless campaign.

The fact that, by the late 1950s, the remnants of Iroquois Louis's brave band of freedom-seekers should have ended up the way they did – shattered by disease, drugs, environmental collapse, police-state domination, generation after generation – was scarcely surprising. The surprise was that anybody had survived at all, even though they were, as one might expect, punchy, battered wrecks. It's very hard to keep your dignity when you have been down that long.

When Royer thought about the big picture, he could be almost objective. What he was doing was looking at a map of a battlefield a century after the battle, and seeing what had happened as a result of the conquest. The mop-up operation was all but complete. The conquered people were thoroughly, utterly crushed.

Well. Not quite. Maybe.

It had taken a long time for him to see through the cloak of lies that had been spread over Canada's colonial history, the greatest lie of which was that the colonial period was somehow over. If anything, it had reached some kind of apogee, yet Canada managed to pass itself off as a liberal democracy, and hardly anybody ever quibbled with that. But so long as Royer was angry, there was a goal. Any young man could see it clearly. You were oppressed, you fought. It was the oldest story.

He wasn't quite sure just when the dream ignited, but there came a point shortly after he saw that word "Extinct" stamped over the history of his clan when he knew suddenly what it was he must do.

That reserve: it had been the fulfilment of great-great-great Grandfather Louis's dream. The war against the Europeans had been lost in the east, and his people had been herded together around a mission at Caughnawaga for generations, but he still piled his family into a birch-bark canoe and led them west to an unclaimed Promised Land, where they could live as free men again, in the tradition of their ancestors. It was a stirring example of somebody not accepting the verdict of history as written by the victor. The Iroquois, in Louis's time, had been whipped. Yet somebody had decided it wasn't over. Louis and Bernard Karhiio set off on their own small exodus – and found what they were looking for. And they prospered for a while before the holocaust came, with the police state in its wake.

Louis begat Michel who begat Louis who begat Sam who begat Albert who begat Bob . . .

He knew something of his roots. He knew where they led. He knew there had been much more to the Indian civilizations that had been crushed than white nationalist historians were willing to admit. He knew something of the incredible influence that the political ideas of those Indian societies had had on the world at large. He knew what his people had stood for when the merchants and soldiers from the monarchies arrived. The worst outrage of living in Canada, from an

Indian point of view, Royer mused, was that the defeat of Indian democracy and the triumph of the European dictatorships was turned on its head. The history books made it sound as though the country had been "liberated" from barbarism.

So long as he was merely fighting the Indian Affairs bureaucracy, he was skirmishing, sniping, practising the sort of guerrilla tactics that had served the Métis well for only so long before they had had to yield to the inevitable, and had served the Beothuks so poorly that they had been swallowed entirely. After sifting through the wreckage of his people's history, it finally occurred to Royer that he needed a place to stand. So did his sons. So would all those relatives who didn't have anything to call their own, and who were strictly limited to a lower-working-class fate. Canada was not their home. They would be forever outcasts.

If he could come back from legal death, why couldn't the Michel Calihoo reserve itself? When he had been struck from the Indian List so many years ago, it had been illegal, and it had proved to be reversible. Michel Calihoo Reserve No. 132 had started in 1878 with 22,784 acres and had belonged to Michel Calihoo and his descendants for "as long as that sun shines and yonder river flows." But the last bits of land had been dismembered and sold off in 1958 under the guise of "enfranchisement." The sun had shone and the river had flowed for exactly eighty years.

He had a case. He had a hell of a case. And he had a lot of the documentation – even if he was barred from most of it because it pertained to him. Extinct, eh?

If he could come back, so could the reserve. All it would take was a horrendous effort. The trouble with pushing at a bureaucracy was that, the moment you eased off to take a break, it pushed back. It always had another clerk to throw in to replace the one who had fallen. There was no way around the fact that any serious effort to turn the tide on the fate of the Michel Calihoo Reserve was a mammoth undertaking.

Yet supposing he succeeded? Then *they* succeeded, for all

the Calihoos would have to be involved. It would have to be very consensual. He'd have to remember that if he wanted to be a leader he would have to truly serve, and he would not have much autocratic power. That was the way it was with Indians, Iroquois in particular.

There was one factor in their favour. The Michel Band was the only band in Canada whose land disappeared purely and simply as a result of enfranchisement. What were involved in the final paperwork stages of the deal were "certificates of possession," which had been issued in the idealistic name of encouraging individual initiative. What they did was promptly to compromise the entire land-tenure system under the Indian Act. A man with a certificate of possession could ignore Band by-laws and do what he wanted with his portion of community-held land. Planning on reserves became impossible. The entire hereditary land-holding system – rather, what was left of it – was rendered ineffectual. It was because they had such certificates that the remaining Calihoos were able to sign away their sections of the reserve.

No bureaucrat was ever going to issue a certificate of possession again. Tacitly, over the years, one bureaucrat after another had admitted to Royer that things had changed too much. To attempt such a move nowadays would be to risk being branded with all sorts of horrible labels – imperialist reserve-wrecker, for instance. The swallowing of the Michel Reserve had been seen retrospectively by just about everybody connected with Indian matters today – the bureaucrats, the politicians, the lawyers, and the judges – as an example of massive error. They were all amazed that it was referred to as involving the granting of a great privilege: Canadian citizenship.

To resurrect the Michel Calihoo Reserve would really be something. It would bring an old dream back to life. It would follow through on a vision, pull off "a Phoenix," as it were. He could see a caravan of people moving back into the reconstituted reserve . . .

The long unravelling would end. Colonial history, which

had gone on far too long, would have to be stopped. That spot you Canadians rubbed out there? Please just go into reverse for a second and we'll put that back on the map. Once it was a repository of a dream that was being kept alive despite a Dark Age. Let it be so again.

This was Bob Royer's secret ambition.

Chapter 28

The Invisible Wall

IT WAS AN AMBITION HE KNEW PERFECTLY WELL HE HAD TO KEEP quiet about for a while. The task at hand, in 1978, was to try to bring off a quiet revolution in the paper-shuffling world of Indian Affairs. As chief of the Indian-Inuit Employment Section, Royer's work was cut out for him. However – ever so briefly – it looked as though he was finally going to be able to move the mountain.

The name of the game was *affirmative action*. He was under explicit orders to bring natives into the civil service. This was supposed to be a number-one-priority program. The political timing seemed right. The necessary background of unrest had manifested itself through the growth of articulate native-rights organizations, unrest on the reserves, picket lines and sit-ins in cities, and, perhaps more potently than any of the bureaucrats or politicians wanted to admit, by such actions as the suicide of Nelson Small Legs, Jr.

Officially, everyone was in favour of affirmative action. Absolutely everyone. But it didn't take long for Royer to realize that he was up against an invisible barrier. While his fellow civil servants were careful to nod solemnly whenever the subject came up, and to pledge their allegiance to the plan, there was a subtext to everything they said. While they were swear-

249

ing up and down that they would do their best to help him in his mammoth undertaking, what was being said behind his back, he learned, was simply this: "There is no way I'm going to teach an Indian to do my job so I can be booted out on the street." More subtly, convincing memos came back, arguing that, while affirmative action made sense in every other department, it didn't make any sense at all in the one particular department in which the one particular bureaucrat writing the memo happened to work. His or her task happened to involve a unique expertise accumulated over the decades, something that just couldn't be passed on like that. One after another, like leaves coming down in the fall, the memos landed on Royer's desk, and when he had gone through them all, it was to discover, lo and behold, that there was absolutely no place in Indian Affairs for actual Indians.

Another roadblock quickly emerged: civil servants, being the good guardians of the *status quo* that they were, had to be on the alert at all times for "political interference." This was something that arose whenever an Indian Band Council tried to make a decision on its own, or, worse, when an "appointee" tried to interfere with the seamless flow of departmental paperwork. For appointees, read: Bob Royer. Thus, affirmative action itself became a particularly dangerous form of political interference, and had to be nipped in the bud. Similarly, a certain upstart half-breed ex-con social-worker named Bob Royer had to be taught where his place was, and how to remain in it. When it came down to the crunch, Royer soon enough realized, there was no way – regardless of what the official line was – that Indian Affairs was about to help in its own dismemberment.

Royer could have sat there in his senior manager's office until cobwebs gathered, sending out directive after directive, and nothing would have changed. All that happened when he sent a directive out was that a memo came back, patiently and condescendingly explaining that, while the idea was terrific, it simply wouldn't work in the context of his particularly unique job-function. When directives failed, he tried calling for reports that could then lead to directives, but everyone was so busy shuffling papers that the requests for reports kept going to the bottoms of "Incoming" baskets and never got out. When directives and requests for reports failed, he tried sending out instructions for the development of individual comprehensive training programs. However, people in the department kept failing to meet deadlines, what with one person off sick, and another person on leave, and somebody else busy with another project. Instructions, requests and directives alike kept getting lost – well, not actually lost, but presumably misfiled – and it would take time to dig them out. This, of course, couldn't be done until next week or next month because such-and-such filing clerk was on holidays or the manager of such-and-such a sub-department was on loan to another sub-department. Excuses, excuses, excuses.

After six months of being stonewalled at every turn, Bob decided in desperation to try to go over the heads of the people surrounding him. He needed to get a serious directive moving downward from the top. So he went to the Deputy Minister, Rod Brown, told him what was happening, and asked Brown to play the one remaining trump card, which was to allow Bob to take the "increments" away from any civil servants "who did not meet their target program objectives." If something like this didn't happen, Royer warned, he would take his case outside the department to native groups, so that the issue could become public and political.

Brown warned him then and there that if he did anything like that, he would be violating his Oath of Allegiance and would be out on the street. Bob's temper got the better of him, and the discussion turned into a shouting match that ended with Royer stalking out of the Deputy Minister's office, slamming the door behind him. He took no further action for the moment, even though he knew that if he did nothing, the entire effort of the past decade of his life would be out the window. On the other hand, if he continued to be frustrated in his efforts at every turn, the exercise would have been in vain anyway.

Finally Bob decided, at the risk of losing his hard-earned job, to go over Brown's head indirectly. He set up a confidential meeting with Harry Daniels, then the President of the Native Council of Canada, and told him what was going on. Daniels had no power over Brown or anyone else at Indian Affairs, but he did have access to Robert Andras, then the head of the Treasury Board. After a couple of weeks, Daniels got an audience with Andras, who agreed to try to speed things up.

In due course, an edict came down from Andras's office to the effect that, if the affirmative-action-program objectives in Indian Affairs weren't met, raises and additional benefits for the various managers and staff involved would not be forthcoming. The Chief of the Indian–Inuit Employment Section, Bob Royer, would be the judge. In the civil service, where the bureaucrat is king, true power resides purely in control over the rate at which paycheques expand. Bob finally had the whip hand, and no one could prove that he had gone behind Rod Brown's back. The trouble was, Brown was no fool. He and everyone else in the department could figure it out for themselves. From that point on, even though he was at the apex of his power, Royer was a marked man.

In the following six months, there were small signs that the department was beginning to move. There was nothing so concrete as the actual hiring of Indians, but the requested reports began to slowly filter in, plans seemed to advance to the program-outline stage, and directives were at least acknowledged. However, for all the effort Bob put in, the pace of metamorphosis left no room for any feelings of triumph. A glacier would have moved faster, and by now, Royer found himself surrounded by white mandarins who were just waiting for him to make a slip so they could stab him in the back.

The laying-on of the whip by the token half-Indian in front office wasn't something taken lightly by the lower ranks. In no uncertain terms, Royer was advised by fellow managers that, like them, he was supposed to understand the "practical limits" to which he could go in his reforms. If he continued to demonstrate that he didn't understand those limits at all, he would be "finished" in the department. That is, he would be trapped in a dead-end ceremonial position, ignored by everyone around him, and he could send out a million memos, directives, requests, and instructions, but it would be to no avail. He might as well be an organ-grinder on the street. The absolute bare minimum of his programs would eventually be developed, but at a snail's pace. He would, indeed, be long dead before his dream of Indians taking over Indian Affairs could be achieved.

Bob's position had become untenable. He had no desire to stay pinned down at a desk, stonewalled on all sides, his effectiveness reduced to near-zero. After barely a year in Ottawa, he had explored the parameters of his range of action, and found them to be effectively not much greater than when he was in a prison cell. His isolation set up memories of the long-ago days in solitary.

His unhappiness showed. During a luncheon meeting with Walter Twin, Grand Chief of the Lesser Slave Lake Region, and Frank Helcrow, the vice-chief, some of his frustration leaked out. Twin and Helcrow exchanged looks. It so happened, they told him, they were looking for some way of taking over the District Office of Indian Affairs at High Prairie, Alberta. If Royer figured he was getting nowhere trying to bore from within the department in Ottawa, why not come and work with them? Knowing the lay of the land called Indian Affairs, he would be just the kind of guy they needed, someone who knew where the buttons and whistles were, someone with intimate knowledge of just how the stonewalling was done. As the discussion went on into the afternoon, the idea took hold. Indeed, why not? He was going nowhere in Ottawa, that was for sure.

Also, there was another angle. Bob had let Twin and Helcrow in on the story of the destruction of the Michel Calihoo Reserve and his secret dream of having the reserve reconstituted. If he came to High Prairie, Grand Chief Twin promised, he would have Royer adopted as a status Indian on one of the reserves within the Lesser Slave Lake Region. As a status – as opposed to general – Indian, he would be in a stronger position to launch his campaign, especially among the various native groups whose support he would eventually need.

It didn't take long for Bob to make up his mind. Nor was there much resistance when he asked Rod Brown for a lateral transfer to High Prairie. Although the people who had resisted his every reformist move were careful to smile politely and wish him well, it was plain that they were all relieved to see the thorn in their side remove itself. Little did they realize that he was simply repositioning himself to come at them from another direction.

In Ottawa one afternoon shortly before he left in 1979, Bob stepped into a shop to pick up a magazine and noticed a particularly beautiful Indian carving hanging from a hook by the cash register. He picked it up to admire it. Turning it over to see who had carved it, he saw a sticker he had never seen before, but which crystallized a lot of things – maybe everything – for him. The sticker said: MADE IN OCCUPIED CANADA. He had never really quite thought about it in such simple terms, but that said it all.

In High Prairie, his task was to assume responsibility for all the various Indian Affairs programs and administer them, while the Lesser Slave Lake Regional Council worked out a takeover agreement with the department – the very first of its kind. Within nine months, most of the mission was accomplished. Of twenty-eight white federal civil servants involved in running the programs, half had accepted lateral transfers elsewhere, clearing the way for their jobs to be assumed by natives. It wasn't quite the 100-per-cent solution that Royer had envisioned, but 50 per cent was a lot better than anything he'd been able to accomplish in Ottawa. The satisfaction was there. He was on the offensive. And while in High Prairie, he and his family were adopted as members of the Grouard Band

Reserve in order to give him rights such as land usage and exemption from taxation until such time as he could set to work full-time trying to get the Michel Calihoo Reserve reconstituted.

As the Indian Affairs job at High Prairie was winding down, an advertisement for a band manager at the west-coast community of Alert Bay caught Bob's eye. There had been a scandal at Alert Bay over the death of a Kwakiutl Indian child, caused by negligence on the part of a drunken doctor. The situation was far from unusual, but some of the statistics that had come out during an inquiry headed by Dr. Gary Goldthrope had drawn the attention of the national media. The average life expectancy among Kwakiutl males, it was found, was only fifty years. The entire health-care system at Alert Bay was found to be woefully inadequate – though not really that much worse than the situation on any other reserve in the country. Royer applied for the band-manager job, landed it, resigned from Indian Affairs, and promptly moved his family to Alert Bay, a village on Cormorant Island, just offshore from the northeastern tip of Vancouver Island.

When he arrived, it was to find not just the health-care system in disarray, but nearly everything else as well. The Nimpkish Band, which controlled the reserve, was a half-million dollars in debt, thanks to mismanagement. Bob took the job on the understanding that he would stay a year, place the band on a deficit-recovery program, and straighten out the Indian Affairs-administered programs that were in need of repair.

He stayed eight years, and they were productive years. After the hostility of Ottawa and the cold of High Prairie, the moist west-coast climate was as agreeable to Mary and the boys as it was to Bob. There, among the sagging totem poles and the lush rain forest, they found a niche that seemed to work. In the time that he was there as band manager, Bob managed to significantly reduce the deficit, attract more government funding, and set up a drug- and-alcohol-rehabilitation centre, a health complex, a museum, and a social-development program that saw a substantial reduction in the number of juveniles appearing in court per month. By 1987, when he decided to move on, the Nimpkish Band had $5.5 million worth of programs operating annually, with 160 mainly native employees at work running their own school, housing programs, two salmon-enhancement programs, two hatcheries, a river-reclamation program, and an extensive forestry program. They had succeeded in bringing the nearby Nimpkish River back from the edge of death by pollution, had fended off development projects that would have wrecked all their work, and had made the reserve into the second-largest oyster-producer on the coast. As for alcoholism and drug abuse, the situation had been effectively turned around. By the time Royer left, a majority of the Nimpkish Band people were sober and hard at work. This was not solely thanks to any one man or woman, but Bob Royer's contribution had been considerable.

In the back of his mind, however, the idea of bringing the Michel Calihoo Reserve back to life had never faded. And however magnificent the scenery at Alert Bay, it wasn't his home, nor would it ever truly be. Still restless, he decided to move to Vancouver, where he signed a short-term contract with the B. C. Municipality of Chiefs to wind down a program in the city's notorious "Blood Alley," the Gastown section, where most natives ended up when they drifted into town and found it impossible to get jobs. Bob's task wasn't to save the program, which had tried to place female social-workers on the streets to help native women, but to put the organization into receivership, making sure that the files were preserved. It was far from an upbeat job, the Gastown section being famous as the toughest part of Vancouver, with a level of despair and hopelessness – so far as the natives who arrived there were concerned – that went as deep as any place in Canada. After a few months of this, having done the administrative deed that needed to be done, Bob latched on to work that was closer to his heart.

He was invited up to Village Island, near Campbell River,

on the eastern shore of Vancouver Island, about halfway between Vancouver and Alert Bay, to take on the role of band planner. After the smallpox plagues had run their course along the coast, village after village had been deserted and left to the moss and the rain. Now a group of Kwakiutl Indians had decided that they wanted to re-establish a community at Village Island, a particularly scenic and well-located settlement, which had existed for centuries, if not millennia, before the arrival of the white man. The assignment meant harnessing the energies of specialists as diverse as hydrologists and lawyers, as well as town-planners, to lay out the streets, figure out electricity requirements, and in general to establish the entire infrastructure of a modern village in the middle of a rainy "nowhere." As usual, he found himself at odds with Indian Affairs, which did not recognize the abandoned village site as reserve land, and wanted nothing to do with setting it up as such. But the land, which had technically fallen into the hands of the United Church, had been offered back to the Indians by the church as a conciliatory gesture.

When the Village Island project was up and running, Bob decided to move back to High Prairie, where he took a job as director of native child welfare. Thanks to the success of his earlier campaign, the Lesser Slave Lake Regional Council now had complete control over the custody of native children, over health, and over alcohol- and drug-abuse programs.

Here he worked until the spring of 1990, when he quit to concentrate full-time on the resurrection of his own reserve. By this time, he had all the expertise it was possible to have concerning the rebuilding of broken Indian lives and communities, and knew precisely how to win independence from Indian Affairs. The main goal of his life now lay before him. Whether it was truly within reach or not was something he couldn't say for sure, but he knew that to give up without pushing the issue as far as possible was to forfeit any chance at all.

Chapter 29

The Long Road Home

THUS, BOB ROYER, A.K.A. ROB ROY, A.K.A. ROBERT CALIHOO, SET out on what some might call a quixotic quest. It was something nobody had ever tried before. And of course he wasn't setting out alone. The boys, Robbie and Jamie, were getting to the ages where they resented being uprooted and moved around. Without the stability of either Bob's civil-service job or his administrative work for various bands, Mary was forced to work, taking odd jobs as a waitress, and for a while, when they were in Vancouver, caretaking a small apartment block. There was disruption, insecurity, and the spectre of poverty looming at every turn.

And all to bring back a dead reserve? There were horror stories galore about reserves and how they had come to be. One definition, in fact, had served very well for a while. A reserve, people said, was simply land which had been rejected by settlers, and therefore had reverted to the Crown and could be offered to Indians, except, of course in the Northwest Territories, where not an inch of land is controlled by either Indians or Eskimo – only by Ottawa. Against this dismal backdrop, why would anyone *want* to resurrect a reserve?

These were new times, Royer reasoned. It was just possible that a serious apotheosis was in the works. Indians weren't taking it any more. They weren't following the white man's path. They were groping toward a kind of pan-Indian agreement-in-principle about what they wanted, with the common goal of re-establishing democracy on their soil after a century of oppression.

So far as the case of the Calihoo Reserve was concerned, there was a particular factor at work that made it difficult. It was not *quite* history. The selling of the Calihoo reserve, a political act with cultural-genocide overtones, had occurred at the end of the 1950s – just before the 1960s, that decade of discovery and awakening – in the heart of Canada. If what had happened to the Calihoos had been allowed to happen to – had been inflicted upon – all the other reserves in Canada, the reserve system would have broken down completely, leaving homeless, unprepared Indians to wash up on hostile urban shores, destitute, illiterate, unhealthy, with a totally negative self-image, many not speaking the language at all, aliens and outcasts in what had once been their own land.

For Royer, the road to the resurrection of Michel Calihoo Indian Reserve No. 132 began the day he sat down to write his first letter to all his scattered relatives to tell them his belief that, indeed, they had been bilked and defrauded and conned and betrayed, just as they had all suspected.

That was the bad news. The good news was that the evidence was still in existence. And since, essentially, what was involved in the eradication of the Michel Reserve was the violation of a political pact, this could in no way be considered an ordinary land deal. The pact upon which the existence of the Calihoo Reserve ultimately rested had been an Adhesion to Treaty Six. As such, it was part and parcel of Treaty Six, just as Treaty Six was part and parcel of all the other numbered treaties and all the other settlements and proclamations involving Indians, through which Canada had backed into ownership of all the land.

To the extent that Canada existed as a legal entity – as opposed to a bandit empire – it had a national obligation to honour its treaties. A nation that abrogated one treaty here

and another there could simply not be trusted, and that reputation would stick. So, as long as the pursuit of the resurrection of the Calihoo Reserve followed the channels of
legitimacy leading back to the British North America Act,
and as long as Royer came forward step by step to the present,
and assuming the case could indeed be made, there was no
immutable legal barrier to the political miracle of Canada's
"lost" reserve being brought back to life.

And there was a certain symbolism, wasn't there? Royer
was probably hopelessly romantic at heart, but the idea of
Canada being big enough to back up a few inches, to say
"sorry about that," make amends, and then start forward
again together with the Indians, was enormously appealing.

This was the thought Royer had to keep foremost in his
mind when he contemplated the awesome array of the five
thousand massed Indian Affairs bureaucrats he was up
against, with their legions of lawyers and cops standing by.

Indian Affairs wouldn't be there forever, Royer fervently
believed. It couldn't be. Sooner or later, Canada would have to
shed its neo-colonial habits, grow into a truly free country.

It was strange, perhaps, that it should be in the hinterland
of Canada that the largest remaining colony in the world
existed – the Northwest Territories. And strange it was that in
Canada, of all places, more than half a thousand captive
nations continued to live under imperial rule. It was simply
because Canada had avoided certain words, like *apartheid*,
and had allowed the natives to vote (after waiting until they
were reduced to a tiny minority) that the country was able to
present such a happy face of liberalism to the world, while an
occupation army of five thousand sat on top of every Indian
man, woman, and child.

But all this would pass. If Indian Affairs wasn't torn down
by its own contradictions, it would someday be infiltrated, of
this he was sure. He had pushed his way in ahead of time. As
an instrument in the hands of natives, Indian Affairs wouldn't

be such a bad thing. If it was utopian to think of a native-run Indian Affairs, he remained a utopian.

A reserve, then, on the day when democracy, after its long outward journey, finally came back to the Indian people, might be something very much worth having. Small was going to look even more beautiful. And if worst came to worst, it would be nice to be able to run to the hills, just as his ancestor, Iroquois Louis, had known all along.

Epilogue

THE SUMMER OF THE MOHAWK UPRISING AT OKA AND
Chateauguay came and went. From the distance of northern
Alberta, the Calihoos watched the Quebec barricades go up
on television, saw the Canadian Armed Forces move in, and
heard politicians like Robert Bourassa dismiss the Mohawk
demands for self-determination at the very time that he was
orchestrating some form of the same thing for French-
Canadians. No one among the Calihoos was surprised. Why,
after all, had Iroquois Louis left his ancient home? It was all
painfully familiar, except for the fact that the Mohawk
Warriors – their cousins – were now better armed than they
had been at any time since the days when Champlain's men
had opened fire on them. In five hundred years, from the
point of view of the Iroquois descendants, Canada had
changed hardly at all.

For Bob Royer (who was tending more and more to think of
himself as Bob Calihoo, even though the mental habits of
most of a lifetime died hard) the battle at Oka was decisive.
Whether the majority of Canadians ended the summer of
1990 feeling negative about native aspirations because
the Mohawks had dared to make their claims at gun-point
(which, previously, the whites had always done), or because a

Cree, Elijah Harper, had stood against the Meech Lake Accord, bringing the possibility of English- and French-Canadian *rapprochement* crashing down around the head of Prime Minister Brian Mulroney, was neither here nor there. On the political agenda of what seemed like a rapidly disintegrating Canadian Empire, the questions of land claims, native grievances, and outstanding cases of injustice had moved forward a giant step. It was a time for action.

By November, after a summer of preparing his case, Bob was in Ottawa, seeking a resolution from the Native Council of Canada endorsing his motion to have the Michel Calihoo Reserve reconstituted. An endorsement from the Native Council had no legal status – but considerable political value. When he got it, his campaign became not just one man's dream, but something within political reach. The resolution, unanimously passed by the Council, said:

Whereas the Michel Indian Band of Alberta is the only Indian Band to have been enfranchised, on August 5, 1958, by Order-In-Council, under Section 112 of the Indian Act, in direct contravention of Treaty Six, therefore be it resolved at the 18th General Assembly of the Native Council of Canada, to support the Michel Indian Band of Alberta in pursuing a specific land claim and its justified demands that the Minister of Indian Affairs immediately recognize and reinstate the Michel Band to its full rights as a Band under the Indian Act.

The resolution also approved the release of council funds to Bob Royer to begin preliminary research into the Michel claim, including "legal analysis, fiduciary trust issues, history, Bill C-31, and enfranchisement of the band."

By coincidence, Royer happened to be in Ottawa meeting with the Native Council when the Canadian Human Rights Commission, headed by Max Yalden, released its landmark report calling on the federal government to scrap both the Indian Act and the Department of Indian Affairs. "The department, like the legislation it administers, is a relic of the past that must be put behind us," the commission stated in the most hard-hitting and sweeping attack on federal aboriginal policy ever issued by so highly placed a Canadian body. "The Indian Act is fundamentally and irreparably flawed," the commission added. "No amount of tinkering can alter that, and the long-range objective must be to remove it from the laws of Canada."

The Globe and Mail called the nine-page report, issued November 21, 1990, "a devastating critique of almost every aspect of Ottawa's policy on aboriginal issues, from land claims and self-government to housing and economic development." In it, Human Rights Commissioner Yalden called the government's current land-claims policy outdated and "heavily weighted in favour of the government." Under the current regime, only three comprehensive land claims have been settled in the past twenty years. "The pace of change is simply too slow," he added. "For every community where headway has been made on land claims, self-government or economic development, there are dozens of others with grievances still outstanding and aspirations yet to be realized."

There was nothing new in what the Human Rights Commission had to say, nothing at all. What was new was the background against which the commission's views were aired. At Oka, it had cost the Canadian government a total of $60 million to conduct a single military exercise against a relative handful of armed and isolated Mohawks. Throughout the world, Canada's vaunted – and undeserved – reputation as a land of tolerance had been stripped away, revealing the naked reality of oppression and racism. The blockades that went up around reserves across the rest of the country offered Canadians a glimpse of the abyss into which they could be plunged should it ever come to all-out civil war with dispossessed, militant native people fighting back against a crushing, centuries-old occupation.

Bob Royer/Calihoo, looking back deeply into the past,

thought he could detect a glint of the future. He was not, he reflected, very different at all from the distant ancestor who had set out by canoe to carve a small circle of freedom for his family out of the darkness created by an implacable, omnipotent foe.

Selected Bibliography

A BOOK LIKE THIS, WHICH ATTEMPTS TO ENCAPSULATE SOME FIVE
hundred years of history in a relatively short space, necessarily skims the surface. For the reader who would venture more
deeply into the dark tale of what happened to Canada's native
people in the course of their long resistance to invasion – a
resistance which the armed uprising at Oka in the summer of
1990 demonstrated is far from over – the works of a new generation of historians who do not flinch from revealing the mag-
nitude of Europe's genocidal rape of "our home and native
land" are available. They are a good antidote to the
whitewashed history most of us were offered in school.

The likes of Harold Cardinal and Heather Robertson unveil
the present political and social reality equally unflinchingly,
while Edmund Wilson and Felix Cohen offer a legal and
moral framework for contemplation of the meaning of what
transpired in the course of the "civilizing" of this continent.

For details of historical French (and particularly Jesuit)
duplicity in dealings with Hurons, Montagnais, Algonquins
and Five Nations Iroquois, Bruce G. Trigger is masterful and
chilling. Calvin Martin and L. F. S. Upton pull no punches
about the devastation of the Beothuks and Micmacs, along

with the entire Maritime ecosystem, bringing powerful new perspectives to bear. John L. Tobias likewise details the despicable (and nowadays utterly illegal) tactics used in the campaign against the Plains Indians. Ruth Kirk lays bare the holocaust inflicted on the peoples of the west coast, while the venerable Diamond Jenness rounds out the bleak picture of the running-to-ground of the tribes of the far north.

Here are the books, essays, papers, studies, and articles upon which we drew for the background to the story of the descendants of "Iroquois Louis" Karhiio and their unfinished, centuries-long search for freedom.

Bissonnette, Alain, Serge Bouchard and Jacques Pregent. *Native Juveniles and Criminal Law: Preliminary Study of Needs and Services in Some Native Communities of Quebec.* Ottawa: Department of Justice, Research and Statistics Section, 1985.

Boas, Franz. *Kwakiutl Ethnography.* Edited by Helen Codere. Chicago: University of Chicago Press, 1966.

Brown, George and Ron Maguire. *Native Treaties in Historical Perspective.* Ottawa: Department of Indian and Northern Affairs, Research Branch, 1979.

The Calahoo Women's Institute, comp. *Calahoo Trails.* Edited by Mrs. K. Dalheim and Mrs. M. Kerr. Calahoo Women's Institute, n.d.

Calihoo, Victoria. "Early Life at St. Anne and St. Albert." *Alberta Historical Review* (November 1953).

Canada. Department of Indian and Northern Affairs. *Adoption and the Indian Child.* Ottawa: Department of Indian and Northern Affairs, Indian and Inuit Affairs Program, Membership and Entitlement Directorate, 1987.

——. *The Canadian Indian*. Ottawa: Department of Indian and Northern Affairs, 1986.

——. *Comprehensive Land Claims Policy*. Ottawa: Department of Indian and Northern Affairs, 1986.

——. *Indian Band Membership: An Information Booklet Concerning New Indian Band Membership Laws and the Preparation of Indian Band Membership Codes*. Ottawa: Department of Indian and Northern Affairs, 1986.

——. Parliament. House of Commons. Report of the Special Committee. *Indian Self-Government in Canada*. Ottawa: Report of the Special Committee, House of Commons, Issue No. 40, 1983.

Cardinal, Harold. *The Unjust Society: The Tragedy of Canada's Indians*. Edmonton: Hurtig, 1969.

——. *The Rebirth of Canada's Indians*. Edmonton: Hurtig, 1977.

Cohen, Felix S. *The Legal Conscience: Selected Papers of Felix S. Cohen*. Edited by Lucy Kramer Cohen. Hamden, Connecticut: Shoe String Press, Archon Books, 1970.

de Trémaudan, Auguste-Henri. *Hold High Your Heads: History of the Métis Nation in Western Canada*. Translated by Elizabeth Maguet. Winnipeg: Pemmican, 1982.

Dunn, Marty. *Red on White: The Biography of Duke Redbird*. Chicago: Follett, 1971.

Fellegi, Dr. Ivan. *Indian Demographic Workshop: Implications for Policy and Planning*. Ottawa: Department of Indian and Northern Affairs and Statistics Canada, June 20, 1980.

Fisher, Robin and Kenneth Coates, eds. *Out of the Background: Readings on Canadian Native History.* Toronto: Copp Clark Pitman, 1988. (The following chapters were of special interest: "Canada's Subjugation of the Plains Cree, 1879-1885" by John L. Tobias; "The Extermination of the Beothuks of Newfoundland" by L. F. S. Upton; and "The European Impact on the Culture of a Northeastern Algonquian Tribe: An Ecological Perspective" by Calvin Martin.)

Francis, Daniel. *A History of the Native Peoples of Quebec, 1760-1867.* Ottawa: Department of Indian and Northern Affairs, 1983.

Jenness, Diamond. *Indians of Canada.* 7th ed. Bulletin 65, Anthropological Series No. 15. Ottawa: National Museums of Canada, 1967.

Johansen, Bruce E. *Forgotten Founders: How the American Indian Helped Shape Democracy.* Boston: The Harvard Common Press, 1982.

King, Thomas, Cheryl Culver and Helen Hoy, eds. *The Native in Literature: Canadian and Comparative Perspectives.* Toronto: ECW Press, 1987.

Kirk, Ruth. *Wisdom of the Elders: Native Traditions on the Northwest Coast.* Vancouver: Douglas & McIntyre in association with the British Columbia Provincial Museum, 1986.

Leslie, John and Ron Maguire, eds. *The Historical Development of the Indian Act.* 2nd ed. Ottawa: Department of Indian and Northern Affairs, Treaties and Historical Research Centre, Research Branch, Corporate Policy, 1979.

Little Bear, Leroy, Menno Boldt and J. Anthony Long, eds. *Pathways to Self-Determination: Canadian Indians and the Canadian State.* Toronto: University of Toronto Press, 1984.

MacEwan, Grant. *Métis Makers of History*. Saskatoon: Western Producer Prairie Books, 1981.

Madill, Dennis. *British Columbia Indian Treaties in Historical Perspective*. Ottawa: Department of Indian and Northern Affairs, Research Branch, 1981.

Manual, George and Michael Posluns. *The Fourth World: An Indian Reality*. Toronto: Collier Macmillan, 1974.

Morris, Alexander. "Treaties of Canada with the Indians of Manitoba and the North-West Territories." Paper in Public Archives of Manitoba.

Morrison, R. Bruce, and C. Roderick Wilson, eds. *Native Peoples: The Canadian Experience*. Toronto: McClelland & Stewart, 1986. (Virginia Miller's chapter "The Micmac: A Maritime Woodland Group," is quoted in the text.)

Petrone, Penny, ed. *First People, First Voices*. Toronto: University of Toronto Press, 1983.

Redbird, Duke. *We Are Métis: A Métis View of the Development of a Native Canadian People*. Willowdale, Ont.: Ontario Métis and Non-Status Indian Association, 1980.

Robertson, Heather. *Reservations Are for Indians*. Toronto: James Lorimer, 1970.

Sewid-Smith, Daisy (My-yah-nelth). *Prosecution or Persecution*. Alert Bay, B.C.: Nu-Yum-Baleess Society, 1979.

Tanner, Ogden. *The Old West: The Canadians*. Alexandria, Va.: Time-Life Books, 1977.

Taylor, John Leonard. *Treaty Six (1876): Treaty Research Report*. Ottawa: Department of Indian and Northern Affairs, Treaties and Historical Research Centre, 1985.

Trigger, Bruce G. *Natives and Newcomers: Canada's "Heroic Age" Reconsidered.* Montreal: McGill-Queen's University Press, 1985. (Pages 226-97 are especially interesting.)

Weatherford, Jack. *Indian Givers: How the Indians of the Americas Transformed the World.* New York: Crown, 1988.

Weaver, S. M. *Making Canadian Indian Policy: The Hidden Agenda, 1968-1970.* Toronto: University of Toronto Press, 1981.

Wilson, Edmund. *Apologies to the Iroquois.* New York: Farrar, Straus & Cudahy, 1959.